MEISTER ECKHART
Mystic and Philosopher

Studies in Phenomenology and Existential Philosophy

MEISTER ECKHART

Mystic and Philosopher

Translations with Commentary by
Reiner Schürmann

INDIANA UNIVERSITY PRESS / BLOOMINGTON & LONDON

Published by arrangement with Editions Planète, Paris,
publishers of the French edition of this work, *Maître Eckhart ou la joie errante,*
copyright © 1972 Editions Planète-Denoël.

Copyright © 1978 by Reiner Schürmann

Published in Canada by Fitzhenry & Whiteside Limited, Don Mills, Ontario

Manufactured in the United States of America

Library of Congress Cataloging in Publication Data

Schürmann, Reiner, 1941-
Meister Eckhart, mystic and philosopher.

(Studies in phenomenology and existential philosophy)
Translation of Maître Eckhart ou la joie errante.
Bibliography
Includes index.
1. Eckhart, Meister, d. 1327.   I. Eckhart, Meister,
d. 1327.   Selected works.   English.   1977.   II. Title.
B765.E34S3813 1977   193   76-26416
ISBN 0-253-35183-9   1 2 3 5 82 81 80 79 78

Was scheint leichter, als das Seiende eben das Seiende sein zu lassen, das es ist? Oder kommen wir mit dieser Aufgabe vor das Schwerste, zumal wenn ein solches Vorhaben, das Seiende sein zu lassen, wie es ist, das Gegenteil darstellt von jener Gleichgültigkeit, die dem Seienden einfach den Rücken zukehrt? Wir sollen uns dem Seienden zukehren, an ihm selbst auf dessen Sein denken, aber gerade so es in seinem Wesen auf sich beruhen lassen.

MARTIN HEIDEGGER

What seems easier than to let a being be just the being that it is? Or does this turn out to be the most difficult of tasks, particularly if such a project—to let a being be as it is—represents the opposite of the indifference that simply turns its back upon the being itself? We must turn towards the being, think about it in regard to its Being, but by such a thinking at the same time let it rest upon itself in its way to be.

Contents

INTRODUCTION

MEISTER ECKHART'S attempt, over six centuries ago, to reconcile philosophical thought and a certain type of experience of life continues to arouse much interest in modern readers. Many of these readers, however, find Eckhart a confusing author. One may turn for help to the numerous, mostly German, commentaries and interpretations of Eckhart's thought, but this will only increase the confusion, for they are so diverse, their renderings so contradictory, that one hesitates to choose any one of them for a guide.

Each generation has produced its own interpretation of Eckhart's works in accordance with its own ideological movements. German philosophy of the nineteenth century adopted Eckhart as an ancestor and called him the "father of German speculation" (Joseph Bach, 1864). Hegel regarded Eckhart as the reconciler of faith and science; Schopenhauer saw him as the founder of transcendental idealism; and Schelling found in Eckhart's works a close similarity to his own philosophy of Revelation. Schelling and Franz von Baader undoubtedly reflect most accurately the thought of Meister Eckhart. Because of this appropriation of Eckhart's philosophy by the Idealists, credit is due to Franz Pfeiffer and Henri Denifle for having established in this period the letter of his text. In the twentieth century the National Socialist pseudomythology glorified the Arian man as "Eckhartian man." It is not only the *Myth of the Twentieth Century* by Alfred Rosenberg which demonstrates these aberrant interpretations of the Rhineland master: the racist abuse, which renders Eckhart unrecognizable, is found even in academic works of these years.

A return to the sources was necessary. In 1936 a critical edition of the Latin and German texts of Meister Eckhart was begun. This work is still in progress. Many historical studies of Meister Eckhart have also appeared. However, philosophical interpretations of his thought are still rare. This is the task that this work will undertake: to uncover the philosophical articulation of Eckhart's fundamental intuitions through a careful reading of his German sermons. For this purpose, a close examination of the texts will be the primary method used.

Strangely enough, for several years it has been authors far removed from the Christian tradition who have found in Eckhart a spiritual master. Some Buddhists discover in his preaching elements of their own teachings. In the United States, in Germany, and in Japan Meister Eckhart is sometimes considered a point of encounter between Eastern and Western traditions. Marxists have also adopted Meister Eckhart. To some he appears as the theoretician of the class struggle in the Middle Ages. This "mystic of the left" would have fought to free the proletariat from the oppressive force of the feudal Church, indeed from God. Meister Eckhart speaks of a "breakthrough" of man beyond God; to the Marxist Ernst Bloch, this is the act by which man takes possession of his native good, alienated by dogma in an inaccessible heaven.[1]

In the English-speaking countries, Meister Eckhart is still relatively unknown. This book attempts to make Eckhart himself speak through translations and analyses of his sermons. The final chapter, however, will introduce a comparison between Eckhart and Martin Heidegger. It has frequently been stressed, especially by Heidegger himself, that the study of Eckhart's sermons has contributed to the development of Heidegger's thought. I shall limit myself in the last chapter to an examination of what both authors call *"Gelassenheit."* This key term has been translated by "serenity," "letting be," "abandonment"; the most appropriate translation seems, however, to be "releasement."

I shall concentrate primarily on the German works of Meister Eckhart. In accordance with Pfeiffer, and in opposition to Denifle, the German works should be recognized as the most significant reflection of his thought and of the creative genius of his language. The Latin work was written for academic purposes; it consists mostly of commentaries, designed for students of theology and composed according to rules already three centuries old. When Eckhart addressed himself to the nuns of the Rhineland (who preserved these sermons for us) in his mother tongue, he was more original and more personal; he spoke to them without the confining apparatus of late scholasticism. It is true that Meister Eckhart teaches basically the same thing in both languages. The Latin work constitutes the doctrinal basis for the understanding of his thought. It will draw the limits within which interpretation remains safe. Thus we shall not pass, once again, into fantastic theories. The Latin works mark the road, but the German works invite us on the journey.[2]

Here are translated three German sermons. Each of these translations is followed by an analysis of the argument, then by a commentary on the principal themes in the sermons. The commentary does not employ the same methods in all three cases. For the first Sermon, "Jesus Entered," we have combined it with the analysis itself. Our purpose, indeed, is to understand this sermon through the sources used by Meister Eckhart and through his testimony before the tribunals of the Inquisition. It would have been artificial to separate this historical inquiry from the analysis of the text itself.

For the second sermon, "Woman, the Hour Is Coming," the analysis and the commentary have different orientations. The analysis elucidates the philosophical implications of the spiritual experience which the text exhibits. For this Meister Eckhart will be studied within the setting of the intellectual tradition which he represented in the chairs of Cologne and Paris. Some of his more controversial statements will be compared to the theology that had become predominant in his time. The commentary on this sermon will trace what we call the way of Meister Eckhart: through *Dissimilarity, Similarity, Identity,* and *Dehiscence,* leading into the ineffable desert of the Godhead. The four paragraphs so entitled constitute a whole that can be read independently of the rest. The fundamental themes of Meister Eckhart are arranged in it according to their order in his philosophy, or rather according to the order of a life in whose midst is born the Word, the Son of God.

Meister Eckhart can be understood in his entirety only through a philosophical interpretation. The third sermon, "See What Love," has been chosen as an example of the most traditional philosophical problem, the understanding of being. The analysis of this text tends to make clear what moderns would call the ontology of Meister Eckhart. The commentary proceeds to a double explanation of his approach to the question of being: first according to the Aristotelian theory of analogy, then according to Heideggerian thought on the difference between Being, which "lets be," and the beings.

These sermons have been selected as illustrative of the central theme of Eckhart's preaching: releasement. His thought fluctuates between the demands of a law: voluntary disappropriation and impoverishment; and the description of a state: the original liberty which man has never lost at the basis of his being. The concept of releasement includes these two aspects. For Eckhart, learning how to give up everything, and understanding perfect identity with God, which is already given, are the two aspects, legislative and manifestative, of releasement. Bringing together the imperative of a moral course: "You will detach yourself" and the infinitive of a metaphysical discourse: "To be of the nature of God"— this is grasping Meister Eckhart. These two aspects will be joined under the designation, wandering identity.

When this dialectic is transferred onto the daily plane on which existence is carried out, it will be expressed differently. A detached man, Eckhart says, experiences such a joy that no one would be able to tear it away from him. But such a man remains unsettled. He who has let himself be, and who has let God be, lives in wandering joy, or joy without a cause.

So entering into Meister Eckhart's universe with a strict dependence on his texts gives one a triple advantage. There is, first of all, less risk of going astray. Also, in a mosaic of quotations many things can be said, while an integral text allows for constant verification by the reader of the hypotheses advanced. Finally, this method has produced a new translation: in addition to the three sermons analyzed and commented on, five more have been added, in each of which a central idea of Eckhart's philosophy is developed. These five sermons follow and illustrate the chapters devoted to their theme. Altogether we present here new translations of eight sermons.

There is one interpretative option in the translations that requires an explanation. We have consistently rendered Eckhart's *sêle* not as "soul," but as "mind." One could object that this translation disregards the etymological evidence. But Eckhart's vocabulary in this case is Augustinian.[3] *Sêle* mostly stands for Augustine's *mens* or *animus*, both of which are usually translated as "mind." Only when *sêle* is used in the sense of *anima*, designating the animating principle of the body, have we used "soul." In Eckhart's Latin writings, though, he follows Scholastic terminology, and there even *anima* is often to be translated as "mind."[4]

Contradictions and fluctuations in the reasoning of Meister Eckhart are not lacking. We must remember, however, that these sermons are an attempt at a double translation: on the one hand, an ineffable experience ("mystic" comes from μύειν, "to close one's eyes, mouth") is translated into daily language so as to become communicable; on the other hand, the hearer of this communication is himself translated before the source which grants such an experience. It is probably possible to reproduce Eckhart's experience of being, but only on one condition: "He who wants to understand my teaching of releasement must himself be perfectly released." An attitude is required for thinking to succeed. We propose to define mysticism as this reciprocity between existence and thought: to think of being as releasement one must first of all have a released existence. This appears to be a more satisfactory approach to the phenomenon of mysticism than all definitions that derive the mystical experience from the arrival in consciousness of an all-encompassing being that submerges us.

Each line of Meister Eckhart testifies to an uneasiness about the fundamental inadequacy of language when confronted by the joy without a cause. There are perhaps illogical murmurings which mobilize deeper forces in us than does the rigor of constructed discourse. Meister Eckhart undertakes the risk of "speculative mysticism," explaining under philosophical guise the overwhelming closeness of the origin beyond God. That this clothing is full of holes suggests to us the fire that consumed him. The struggle for the right concept, when it has recourse to paradox, turns into combat, and, *after* reasonings and commentaries, at last invites silence.

I gratefully acknowledge the help I have received in the preparation of the American edition of this book, and especially wish to thank Leonard Bushinski, who prepared the first draft, and Alan Kusinitz, who revised my own translation. I also thank Professor Bernhard Welte of Freiburg, Germany, for decisive insights into Meister Eckhart's thinking at a very early stage of this work. The book is gratefully dedicated to Professor Jeanne Ancelet-Hustache of Paris for her enthusiastic encouragement.

MEISTER ECKHART
Mystic and Philosopher

Chapter
One

SERMON,
"JESUS ENTERED"

(INTRAVIT JESUS IN QUODDAM CASTELLUM ET MULIER
QUAEDAM, MARTHA NOMINE, EXCEPIT ILLUM IN DOMUM SUAM,
Luke 10:38)

[1] I have spoken a word, first in Latin, which is written in the Gospel and which is translated so: "Our Lord Jesus Christ went up into a little castle and was received by a virgin who was a wife."

Now then, pay close attention to this word: it was necessary that it be a virgin by whom Jesus was received. "Virgin" designates a human being who is devoid of all foreign images, and who is as void as he was when he was not yet.

Observe that it could be asked how it is possible that a person already born and already using reason could be as devoid of all images as when he was not yet; in fact he does know many things, and all these are images. How then can he be so void?

[2] Listen closely to the instruction that I am going to give you. I could have so vast an intelligence that all the images that all human beings have ever received and those that are in God himself were comprehended in my intellect; however, if I were in no way attached to them, to the point that in everything I do or neglect to do, I did not cling to any of them with attachment —with its before and its after—but if in this present now I kept myself unceasingly free and void for the beloved will of God and its fulfillment, then I should indeed be a virgin, without the ties of all the images, as truly as I was when I was not yet.

[3] I say besides: for man to be a virgin does not take away any of the works he has ever done; of all this he keeps himself virginal and free, without any impediment to the supreme truth,

3

just as Jesus was free and void and virginal in himself. Since the masters say that only the likeness of the like establishes union, he who is to receive the virginal Jesus must himself be virginal and free.

[4] Now pay attention and look! If a human were to remain a virgin forever, he would never bear fruit. If he is to become fruitful, he must necessarily be a wife. "Wife," here, is the noblest name that can be given to the mind, and it is indeed more noble than "virgin." That man should receive God in himself is good, and by this reception he is a virgin. But that God should become fruitful in him is better; for the fruitfulness of a gift is the only gratitude for the gift. The spirit is wife when in gratitude it gives birth in return and bears Jesus back into God's fatherly heart.

[5] Many excellent gifts are received in virginity but are not born back into God with wifely fruitfulness and thankful praise. These gifts spoil and perish, so that man becomes neither happier nor better through them. His virginity does not avail him anything, for he is only a virgin, but not also a wife with total fruitfulness. Here is the damage. This is why it is said: "Jesus went up into a little castle and was received by a virgin who was a wife." It must necessarily be so, as I have just said.

[6] Spouses rarely bear more than one fruit in a year. But it is another kind of spouse that I have in mind this time: all those who with attachment cling to prayer, to fasting, to vigils, and to all kinds of exterior exercises and mortifications. Attachment to any work, which deprives you of the freedom to serve God in this present now and to follow him alone in the light by which he instructs you what to do and what not to do, free and new in each now, as if you did not possess, nor desire, nor indeed could do anything else; every such attachment or every premeditated work which deprives you of this ever new freedom, I now call a year, for your mind does not bear fruit as long as it has not accomplished the work that you held with attachment. You have confidence neither in God nor in yourself, until you have carried out the work that you have grasped with attachment; otherwise you

will not have peace. This is why you do not bear fruit unless you are finished with your own work. This is how a "year" should be understood. Even then the fruit is still small, for it is born from attachment to the work and not from liberty. These I call spouses, because they are tied to attachment. As I have just said, they bear few fruits, and even these are quite small.

[7] A virgin who is a wife, free and disengaged from attachment, is at all times equally close to God and to herself. She bears many fruits, which are big, neither more nor less than God himself. This virgin who is a wife produces this fruit and this birth, and she bears fruits, a hundred or a thousand times a day, yes incessantly, by giving birth and by becoming fruitful from the most noble ground. To say it even better: truly, she is fruitful out of the same ground from which the Father begets his eternal Word, and she begets together with him. For Jesus, the light and the reflection of the fatherly heart—as Saint Paul says, he is an honor and a reflection of the father's heart, and his radiance shines through the father's heart with power—this Jesus is united to her, and she is united to him, and she shines and is resplendent with him, one identical unity, a pure and clear light in the father's heart.

[8] I have already said often: there is a power in the mind which touches neither time nor flesh: it emanates from the spirit and remains in the spirit and is totally spiritual. In this power, God is fully verdant and flowering, in all the joy and all the honor that he is in himself. There reigns such a dear joy, so incomprehensibly great a joy, that no one can ever fully speak of it. For in this power, the eternal Father is ceaselessly begetting his eternal Son, in such a way that this power begets the Son of God together with him, and begets itself as this selfsame Son in the identical power of the Father.

[9] If a man possessed an entire kingdom or all the goods of the earth, and abandoned them totally for God and became one of the poorest people who had ever lived on earth; if with this God sent him so much to suffer as no one had ever suffered; if he endured all this even to death; and if then God granted him

only once to contemplate in a glimpse what he is like in this power, his joy would be so great that all this suffering and this poverty would still be too small a thing. Furthermore, if afterwards God never granted him the kingdom of heaven, he would still have received a reward too great for what he had suffered.

[10] For God is in this power as in the eternal now. If the spirit were at all times united to God in this power, a man could never grow old. Indeed, the now in which God made the first man, and the now in which the last man is to perish, and the now in which I am speaking are all equal in God and are nothing but one sole and same now. Look! This man dwells in one sole and same light with God: this is why there is in him neither suffering nor succession, but only an equal eternity. In truth, this man is bereft of all wonder, and in him all things are present in their essence. Therefore he gets nothing new from things to come nor from any chance: he dwells in a single now which is in all time and unceasingly new. Such a divine sovereignty is in this power.

[11] There is another power, equally incorporeal; it emanates from the spirit and remains in the spirit and is totally spiritual. In this power, God glows and burns without ceasing, in all his riches, in all his sweetness, and in all his delight. Truly, within this power is so great a joy and so great an unmeasurable delight, that no one can fully tell nor reveal it. I say it again: if there were a single human whose intelligence, were it only for an instant, could see according to the truth the delight and the joy which reign therein, all he may ever have suffered or that God may have wished him to suffer would be a trifle, indeed a nothing; even more, it would be for him entirely a joy and a pleasure.

[12] Do you want to know correctly if your suffering is your own or God's? You can tell it in this way: if you suffer for the love of yourself, in whatever way it be, this suffering hurts and is hard for you to bear. But if you suffer for the love of God and for God alone, that suffering does not hurt and is not hard to bear, for it is God who carries the burden. In all truth! If there were a man who liked to suffer for God and purely for God alone, and if on this man fell in a single blow all the suffering that all men

have ever suffered, and all the suffering the entire world bears, it would not hurt him and would not weigh him down, for it is God who would carry the burden. If a hundredweight were placed on my neck, but someone else supported it above my neck, I should load myself with a hundred hundredweights as willingly as with a single one, for this would not weigh me down and would not hurt me. Briefly, those things a man suffers for God and for God alone, God makes light and gentle for him. As I have already said at the beginning of the sermon: "Jesus went into a little castle and was received by a virgin who was a wife." Why? It was necessary that she be a virgin and at the same time a wife. Now I have told you that Jesus was received. But I have not yet said what this little castle is. So at present I wish to speak of it.

[13] I have sometimes said that there is a power in the mind, the only one that is free. Sometimes I have said that it is a guardian of the mind; sometimes I have said that it is a light of the mind; sometimes I have said that it is a spark. Here is what I say now: it is neither this nor that, and yet it is a something. It is raised above this and that, higher than the sky is above earth. This is why I designate it now in a nobler way than I have ever done before, though it resists nobleness and fashion, and sur- passes them by far. It is free of all names and devoid of all forms, entirely bare and free, as void and free as God is in himself. It is perfect unity and simplicity as God is unity and simplicity, so that in no way can one peer into it.

[14] In this same power of which I have spoken, in which God is verdant and flowering with his entire divinity, and the spirit in God—in this same power, I say, the Father begets his only Son as truly as in himself, since he truly lives in this power; and the spirit, in harmony with the Father, begets the same sole Son and itself as this same Son, and it is this same Son, in this light, and it is the truth. If you could grasp this with my heart, you would understand well what I say, for it is true, and the truth says it itself.

[15] Look and see: this little castle in the mind of which I am speaking and which is my intention, is so one and simple, ele-

vated above every fashion, that the noble power of which I have
spoken is not worthy to pry, were it only once for a moment, into
this little castle; and also the other power of which I have spoken,
in which God does not cease to glow and burn with all his riches
and all his delight, would not dare to ever cast a glance into it:
this castle is one and simple, an identical unity so highly elevated
above every mode and above every power that no power nor any
mode can ever look into it, not even God himself. In all truth and
as truly as God lives! God himself will never peer into it, not even
for an instant, and has never looked into it insofar as he possesses
attributes and according to the propriety of his Persons. This is
easily understood, for this identical unity is without mode and
propriety. This is why, if God is ever to catch a glimpse of it, it
will cost him all his divine names and the propriety of his Persons; he will have to leave all this outside, if he ever wishes to
look inside. Rather, insofar as he is simple and one, without any
mode or propriety, he is neither the Father, nor the Son, nor the
Holy Spirit in this sense, and yet he is something that is neither
this nor that.

You see, insofar as he is one and simple, he penetrates into this
unity that I call the little castle in the mind, but otherwise he will
not enter into it in any way; it is only thus that he penetrates into
it and is already within. With this part of itself the mind is equal
to God and not otherwise. What I have told you is the truth; I
give you truth itself as witness and my soul as pledge.

May we so be a little castle in which Jesus ascends and is
received and abides eternally with us the way that I have said:
may God help us in this. Amen.

ANALYSIS AND COMMENTARY

The text of Meister Eckhart which we have just read[1] is very representative. In a careful, but also necessarily interpretative, reading we are going to repeat one by one the paragraphs of this sermon. The content of Eckhart's statements will be revelatory of his thought, but so will be the order of their progression itself. However, this order reveals its inner necessity only to a thoughtful reading. Exegesis and interpretation; *lexis*, listening to the words, and *theoria*, listening to the unique thought addressed to us, will mark out the path. Only in this manner will the understanding of the text be given to us.

[1] What Does It Mean "To Be Virgin"?

I have spoken a word, first in Latin, which is written in the Gospel and which is translated so: "Our Lord Jesus Christ went into a little castle and was received by a virgin who was a wife."

Now then, pay close attention to this word: it was necessary that it be a virgin by whom Jesus was received. "Virgin" designates a human being who is devoid of all foreign images and who is as void as he was when he was not yet.

Observe that it could be asked how it is possible that a person already born and already using reason could be as devoid of all images as when he was not yet; in fact he does know many things, and all these are images. How then can he be so void?

The title and its translation. After having read in Latin the gospel of the day, Meister Eckhart translates into German the phrase which serves as a starting point for his sermon. This translation is loose: the English (and German) "went up" adds a nuance that the Latin verb *intravit* does not have; *Jesus* becomes "Our Lord Jesus Christ"; the active of the Latin version *excepit* is turned into the passive, "was received"; and the mention of the *domus* is omitted altogether. The translation is even erroneous, as *mulier quaedam, Martha nomine* does not signify "a virgin who was a wife." Besides, we should not know how to determine if the

9

preacher wants to make "virgin" correspond to *mulier* (woman) or to *Martha*. In both cases, Eckhart translates the name of Martha either by "virgin" or by "wife." However, the equivalence between *Martha* and "wife"—more precisely "mistress of the house"—is authorized by the traditional exegesis of this passage. The procedure of translating proper names is as ancient as Chrisian revelation.[2] In his sermons, Meister Eckhart frequently establishes more or less arbitrary connections between biblical names and philosophical concepts. He himself explains this hermeneutic principle: in interpreting the Scripture, he says, it is always important to elucidate the hidden meaning under the letter.[3] Therefore this translation of the verse from Luke should not surprise us. As the following will show, all the terms in this verse contain unexpected significance: beginning with "virgin," the text of the Scripture undergoes a modification and becomes more profound. However, the question remains open as to whether and to what extent a thought can be called of biblical inspiration if the elaboration of the new meaning of the sacred text cannot but do violence to its letter.

Detecting the architectural pattern of the sermon has been made easier by the preacher himself, who almost always introduces each new step in his train of thought by some oratory formula or through brief imperative phrases directed to his audience. For instance, he says, "Now then, pay close attention to this word"; later he says, "Look," "Listen well," "I say besides," "Now pay attention and look."

> It was necessary that it be a virgin by whom Jesus was received. "Virgin" designates a human being who is devoid of all foreign images and who is as void as he was when he was not yet.

This interpretation of the word "virgin" calls upon a philosophical rather than a biblical tradition. The "necessity" which Meister Eckhart evokes contains an allusion to the theory of the imprint which a representation places upon the intellect.

The reception of Jesus by a "virgin" can be compared to that of an image by the intellect: if the intellect is to receive an image, it is necessary that it be empty of the determination that the image brings: *entbildet*. When the image enters into you, God must withdraw with all his divinity; then you belong to the images, and no longer to God. The adult "knows many things, and all these are images." This is why the intellect must be entirely empty, in a state of pure receptivity, to completely accommodate the whole Jesus. This receptivity is the meaning of Eckhart's concept of virginity.[4]

Whoever wants to receive Jesus must become as free of all representations "as he was when he was not yet." Before I was, before my birth on earth, I existed according to a mode before every mode. I was not yet that being who knows things by mediation of representations or phantasms: I was entirely free of every image taken from the world, since I was not of the world. In this original existence, when I was and was not yet, I had no need attaching me to the knowledge of sensible things by representations drawn from the sensible: no images were in me. The totality of things was not foreign to me as are representations, for everything held together in me through its "idea." In this preexistence, each idea was equally near all the others; thanks to their simultaneous possession, I was entirely "free," *ledic,* "virgin" of all images.

Whoever wishes to receive Jesus must be freed of all exterior images and become as free as he was before coming into the world.

Meister Eckhart does not dwell on this eternal existence of man before his coming into the world. He rather describes for his hearers the way which leads them to a commitment, proposing to them a way of liberation and of recovering original freedom, for this alone matters. The remainder of the sermon repeats in many forms this invitation to a path open to existence, so that the hearer may commit himself to such a path and pursue it.

Undoubtedly this first paragraph contains an allusion to the Virgin Mary, since it can be equally translated: "it necessarily had to be a virgin by whom Jesus was conceived." The word used by Eckhart, *enpfangen,* means "to conceive" as well as "to receive." But this allusion is of secondary importance, since from the beginning the preacher puts forward his own understanding of virginity, which we shall call "wandering."

This meaning, apart from the influence of Augustine, is inspired by what can be termed Platonist Albertinism, which flourished in Germany during the 14th century. It held that creatures preexist from all eternity in God, by their ideal being. The theory of eternal preexistence of man and of things before their appearance in this world is not, then, an invention of Meister Eckhart.

Plato outlined this doctrine in his dialogue "Meno." In it Socrates asks the question concerning the origin of truth: How is a true opinion possible? From where does the tenor of the truth of a proposition stem, what means are at man's disposal to find solutions concerning things of which he has no previous knowledge? Socrates demonstrates that the human being through recollection finds truths buried within himself just like traces and seeds of an otherwise forgotten state. To illustrate his theory, he brings forth from a slave who does not know geometry the elementary principles of this discipline. Thus proof is given of the preexistence of the soul, and Socrates is satisfied that this ancient doctrine, which he now adopts, is adequately explained: "They say that the soul of man is immortal, and at one time has an end, which is termed dying, and at another time is born again, but that it is never destroyed."[5] Through its successive immersions into the world of bodies, the soul reveals that it is of the family of ideas, naturally inhabiting the intelligible world which is its fatherland. Elsewhere Plato explains that in this other world it is the soul "which dispenses and procures truth and intelligence."[6] Before its birth here on earth, it contemplated all things in their ideas, hence remaining marked with truth and intelligence.

Even though Meister Eckhart had not read the Greek philosophers, their thought had become in many ways common doctrine in Christianity since the age of the Fathers. Without a great risk of error we can state that the true source behind the paradoxical expression "as free as he was when he was not" is the Platonic doctrine of the preexistence of the soul, which Eckhart knew perhaps, though somewhat altered, through Origen. In this existence before existence, man was free of every image or representation coming from things; everything that is was near him just as an idea is "near" another idea.

Eckhart, however, modifies in an original and decisive manner this traditional doctrine. " 'Virgin' designates a human being who is devoid of all foreign images, and who is as void as he was when he was not yet." This original freedom appears not as lost, but as something to be discovered: it is ahead of us as the goal of a liberation, i.e., of a becoming which consists of detachment from images. What does this mean?

Neither the theory of the images in the intellect nor the theory of the preexistence of the soul is Meister Eckhart's own device. The latter is Platonic. The former has been amply developed by Aristotle in his treatise on the soul, and like the theory of ideas was well known in the period in which Meister Eckhart taught. It is probably through Thomas Aquinas's commentary on Aristotle that Eckhart came under the influence of this current of thought.

As the eye must be without any color in order to be able to register

all colors, and as the palate must be without any specific taste in order
to be able to savor all flavors, so the intellect must be entirely receptive,
virgin of all images, if it is to know all images.[7] Thus the necessary bond,
according to Meister Eckhart, between virginity and the reception of
Jesus in the mind is based on the Aristotelian philosophy of the receptive intellect.

Meister Eckhart integrates both traditions, the Platonic and the Aristotelian, into a new context by blending the theory of the preexistence
of the soul and that of the receptive intellect. From this amalgam results
the Eckhartian dictum that man become "devoid of all foreign images,
as void as he was when he was not yet." In Meister Eckhart's interpretation of Plato and Aristotle the absence of determination, which characterizes both the soul in its first principle and the receptive intellect,
becomes an imperative. Man has been virgin, ledic, in his preexistence,
he is always thus in his intellect, and he must become so again in his
entire being.

Both elements of doctrine are thus recast not in a theoretical dogma
of what man is, but as a practical guide to what he must become.
Somehow man is invited to retrace the growth of his rational life.

[2, 3] A New Commerce with Things: Detachment

Listen closely to the instruction that I am going to give you. I could have
so vast an intelligence that all the images that all human beings have ever
received and those that are in God himself were comprehended in my
intellect; however, if I were in no way attached to them, to the point that
in everything I do or neglect to do, I did not cling to any of them with
attachment—with its before and its after—but if in this present now I
kept myself unceasingly free and void for the beloved will of God and its
fulfillment, then I should indeed be a virgin, without the ties of all the
images, as truly as I was when I was not yet.

The key word of the second paragraph is *eigenschaft,* attachment. It
can also mean ownership. To be attached to images, and through them
to be attached to things as to a property, leaves the mind stupefied and
forms an obstacle to receptivity.

I could have so vast an intelligence that all the images which all men have
ever received and those which are in God himself were comprehended in
my intellect. . . .

This oratorical hypothesis of someone who would have knowledge of all things together is reminiscent of the beginning of the "Hymn to Charity" by Saint Paul.[8] Meister Eckhart adopts it here to suggest the dimensions of his teaching: even from the highest knowledge we must be detached if we want to be as free and as void as we were in our preexistence and as we still are in our intellect. Whatever my knowledge may be, I can nevertheless become "virgin," for all my knowledge will not hinder the reception of Jesus in me unless I possess that knowledge avidly. Attachment wounds liberty. We see that what encumbers the mind and is opposed to spiritual virginity is not representation as such, but avid attachment to representations.

One thing alone matters: to loosen the grip over things and to dispossess oneself. Leaving behind all attachment, I shall receive in exchange serenity; having attained this I shall be as free as I was when I was not. The path of Meister Eckhart is the path of detachment.

This same paragraph establishes a link between what Eckhart calls attachment and temporality. A man attached to things is stretched between a "before" and an "after," or between past and future. He lives in duration, while detachment dwells in "this present now" (*in disem gegenwertigen nû*). A detached man lives in the instant. The text speaks of "everything I do or neglect to do," that is, of works. The works are paralleled with the intellectual representations: we may cling to both of them as to a property. Having a culture and undertaking works are obstacles insofar as this culture and these works are acquired or carried out in duration, i.e., projected, realized, possessed. The "before" of a work is its project (further on we shall meet the expression "premeditated works"), the "after," its recompense. Project and recompense are marks of ownership and cannot be reconciled with the "beloved will of God." Duration is the mode of temporality corresponding to attachment.

The temporality of detachment, the instant, annihilates the project as well as the recompense. It is only itself. Whatever my knowledge may be and whatever my works may be, if in this present instant I dedicate myself to them without making them mine, if I remain as open and as free from entanglements as I was in the beginning, then I am truly detached. Detachment arises and is verified in such a "now" which is always new.

What exactly is the significance of this link between detachment and the instant? Numerous authors, pagan and Christian, have left descriptions of an instantaneous "raptus" in which the soul rejoins, in a happy ecstasy, the original fullness from which it comes. By practice or by sudden illumination, it runs away from the constraints of the here-below and, like a prisoner escaping from a dungeon, it savors the delights of the fatherland. It may seem that our text relates a similar experience: Meister Eckhart, having first spoken of the world of ideas from which we come, would here indicate the way of return for the time of ecstasy. However, nothing of the kind is meant here. Eckhart, in speaking of "this present now," indicates not any departure from time, but its acceptance with equanimity. He points towards a type of communion with things: what he says here of the instant, opposed to duration, describes a manner of moving in this world, not of evading it. Detachment carries a mark of "worldliness," since it designates a being among things, without restraint.

In contrast, a text of Plotinus will show in what terms the mystique of ecstasy is expressed:

> Many times it has happened: lifted out of the body into myself; becoming external to all other things and self-encentered; beholding a marvellous beauty; then, more than ever, assured of community with the loftiest order; enacting the noblest life, acquiring identity with the divine; stationing within it by having attained that activity; poised above whatsoever within the Intellectual is less than the Supreme: yet, there comes the moment of descent from intellection to reasoning, and after that sojourn in the divine, I ask myself how it happens that I can now be descending, and how did the Soul ever enter into my body, the Soul which, even within the body, is the high thing it has shown itself to be.[9]

In Eckhart there is no appeal to a privileged experience, no regret of falling back into the body after a repose in the divine, and above all no opposition between a higher world and a lower world into which the soul is resigned to redescend.

If in his comprehension of time Eckhart is indebted to Neoplatonic mysticism, he modifies its meaning throughout, moving away from an "ecstatic" comprehension to a "worldly" comprehension of the instant: flight from the present situation turns into a way of being with it. The apprenticeship to detachment has no other purpose than to make man "free and void for the beloved will of God and its fulfillment." And to the extent to which a man triumphs over attachment, Christ is received in a virgin spirit.

One of the key terms in the very rich vocabulary of detachment is *gelâzenheit,* in modern German *Gelassenheit.* We shall encounter this word again in another context, but its first significance is moral. It designates the attitude of a human who no longer regards objects and events according to their usefulness, but who accepts them in their autonomy. This attitude makes him renounce influences, and it produces equanimity. We can translate this word by "infinite resignation" and by "serenity." These two translations imply breaking the habit of possessing things and also oneself. *Lâzen, lassen,* signifies "to let" or "to let be," hence to restore freedom, to untie. It is only secondarily that the word means "to abandon," "to reject," or even "to ignore." He who has learned how "to let be" restores all things to their primitive freedom; he leaves all things to themselves. He has learned not to subject them to his projects; he has rid himself of any self-affirmation in which mixed curiosity and ambition inhibit him.

The teaching of Eckhart concerning detachment seems to come closer to the Stoic doctrine of apathy than to Plotinian descriptions of ecstasy. Both Eckhart and the Stoics speak of serenity, and both consider attachment as serenity's most formidable shackle. Attachment is sympathy; to such an attitude Epictetus precisely opposes that of apathy:

> Do not hestitate to sympathize with him who suffers as far as words go, and if it so chance, even to groan with him; but take heed that you do not also groan in your inner being.[10]

Epictetus advises his readers to deliver themselves from the deepest of all affections, sympathy for a friend who suffers, so they can fully exercise their reason. The wise will be so free that even his own sighs and tears will not affect his innermost lack of sympathy. If all emotions are thus eradicated from the inner being, even the exterior attitudes of sympathy will not disturb our apathy. This teaching assuredly suggests a trait that applies to both $\dot{\alpha}\pi\dot{\alpha}\theta\epsilon\iota\alpha$ and *gelâzenheit.* However, Eckhart cannot have had a great knowledge of the authors of the Stoa, and besides this historical difficulty, we shall see Meister Eckhart express an errant joy which is quite different from the Stoic reserve. The way of Stoic liberation passes through a continual and constant effort of the moral will: apathy and sympathy will always remain in struggle. This voluntarism is far from the "letting be" of Meister Eckhart. According to Eckhart, the will ultimately loses all its objects; it will remove rather than erect dams around man's inner being; it opens itself to things and lets them enter, as reflections of the Creator, into its very core.

Neoplatonism and Stoicism certainly brought some elements to Eckhart's teaching concerning detachment and *gelâzenheit,* but it can hardly be reduced to these schemes of thought which had already become the common property of western culture.

> I say besides: for man to be a virgin does not take away any of the works he has ever done; of all this he keeps himself virginal and free, without any impediment to the supreme truth, just as Jesus was free and void and virginal in himself. Since the masters say that only the likeness of the like establishes union, he who is to receive the virginal Jesus must himself be virginal and free.

This paragraph defines the condition that makes possible the union with Christ through his reception or conception. Such union is based on likeness. A man disengaged from all attachment (*eigenschaft*) to images and to works necessarily receives Jesus, to whom his new freedom likens him. Jesus, "free and void and virginal in himself," who without any attachment has accomplished his work of salvation, is the ideal and the reality of a being who has retrieved his original liberty, who is eminently detached.

Jesus, both the model and the goal of this union, defines the condition for us to become one with the Word: freed from all possession of images and works, following him on the way of detachment, we shall be "virgin" in order to receive the virginal Jesus. Exempt from all bonds of property to his own work, Christ has redeemed us; exempt from all attachment to images, the Christian conceives Jesus in a pure receptivity. Man renounces confining things according to their enjoyment. His disappropriated mind, void of images, likens him to the Son of God, uniting him to Jesus as one "virgin" receiving another "virgin."

Eckhart speaks of the end of a becoming: of union, as well as of its condition, likeness. Union on the ground of likeness is found in some classical authors in the proverbial form: "like comes to like."

An early application of this principle is found in the Aristotelian theory of knowledge. In a passage of his book on the soul, Aristotle declares that "like is known by like."[11] Thomas Aquinas, through whom Eckhart received the Aristotelian heritage, comments:

The truth is that knowledge is caused by the knower containing a likeness of the thing known; for the latter must be in the knower somehow.[12]

The starting point for the act of knowledge is otherness, but due to a resemblance between the two terms, namely the knower and the known, otherness is absorbed into unity: that is, the unity of the very act of knowing. In this sense "only the likeness of the like establishes union." Meister Eckhart's way of thinking, formed by the study of commentaries written by Thomas Aquinas, is in this sense then very Aristotelian.

The principle that the like is attracted to the like—"is moved towards the like"[13]—already surpasses the simple case of knowledge in Aristotle. In Plotinus[14] it gives way to a first metaphysics of union, and in Thomas Aquinas to the doctrine of the beatific vision,[15] a true treatise of "wandering identity" between man and God.

Let us now gather our first results. As an Aristotelian, Eckhart transposes to the level of the progressive accomplishment of detachment the birth of a union by which Aristotle had characterized the act of knowing; as a Neoplatonist, he understands likeness as assimilation, as conquered resemblance. The union by which detachment is achieved is more than noetic, it is of the order of existence.

Meister Eckhart transposes to the present life the unendingly growing union with God in which Thomas Aquinas had recognized the dynamism of the eternal vision. Like him, he pushes the Aristotelian theory of knowledge to extremes where, while keeping its terms, it awakes to a becoming; like him, he enriches it with contributions of a philosophy of the One. However, we shall see Eckhart draw some conclusions from this confrontation between the Aristotelian tradition and the Neoplatonic tradition which Thomas Aquinas had still shied away from.

[4-7] The Birth of the Son in Detachment

Now pay attention and look! If a human were to remain a virgin forever, he would never bear fruit. If he is to become fruitful, he must necessarily be a wife. "Wife," here, is the noblest name that can be given to the mind, and it is indeed more noble than "virgin." That man should receive God in himself is good, and by this reception he is a virgin. But that God should become fruitful in him is better; for the fruitfulness of a gift is the only gratitude for the gift. The spirit is wife when in gratitude it gives birth in return and bears Jesus back into God's fatherly heart.

Detachment has been described as a passive attitude: the receptive intellect and virginity—one a philosophical figure of thought, the other a biblical—both speak of the absence of any determination of the mind. Eckhart now exposes the active side of detachment. According to the first figure, borrowed from Aristotle, he treats the active intellect; according to the second, of biblical origin, the active complement of "virgin" is "wife." But behind these schemes of discourse there lies the same appeal to reintegrate the primitive freedom before the self disperses among images.

Meister Eckhart deems the activity that completes detachment superior to passive reception of Jesus in the mind: " 'Wife,' here, is the noblest name that can be given to the mind, and it is much more noble than 'virgin.' "

The reception of God, whom Eckhart here no longer calls "Jesus," in us is a gift which must bear fruit: detachment is completed by fertility. God becomes fertile in a mind deliberately deprived of all images and of all works, so that "the spirit is wife when in gratitude it gives birth in return, and bears Jesus back into God's fatherly heart." By one and the same act a detached mind brings forth the Son in itself and in God. In the supreme emptiness of detachment, man and God are united in fertility; one sole determination joins them together: that of giving birth. United to God in begetting, man returns to God in an act of supreme thankfulness everything that he possesses; he gives back to God what he has received from God, namely the Son. The common determination that joins God and man is operational: a man who has left everything so that he may welcome the Son in turn brings him forth in the paternal heart of God. This is the highest activity into which serenity unfolds. He who has freed himself of all that is his own engenders with the Father the Son whom the Father has made to be born in the mind.

Aristotle said of the active intellect that it "makes" all things: "To the one intellect, which becomes all things, corresponds the other, which makes all things," that is, it makes them intelligible by the production of a word. This intellect, he writes, is "separable and impassive and unmixed, being in its essential nature an activity."[16] Thomas Aquinas repeats these expressions, and he too speaks of a "making" of the intellect.[17]

In their analysis of knowledge the intellect appeared to Aristotle and his disciples as extracting intelligible forms out of the things in which these intelligibles were buried. Because of this type of analysis it is necessary to posit an active power in the mind which effectively confers intelligibility upon that which in itself is only potentially intelligible. In Aristotelian and Thomistic systematizations, the active intellect has the task of conferring intelligibility on the objects. This operation is completed by the production of a word in the mind. In this way the active intellect "produces," "makes" beings by causing them to appear to the mind, and by naming them. As a pure principle of cognition it cannot be mixed with the sensible. The intellectualism of traditional metaphysics entails that attributes such as "separate" (namely from the sensible), "immutable," and "unmixed" mean precisely the same thing as "spiritual" and "in act."

While in Aristotle and Thomas Aquinas this schema of active intellection and of the production of the word is applied only to the knowledge of the world, Meister Eckhart adapts it to the context of his theology of union: the detached man conceives and engenders the Word itself, the Son of God. We never find such identification even in the writings of Augustine, the initiator in the West of the Stoic doctrine of the interior word. Augustine indeed speaks of "the word of man, by the likeness of which the Word of God may be somehow seen as in an enigma." But while stressing the traits common to the word "which is begotten from the knowledge that continues in the mind" and the Word engendered in the bosom of the Trinity, he never tires of recalling the profound dissimilarity between them.[18]

The statement of Meister Eckhart according to which man gives birth to the enternal Word (he "gives birth in return" and "bears Jesus back into God's fatherly heart") should be understood as an original adaptation of Aristotelian and Augustinian doctrinal elements.[19]

Many excellent gifts are received in virginity but are not born back into God with wifely fruitfulness and thankful praise. These gifts spoil and perish, so that man becomes neither happier nor better through them. His virginity does not avail him anything, for he is only a virgin, but not also a wife with total fruitfulness. Here is the damage. This is why it is said: "Jesus went up into a little castle and was received by a virgin who was a wife." It must necessarily be so, as I have just said.

In this paragraph, Eckhart repeats the main themes of the development which has preceded: virginity, fertility, gift, thanksgiving, and bearing fruit in return. Following his preference for sharp and paradoxical expressions, he declares that he who does not become a "wife" has detached himself in vain: "His virginity does not avail him anything, for he is only a virgin, but not also a wife with total fruitfulness." The repetition of the text from the gospel of Luke shows that in all this Eckhart intends to do the work of an exegete.

> Spouses rarely bear more than one fruit in a year. But it is another kind of spouse that I have in mind this time: all those who with attachment cling to prayer, to fasting, to vigils, and to all kinds of exterior exercises and mortifications. Attachment to any work, which deprives you of the freedom to serve God in this present now and to follow him alone in the light by which he instructs you what to do and what not to do, free and new in each now, as if you did not possess, nor desire, nor indeed could do anything else; every such attachment or every premeditated work which deprives you of this ever new freedom, I now call it a year, for your mind does not bear fruit as long as it has not accomplished the work that you held with attachment. You have confidence neither in God nor in yourself, until you have carried out the work that you have grasped with attachment; otherwise you will not have peace. This is why you do not bear fruit unless you are finished with your own work. This is how a "year" should be understood. Even then the fruit is still small, for it is born from attachment to the work and not from liberty. These I call spouses, because they are tied to attachment. As I have just said, they bear few fruits and even these are quite small.

> A virgin who is a wife, free and disengaged from attachment, is at all times equally close to God and to herself. She bears many fruits, which are big, neither more nor less than God himself. This virgin who is a wife produces this fruit and this birth, and she bears fruits, a hundred or a thousand times a day, yes incessantly, by giving birth and by becoming fruitful from the most noble ground. To say it even better: truly, she is fruitful out of the same ground from which the Father begets his eternal Word, and she begets together with him. For Jesus, the light and the reflection of the fatherly heart—as Saint Paul says, he is an honor and a reflection of the father's heart and his radiance shines through the father's heart with power—this Jesus is united to her, and she is united to him, and she shines and is resplendent with him, one identical unity, a pure and clear light in the father's heart.

Taking on oneself a work, and carrying it out well, may be called bearing fruit. Yet, Meister Eckhart says, we must distinguish two kinds of "fruits." The first corresponds to what he calls a "premeditated work"; such a fruit, he says, possesses man. The production of this fruit dulls his serenity, it hinders him from being "free and new in each now." The most eloquent example is procreation: spouses are so entirely attached to their fruit that they do not rest until they have carried out their common enterprise. Moreover "spouses rarely bear more than one fruit a year." The length of time that these works require indicates how poor they are. Worst of all, they overwhelm us: "You have confidence neither in God nor in yourself, unless you have carried out the work that you have seized with attachment." This type of work demands attention. In regard to the nuns to whom the preacher addresses himself, the works—which they believe they possess but which in reality possess them—are prayer, fasting, vigils, and all the exercises and "mortifications" which the religious usually practice.

The second kind of fruit is described in paragraph [7]. It deals with the fruit which is formed in detachment. A series of expressions in this paragraph concerning the relationship between God and the detached man may surprise us. A "virgin" who is a "wife," Eckhart says, is "at all times equally close to God and to herself"; she likewise engenders "out of the same ground from which the Father begets his eternal Word"; her fruit is as great, neither more nor less than God himself; "Jesus is united to her and she is united to him"; "and she shines and is resplendent with him, one identical unity."

These statements should be read with care. They designate something very precise. The key to their comprehension is to be sought in the biblical expression "to bear fruit,"[20] which describes an event. "To bear fruit," "to engender," "to shine and be resplendent," these verbs speak of a process that accomplishes itself. According to the ancient theory of light, when a ray of sun illuminates a colored surface, there are not two things that shine, on the one hand light and on the other the color, but one single thing; there exists, properly speaking, nothing any longer except the event of the shining glare itself; everything shines in an "identical unity."

It is the same between God and the detached man. A free man is at all times equally close to God and to himself: namely, in the accomplishment of the divine will. By his obedience he becomes one with God, whose benevolent will inundates man. The comprehension of the union here set to work is based on an operative identity: disposed to obey the will of God in an always present now, the detached man is as near to God as is the eternal Son. He becomes the Son and penetrates into the fatherly heart of God. It will not surprise us that this identity between the light and the illuminated object, between the Father and the engendered Son, will have consequences for the understanding of being in Meister Eckhart. We see that the context of the expressions of union in Meister Eckhart differs considerably from a mystique of the vision, in which one "contemplates" the divine sovereignty and, "forgetting all things, entirely ignores oneself and penetrates even into God."[21] On the contrary, in the process of detachment, the fruit that man bears is man himself: he is delivered to himself, brought back from dispersion and constituted Son of God in the very being of his mind.

However, Eckhart goes a step further; sonship is not the last stage of detachment. Being reborn in the Father as Son of God, as the unique Son, is becoming fertile "out of the most noble ground." From this brief allusion it appears only that the word "ground" means, in Meister Eckhart's use, some interior region of man, of an unsurpassable intimacy. It is here that receptivity must be changed into fruitfulness. The following says that out of the "same" ground from which the Father engenders his eternal Son, the detached man engenders the same Son at the same time. The "same" ground, the "same" Son, the "same" time: this implies clearly that the identity of God and man is altogether related to the birth of the Son. The Father begets, and man begets jointly with him. The second type of fruit is in the last analysis the Son himself. At each instant the detached man engenders the eternal Son of the Father; and in order to emphasize that he is speaking of the Son in his divinity, Eckhart adds that this fruit is great, "neither more nor less than God himself."

Thus is outlined the doctrine of the operative identity between man and God in the begetting of the Son. To separate these expressions of union from the process of detachment would assuredly result in confusing man and God for some indistinct totality. But the thought of Meister Eckhart is quite different. He is thinking of the identity of the nonidentical. His theory must be viewed as a distant reflection of Aristotle: as "receptive" intellect, man's mind receives the Son; as "active" intellect, it bears him forth in return into God. The identity of the distinct is realized in this reciprocity.

Thomas Aquinas borrowed from Aristotle several surprising expressions of identity, including his tenet that "the thinking and that which is thought are identical."[22] Thomas Aquinas in his commentary on this passage wrote:

> The actually understood object and the actually understanding subject are one being, just as the actually sensed object and the actually sensing subject are one being.[23]

The expression *in actu*, "actually," is repeated four times in this sentence. Broadened by Meister Eckhart into the domain of deification, the identity of the act of knowledge becomes the operative identity in the reciprocity of begetting.[24] This broadening of perspective, in Meister Eckhart, is due to another current of thought to which he is indebted. With regard to his theory of the word, Aristotle, the Neoplatonists, and Augustine are joined in Eckhart by a particular school of eastern patristic tradition.

The birth of the Son in the ground of the heart of the believer is a theme of early Christian instruction which, from the second century A.D., appears in the writings of the Greek Fathers. In the last chapter of the "Letter to Diognetes," we read that the Word is incessantly born in the heart of the saints:

> It is for this that he has been sent: that he may be manifested to the world, he who, despised by his people, has been preached by the apostles and believed by the nations. He who was from the beginning, he has appeared as new, and was found old, and he is always reborn young in the heart of the saints. Eternal, he is today recognized as Son.[25]

Clement of Alexandria develops this same theme in regard to baptism, which he says inaugurates in our hearts the life of the Word:

> The Baptized "in whom dwells the Word, possesses the beautiful form of the Word; he is assimilated to God and he is beautiful himself." It is then rightly that Heraclitus said: "Men are gods and gods are men." This mystery is indeed revealed in the Word: God in man and man, God.[26]

Hippolytus, to whom has been attributed the last chapter of the "Letter" whose authenticity seems contestable, likewise testifies in favor of the tradition that we are tracing. But it is especially to Origen that the theme of the birth of God in us owes its broad diffusion, before being brushed aside by the rational unfoldings of medieval Scholasticism. In the homily by Origen on Jeremiah sentences are found that astonishingly foreshadow the sermon "Jesus Entered" of Meister Eckhart:

Blessed he who unceasingly is born of God. I say indeed: the just is born of God not once, but it is in each good work that he is always reborn, because God through it engenders the just. Our Lord is the brilliance of glory; but a brilliance does not appear once for all and then it ceases to appear: so many times as the light appears from which the brilliance emanates, so many times is born the brilliance of glory. Our Saviour is the wisdom of the Father. The wisdom is the brilliance of the eternal light. If then our Saviour is born incessantly—and it is purposely that is written: "before the hills he begets me" and not, as some translators who read badly: "he has begotten me," no: "he begets me"—if then the Lord is incessantly born of the Father, then to you also God gives birth in him. If you have the Spirit of sonship, he engenders you in each work, in each thought, and you become a child of God incessantly engendered in Christ Jesus.[27]

When Origen develops his theology of baptism he writes:

He who, among humans has not yet felt the Wisdom of God full of all splendors, for him Christ is not yet born, that is, he is not yet manifested, revealed, shown to him. But when even for such people the mystery of grace is disclosed, then for them too, when they will be converted to the faith, Christ will be born: in knowledge and within. And this is why it is rightly said that the Church incessantly forms and gives birth, in the baptized, to the masculine Word.[28]

For Origen, the union of the Word and the soul is accomplished by knowledge: to acquire knowledge is to become one with the Word. Knowledge leads the soul to the union.[29] "He who is known is mingled in a certain way with him who knows."[30]

We should remind ourselves here that it is not on knowledge that Meister Eckhart principally puts the emphasis.

The doctrinal lineage that we trace leads to Maximus Confessor. Some rather stereotyped expressions in his works show him faithful to the ancient teaching: by the practice of virtues, he says, "God comes incessantly to be engendered as a human, in those who are worthy of him."[31] The Word, he writes, descends into "the depths of the heart,"[32] its voice calls out in "the intimacy of the heart."[33]

By grace which calls, Christ comes incessantly to be engendered mystically (in the soul), by taking on flesh, through those who receive salvation: thus he makes the soul, by which he is brought forth, a mother, while allowing its virginity to remain intact.[34]

Each human being, inasmuch as he bears in himself the virtue which makes him "worthy," is called upon to give birth to the Word, to lend him in some way humanity so that he can again be incarnated. Although "virgin" he becomes "mother," that is, mother of the *Logos*, "for always and in every man the Word of God wishes the mystery of his incarnation to be realized."[35]

The tradition in which Meister Eckhart stands with regard to this point probably begins with the writings of Clement of Alexandria, who still used a vocabulary very close to that of the Bible. It underwent a philosophical development with Hippolytus and especially Origen, and it blossomed out into a systematized theology of union with God in Methodius, Gregory of Nazianzus, and Maximus.[36] How could Eckhart have been cognizant of a Greek school of thought from which he was separated by a millennium of Latin culture?[37]

It is believed that on the one hand he assiduously delved into the writings of Richard of Saint Victor and of Scotus Erigena. The latter, translator of "the venerable master and divine philosopher" Maximus, was the first in the West to have studied the writings of Origen. On the other hand, Albert the Great with his rich patristic culture, as well as the "Catena Aurea" of Thomas Aquinas, could equally have served as sources for Meister Eckhart. Nor can contact with the Cistercian monasteries, those centers of fourteenth-century spiritualism, be overlooked. In any case, Eckhart quotes readily from the homilies of Origen.

In conclusion, it seems that if the theology of the Greek Fathers remained faithful to an inspiration and a vocabulary above all biblical, this is not true of Eckhart. His teaching aims to go beyond union with God by the birth in us of the Word. According to him, not only does grace make the Son be born within us in his divinity, but the human being engenders the Son in God. This was the "active" side of detachment.

The preaching of the simultaneous and identical bearing forth of the Word, in the detached human being and in the bosom of the Father, cannot be entirely corroborated by patristic sources. It has been forged out of the Aristotelian theory of knowledge which it in turn surpasses, finally appearing foreign to both the Scripture and Greek philosophy. It is a matter of an originally patristic doctrine, boldly enlarged by the Aristotelian flavor. In this amalgamated form it is original to Meister Eckhart.

[8–10] The Divine Destiny of the Intellect

I have already said often: there is a power in the mind which touches neither time nor flesh: it emanates from the spirit and remains in the spirit and is totally spiritual. In this power, God is fully verdant and flowering, in all the joy and all the honor that he is in himself. There reigns such a dear joy, so incomprehensibly great a joy, that no one can ever fully speak of it. For in this power, the eternal Father is ceaselessly begetting his eternal Son, in such a way that this power begets the Son of God together with him, and begets itself as this selfsame Son in the identical power of the Father.

These lines are the heart of Eckhart's sermon. With the analysis of the first half of the text the broad contours of his original thought have progressively emerged: operative identity, birth of the Son simultaneously with the divine invasion, and strict reciprocity between the acting of the Father and the acting of the detached human being. In the second half of the sermon identity with God is delineated in three directions: in paragraph [8], identity is described as it occurs in the intellect; in paragraph [11], as it is achieved by the will; and at the end of the sermon, as it happens in man's being itself. It was because of this threefold theory of identity that Meister Eckhart was summoned to explain himself to the Inquisition. The text he wrote for his defense consists on this point of an attenuated version of the sermon "Jesus Entered":

It is exactly as it is said [in this sermon] that God, inasmuch as he is true, is received in the intellect, inasmuch as he is good in the will, which are powers in the mind; and that in his being he gives himself to the mind in its essence.[38]

The remaining parts of the sermon are devoted to these three kinds of union.

"There is a power in the mind which touches neither time nor flesh: it emanates from the spirit and remains in the spirit and is totally spiritual." Meister Eckhart speaks of what Franciscan mysticism called the "peak of the spirit,"[39] and what Augustine had called "the head, the eye, the face" of the soul.[40] Eckhart's purpose here is to describe the region of the spirit in which the intellectual union with God is accomplished: the region or power beyond time and flesh. "In that power, God is fully verdant and flowering." In the peak of the intellect, God lives and has always lived.

However, so as not to risk being misled from the true course of Eckhart's teachings, we shall refrain from searching for any assertion concerning the "nature" of the intellect in this passage. The concept of nature, in Meister Eckhart, is very complex. We have stressed that he speaks less of what man is prior to the itinerary of his existence, than of what he is destined to become. His claims are never to be taken as theses or results of analyses; they are not "scientific" in the same sense in which the ancients devoted themselves to metaphysics as a "science." His language is opposed to the language of metaphysics as an exhortation is opposed to verification: Meister Eckhart's words never state facts; rather, they open our eyes to new possibilities and, in making us see, they engage our existence on a new road.

An inquiry into the power in the mind above time and flesh,[41] in which God is verdant and flowering, is an inquiry into the "nature" of man under one condition only—that he let himself be. Man is naturally inhabited by God, but he must also yet achieve this as a task. In this sense man can be said to be naturally divine in his intellect. Divine inhabitation is given and ordained, inseparably. Man is not yet in full possession of his nature; he must first learn to let God carry out in him the birth of the Son, and must beget in turn, in God, this same Son, as the fruit of the union. If he then becomes what he is naturally, the intellectual power in him "begets itself as this selfsame Son, in the identical power of the Father."

On this subject again the theologians investigating the orthodoxy of Meister Eckhart's sayings disapproved of both its formulation and its content. Their objections as well as the responses of the defendant illustrate the positions of the real confrontation: a form of "wandering" thought, concerned with showing a way, is subject to the judgment of the "thetic" thought of late Scholasticism and is rejected as heterodox. Eckhart was summoned to appear before the tribunal of the bishop of Cologne to respond to accusations concerning his teaching. The minutes of the session of September 26, 1326, report that the following statement of his was suspected of being heretical:

> There is a power in the mind whose operation is identical with that of God. It creates and makes all things in union with God, and it does not possess anything in common with anything else; united to the Father it engenders the sole Son himself.[42]

This article of the prosecution, as well as the others that deal with the birth of the Son in the mind and in God,[43] indeed expresses the doctrine of Meister Eckhart as we have just encountered it in the sermon "Jesus Entered." Identity with God is bound to an operation (*werk, ereignis*) whose condition is detachment and whose consequence is the engendering of the Son.

Eckhart was anxious to answer publicly the accusations against this point of his doctrine. He had been a well-known public figure, and his trial was followed with interest, especially since it resulted partly from the intrigues of two of his own Dominican brothers. On February 13, 1327, he declared from the pulpit of the Church of the Preachers at Cologne:

> There is something in the mind of such a kind that, if the mind were entirely thus, it would be uncreated. This I have understood and understand to be true and even conform to the doctors, my colleagues, that is to say, if the mind were intellectual by essence. But I have never said nor felt that there is in the mind anything of the mind which is uncreated and uncreatable, because then the mind would be composed of created and uncreated; I have always written and taught quite the contrary.[44]

Before the bishop, he insisted on his good faith: "I may be in error, but I cannot be heretical, for error is a matter of the intellect, but heresy is a matter of will."[45]

To speak of "something of the mind which is uncreated and uncreatable" is not at all the same as affirming that the operation of the detached mind, "in the mind" and not "of the mind," is identical with the divine operation. The decisive point is this: Meister Eckhart in no way teaches a simple identity between the human intellect and God, but he teaches the imperative of an identity to be accomplished. Identity is not thought of here according to a nominal scheme,[46] but rather a verbal one.

Two forms of thought confront each other. The type of thought that urges a path upon existence can be called "imperative" thought; this is opposed to "indicative" thought, which apprehends the real and establishes a noetics of it. The first type of thought, that of Meister Eckhart, gives special attention to the possible, therefore to the future, or to what is ordained (*aufgegeben, ordonné*); the second pays heed only to the actual, to the present, or to the given (*gegeben, donné*). We can say that imperative thought and indicative thought differ from each other in their understanding of being: according to the first, being is known when a concrete existence assumes the path of detachment, which is the condition and the sole content at the same time of its understanding; according to the second, being is represented as the totality of objects comprehended by the mind. It is not by chance that Meister Eckhart chose to preach. His word calls upon a hearer. The word of his judges hardens into "treatises."

In this confrontation, however, we should grant to the prosecution, whom the defendant suspects of malice and "short and imbecilic intelligence,"[47] that the epistemology of Meister Eckhart, selected as it is from diverse currents of thought, can sometimes make one imagine a formal, entitative, identity between the intellect and God. This notwithstanding, it should nevertheless be recognized that what was at stake at the trial of Avignon was the priority either of Eckhart's "operative identity" or of the Scholastic "ontological identity" (ontology taken here as science of the real).

The Bull of Pope John XXII, *In Agro Dominico,* dated March 27, 1329, officially consecrates the interpretation of Meister Eckhart's texts on the intellect according to a type of an "indicative" rather than an "imperative" mode of thought. The description of a development of Christian existence, that is, of an existential becoming, once it is read in the fixed setting of a body of doctrine, takes on the aspect of a literally fabulous system. The sentence, which arose out of a misunderstanding about the form of thought that is in question, states that the accused "wished to know more than is necessary" and "turned himself from the truth to turn towards fables."[48] The Bull goes on to condemn as heretical the following proposition:

> There is a something in the mind which is uncreated and uncreatable. If the mind were entirely so, it would be uncreated and uncreatable; and that is the intellect.[49]

We recognize this sentence as the one already censured at the Cologne trial, but this time it is truncated. The verbs "to operate," "to create," "to make," "to beget," which alone could assure its correct understanding, are missing. In his defense at Avignon Eckhart is content simply to deny this proposition as "insane."[50] It indeed deals with the intellect as an entity and it ascribes to it attributes which belong only to God. Two families of language confront each other: the ecclesiastical institution at the end of a great period stiffens within an already curdled terminology, which can only lead to the condemnation of the one who breathes a new form of thought into the old body of metaphysical dogmata.

The fate that this point of his doctrine of the intellect underwent illustrates to what extent "the trial against the theses of the Master before the Pope's court at Avignon gives the impression of a trial brought to action by Being itself against the one who daringly forestalled its destiny."[51]

> If a man possessed an entire kingdom or all the goods of the earth, and abandoned them totally for God and became one of the poorest people who had ever lived on earth; if with this God sent him so much to suffer as no one had ever suffered; if he endured all this even to death; and if then God granted him only once to contemplate in a glimpse what he is like in this power, his joy would be so great that all this suffering and this poverty would still be too small a thing. Furthermore, if afterwards God never granted him the kingdom of heaven, he would still have received a reward too great for what he had suffered.

In order to stress the greatness of the human mind, capable of being united to God, Meister Eckhart has recourse here to somewhat artificial comparisons: supposing that a man possessed an entire kingdom, even all the goods of the earth; supposing further that he abandoned all those riches, and that besides his poverty God sent him more suffering than any other human being had ever suffered; if this man could contemplate with his own eyes but for a single instant the core of his intellect where God lives already and always, he would despite everything consider himself happiest of all human beings. His short vision would have overwhelmed him with so many joys that God, even if he excluded him from his Kingdom, could in no way diminish his happiness.

There is in this oratorical development an affirmation that is at the same time a negation concerning the relationship of man's mind to his happiness. On the one hand, beatitude is in man from the beginning. Even today man is blessed, if he follows the call to the union which reaches him. But on the other hand, there is no comparison between the work of man in his detachment and this happiness which is hidden in the intellect: voluntary impoverishment, be it as great as has just been described, in no case will earn him the joys with which he is overwhelmed; the reward of happiness at the term of detachment will be poured out to him without measurement.

The negativity that weakens detachment springs from the radical
inadequacy of man's work with regard to his beatitude. Detachment
proves powerless to procure happiness, hence it, too, is to be left. In this
final letting-be, detachment is abandoned insofar as it is still a "work"
of man. This step approaches regions that are not made by the human
hand. Man is no longer a burden to himself; his doing is identical with
God's. Detachment, the ascetic or moral phase of releasement, has come
to completion. Man is perfectly released, and in him "God is fully
verdant and flowering."

> For God is in this power as in the eternal now. If the spirit were at all times
> united to God in this power, a man could never grow old. Indeed, the now
> in which God made the first man, and the now in which the last man is
> to perish, and the now in which I am speaking are all equal in God and
> are nothing but one sole and same now. Look! this man dwells in one sole
> and same light with God: this is why there is in him neither suffering nor
> succession, but only an equal eternity. In truth, this man is bereft of all
> wonder, and in him all things are present in their essence. Therefore he
> gets nothing new from things to come nor from any chance: he dwells in
> a single now which is in all time and unceasingly new. Such a divine
> sovereignty is in this power.

Meister Eckhart had already distinguised the time of attachment,
duration, from that of detachment, the instant. Now he takes up this
inquiry again with relation to the transconceptual zone of the intellect
and to the representations of things in the detached intellect. The two
themes blend with each other in a development that is significant for
his form of thought.

The instantaneousness of detachment turns out to be a gauge of
eternity. The region of the intellect that is elevated above succession
acts as an incentive of the eternal in the present. "The now in which God
made the first man, and the now in which the last man is to perish, and
the now in which I am speaking are all equal in God, and are nothing
but one sole and same now." This simultaneity of all events in God also
applies in the same way to the human intellect, for "God is in this power
as in the eternal now." We shall presently see what this means.

The entire Aristotelian tradition teaches that time is derived from
movement: "Time is the number of the movement according to a before
and an after," writes Aristotle.[52] Thomas Aquinas interprets this "before and after" as defining the "continuous" movement of a physical

being, as opposed to the "instantaneous," discontinuous, operation of a spiritual being.[53]

In the same line Meister Eckhart distinguishes between continued time or duration and discontinued time or the instant. However, he chooses another criterion for distinction. The two modes of time differ not according to immateriality or materiality of a being, but according to moral attachment or detachment. In Eckhart's view it is not the opposition between a physical creature and a spiritual creature that is essential to the modes of temporality—duration and instant—but rather the opposition between the two ways man exists, attached or detached. It follows from this that only the detached man lives fully within the temporality of the spirit. As early as paragraph [3], Eckhart had denounced attachment as a manner of being which, "with its before and its after," ties us to succession: a man attached to things takes over their temporality. Here this denunciation receives its positive complement: each time and inasmuch as the intellect lets itself be, it enters into the fullness of the instant, which is eternity.

Eckhart certainly does not refuse the traditional teaching according to which the material or immaterial quality of a being determines the temporality of its change. He maintains, on the contrary, that only the intellect, which is the trace of immateriality in man, emerges from succession. But his attention leads him elsewhere; although man has never ceased to be a citizen of the eternal now in his spiritual nature, he must nonetheless, through an apprenticeship, become what he is by nature. Understood in this way detachment appears as the means by which time is humanized and human nature is temporalized: "nature" does not come fully to itself except in a detached being.

This theory of the temporality of detachment is connected by Eckhart to a certain comprehension of representation. To move among things in detachment is to live "in one sole and same light with God"; to whoever leaves everything, "all things are present in their essence." We shall see that this expression leads to a surprising and bold conception of man.

Does "essentially" mean the same thing as "intellectually"? Eckhart said in paragraph [2]: "I could have so vast an intelligence that all images ... were comprehended in my intellect," i.e., that all things are joined together in my intellect according to their phantasms or representations. But, according to this theory of mental schemes, things known do not come together in the human intellect "essentially" but only "accidentally"; representations are only the imprint or the figure of what is known. The different versions that the theory of ideas has undergone have in common that things are joined together "essentially" only in God.

In the vocabulary of the "form," to know is to exist according to the form of the known; but this form received in the intellect is not the form insofar as it gives being to the thing: in the spirit it is represented in a purely noetic mode, not in substance. The "intellectual" representation about which Meister Eckhart spoke earlier (paragraph [2]) therefore designates the mode according to which things exist in man, while in this paragraph he deals with the mode according to which they exist in God, that is, "essentially," or in their idea. Thus Eckhart brings the divine existence of forms down into man.

In a text from Eckhart's Commentary on the Gospel of John, we read: "The intellect is the place of representations or reasons, as it is said in the third book of *On the Soul*."[54] Eckhart is referring to the following text of Aristotle:

> It has been said well that the soul is a place of forms or ideas: except that this is not true for the whole soul, but only of the soul which can think, and again that the forms are there not in actuality but potentially.[55]

This is quite evidently, on the part of Aristotle, a reference to Plato, even a rectification of his theory of ideas.[56] Aristotle restricts the Platonic thesis as follows: it is correct to speak of the ideas of all things as residing in man's intellect, as long as one understands their presence to be potential: the intellect can know all that there is. Its original openness ("virginity") allows it to receive representations of everything, but according to their being the objects that it knows remain strangers to it. This is a profound alteration of the Platonic doctrine. The intellect is no longer, as Plato taught, that part of the human being by which he remains in natural communication with subsistent ideas: now it is defined by its unique capacity of acquiring empirical knowledge through impressions received by the senses and derived from substances foreign to it.

When we read in Meister Eckhart that the intellect is "the place of representations or reasons," he is evidently doing the job of a syncretist: "*species*" or "representation" designates in the Scholastic terminology of his biblical commentaries the intellectual phantasms or the ideas that the mind is naturally open to receive (ideas in potentiality), whereas

"rationes" or "reasons" refers to subsisting divine ideas (ideas in en-
telechy). In other words, according to Eckhart the intellect, being potentially the sum total of all possible representations, contains, inasmuch
as it is detached from what it actually knows, the "ideas" or models of
all things themselves. A detached man is no longer the place of contin-
gent "representations," but of subsistent "ideas." This combination of
the Platonic and Aristotelian traditions permits Eckhart to posit a bold
identification between knowledge by detachment and divine knowledge.

A brief look at a text of Thomas Aquinas will help clarify the importance of this deliberate syncretism. The passage is taken from the article
of the *Summa Theologiae* in which he questions the existence of the
"divine ideas,"[57] an article which Meister Eckhart certainly read during
his student days as well as when he had become a professor in his own
right.

Aquinas gives an enlightening translation of what in his period was
called an "idea": "In Greek one names 'idea' what in Latin is termed
'form.'" However, "idea" designates the form not insofar as it exists in
the thing and confers being on it, but such as it exists outside it. This
separate existence can be twofold: as a principle of knowledge, the form
is found in the human intellect; as a model of the thing, it is in God.
While in the first mode, intelligible, the form can exist in any being
whatever endowed with reason, created or uncreated, in the second it
is by right reserved to a creating cause alone; this latter possesses in itself
the primal image of the thing that will be produced. For Thomas Aquinas the original meaning of the "idea" lies here: it is the title for the
preexistence of an effect in the creating cause. The idea precedes the
created object in the intention of the creator.

It seems that in the sermon "Jesus Entered," Meister Eckhart identifies
the form as the principle of knowledge in a being endowed with reason,
with the form as the preexisting model in the Cause. For the concept,
the principle of knowledge in man, he substitutes the idea, the principle
of creation in God. In the detached intellect, all things are found "essentially," *wesenlich*: this adverb is formed out of the word *wesen*, which in
Meister Eckhart translates *esse*. So it now becomes understandable why
the return of the intellect upon itself is a source of happiness as great
as is the kingdom of heaven.[58]

The very actuality according to which things are in God becomes the
actuality of the detached man, so that he is indeed "bereft of all won-

der" and "gets nothing new from things to come nor from any chance": imbued with divine knowledge he turns away from knowledge by successive representations. "He dwells in a single now which is at all times and unceasingly new." He cannot grow old.

To blend "representations" with "ideas" as Eckhart does here clearly indicates that he intends to identify the activity of the spirit in detachment with the eternal divine actuality. But is that not an excessive and absurd position to hold?

Affirmations of identity—here between the activity of the human intellect and the actuality of the divine intellect; above, in paragraph [7], between the ground of the mind and the ground of God—seem absurd so long as they are separated from the dynamics of detachment. They give a conceptual expression to a calling which is impossible to conceptualize: they invite the instinct of possession to abdicate.

The intellect despoiled of all attachment, Meister Eckhart says, falls into a nothingness of determination which is the abyss filled with the original figures of whatever is. This intellect ceases to cling to things; its fall gives it freedom to obey immediately the will of God; commerce with representations is turned into commerce with ideas. In the present now of this returning, the man belongs to his origin, and his origin belongs to him. The things that he has "let be" in their singular being, he now recovers in their primordial being. The language describing such an itinerary must often have recourse to words loaded with meanings that seem excessive in the face of their common usage.

Is there a reference, in this dialectic between abandoning and recovering, to the gospel which promises hundredfold to whoever, in the name of the Kingdom, leaves everything behind on earth? To dispossess oneself of "representations" would then contain the promise of receiving in God "ideas." A simple exegesis of the sermon does not authorize this connection. Yet the thought of Meister Eckhart appears here to be evangelical in the articulation of its direction, if not in its content. Leaving everything—receiving everything: this is surely a structure of thought faithful to that of Christian preaching. We should be tempted to qualify his reasoning, in this paragraph, as formally biblical and materially philosophical; in that case, the conclusion, "such a divine sovereignty is in this power," before apparently concluding a philosophical analysis on the intellect, would nonetheless express, in the literary form proper to Meister Eckhart, the fullness of the Kingdom where no veil will darken the knowledge that we have of the universe.

Philosophical speculation or biblical meditation—the line of separation is impossible to trace.

The theory of the intellect which we have explained could finally appear as a resurgence of Neoplatonic currents. We have already seen that Eckhart was an eclectic in terms of his philosophical vocabulary, so it is not unlikely that he adopted elements of the Neoplatonic view of the cosmos. Such an influence is particularly verifiable in the manner in which Eckhart connects detachment with the intellect. However, a short explanation is needed here, because the main Neoplatonic philosophers were not Christian, and their texts do not mention the birth of God from man.

Proclus, the last philosopher of this line, whose *Book of Causes*, a then-famous selection of his writings, Meister Eckhart had read, had systematized the different theories of the intellect which claimed Platonic fatherhood into a great scholastic edifice.

According to Proclus, the νοῦς, the first deployment or radiation springing from the One, contains in itself intellectually the multiplicity of sensible forms; like a reservoir of archetypes, it collects the potentialities of all things. With relation to the One, the summit of the universe and source of all existing things, in whose divinity it shares, the intellect is a *henad*: the first "hypostasis" or the first degree of perfection, and of the family of the gods; with relation to existing beings, to which it gives intelligence, it is a "monad," the principle in the quality of which they share. It is the image of the origin, an εἰκονικῶς unity, and it is the cause of beings, a multiplicity κατ' αἰτίαν.[59] It is, one might say, the threshold where the One overflows into the multiple: "One and yet not one."[60]

In the procession, πρόοδος, of beings from their origin and in their return, ἐπιστροφή, towards the origin, the νοῦς assumes a twofold mediation: it derives the multiple from the One, and it leads the multiple back to the One.

On this last point, a certain continuity of teaching from Proclus to Meister Eckhart is undeniable. The reservoir of archetypes in a descending reading, or in genetic emanation, the νοῦς is in Proclus likewise the place of representations in an ascending reading, where it brings the sensible back to the intelligible and gathers into itself the forms or species of things. The field of thought proper to Proclus and that of Meister Eckhart overlap on this margin; for both of them, the intellect contains in itself the "ideas" or archetypes as well as the "representations" or species of knowledge. According to our way of looking at it, it is all things in a twofold manner: potentially insofar as it can know them all, and actually insofar as they reside in it as in their origin, according to their perfection, their truth, their eternity.

The philosophical perspective is nonetheless totally different in Proclus and Meister Eckhart. The Neoplatonic system is a noetic of the cosmos, and if Proclus also proposes a road that leads to the recovery of a certain inner freedom, the spiritual itinerary of the return of the Intellect to the One aims before anything else at a comprehension of the universe; his form of thought is "cosmocentric." The unification of the multiple, in the νοῦς, assures the universal cohesion of the cosmos around the subsistent One. Plato, in the *Parmenides* had already reasoned in this way: if the One is not, all things are dissolved in disorder; but they are visibly regulated according to an order, so the One exists. Proclus, a faithful disciple, imagines the One as the hub of a wheel from which proceed the series of beings in multiple rays. As the origin and guarantee of the order, the One does not mingle with any of these series. But it is the νοῦς which reveals, by its twofold mediation, that universal harmony: the νοῦς is the keystone of the cosmological dogmatic of Proclus.

Something entirely different is at stake in the sermon "Jesus Entered," centered as it is (like Eckhart's thought altogether) on the birth of God in the detached man. The intellect is not thought of as a hypostasis on the threshold of the Deity, dispensing universal knowledge and cohesion, but as a power in man: the power that makes him capable not only of returning towards his origin in forgetfulness of the self and in admiration for the One, but also of engendering himself as the Son of God.

Detachment differs from ἐπιστροφή especially in that it is not oriented towards contemplation. It produces a new birth: the birth of the Son in the intellect or the birth of the intellect as the Son.

Two sources then concur in the theory of the intellect according to Meister Eckhart: the Aristotelian tradition enriched by Neoplatonic themes. Between these two traditions, however, the Aristotelian predominates, because Aristotle's "energetic" conception of knowledge has furnished the basis for the thought of operative identity in Eckhart.

[11–12] The Divine Destiny of the Will

There is another power, equally incorporeal; it emanates from the spirit and remains in the spirit and is totally spiritual. In this power, God glows and burns without ceasing, in all his riches, in all his sweetness, and in all his delight. Truly, within this power is so great a joy and so great an unmeasurable delight, that no one can fully tell nor reveal it. I say it again: if there were a single human whose intelligence, were it only for an instant, could see according to the truth the delight and the joy which reign therein, all he may ever have suffered or that God may have wished him to suffer would be a trifle, indeed a nothing; even more, it would be for him entirely a joy and a pleasure.

This paragraph, dealing with the will, is patterned after the passages that discuss the intellect. It repeats the very words of paragraphs [8–10], so much so that the two developments allow themselves to be written in parallel:

The intellect [8–10]	*The will* [11]
"touches neither time nor flesh"	is "equally incorporeal"
"emanates from the spirit and remains in the spirit and is totally spiritual"	"emanates from the spirit and remains in the spirit and is totally spiritual"
"In this power, God is fully verdant and flowering"	"In this power, God glows and burns without ceasing"
God is there "in all the joy and all the honor that he is in himself"	God is there "in all his riches, in all his sweetness, and in all his delight"
"There reigns such a dear joy, so incomprehensibly great a joy, that no one can ever fully speak of it"	"within this power is so great a joy and so great an unmeasurable delight, that no one can fully tell nor reveal it"
If God sent man "so much to suffer as no one had ever suffered"	All that man "may ever have suffered or that God may have wished him to suffer"
"and if then God accorded him only once to contemplate in a glimpse what he is like in this power"	"if there were a single human being whose intelligence, were it only for an instant, could see according to the truth the delight and the joy which reign therein"

"all this suffering and this poverty would still be too small a thing.

this suffering "would be a trifle, indeed a nothing"

"Furthermore if afterwards God never granted him the kingdom of heaven, he would still have received a reward too great"

"it would be for him entirely a joy and a pleasure"

If we now examine all the sentences that have not found a place in one or the other column, we notice that the only themes on the side of the intellect are the reciprocity of engendering and the theory of the "now" in which detachment is accomplished. These are also the two decisive points around which the whole sermon is organized.

On the side of the will, on the contrary, there appear no new elements except some oratorical variations and the long development on suffering [12], which is a somewhat redundant amplification of themes at the end of paragraph [11]. In other words, Meister Eckhart cites the will only to be complete in his treatment of detachment. The problem of the order between the two faculties of the soul, intellect and will, a question disputed at length in the School, did not raise a particular interest on his part. We do not find any traces in his texts of a genuine philosophy of the will. The terms to which he has recourse in this area are borrowed without exception from the doctrine of the intellect; they do not constitute an original epistemology of the will. It is worthwhile to keep in mind this absence of an elucidation of the relationship between intellect and will. Given the floating, even contradictory, expressions on this subject throughout the sermons, it will be difficult to maintain that the ultimate meaning of detachment and releasement in Meister Eckhart still falls "within the domain of will."[61]

Do you want to know correctly if your suffering is your own or God's? You can tell it in this way: if you suffer for the love of yourself, in whatever way it be, this suffering hurts and is hard for you to bear. But if you suffer for the love of God and for God alone, that suffering does not hurt and is not hard to bear, for it is God who carries the burden. In all truth! If there were a man who liked to suffer for God and purely for God alone, and if on this man fell in a single blow all the suffering that all men have ever suffered, and all the suffering the entire world bears, it would not hurt him and would not weigh him down, for it is God who would carry the burden. If a hundredweight were placed on my neck, but someone else supported it above my neck, I should load myself with a hundred hundredweights as willingly as with a single one, for this would not weigh me down and would not hurt me. Briefly, those things a man suffers for God and for God alone, God makes light and gentle for him. As I have already said at the beginning of the sermon: "Jesus went into a little castle and was received by a virgin who was a wife." Why? It was necessary that she be a virgin and at the same time a wife. Now I have told you that Jesus was received. But I have not yet said what this little castle is. So at present I wish to speak of it.

This passage concerning suffering shows at the very least some candor: suffering, says Eckhart, can be transformed into joy and pleasure on the condition that we suffer for God and not for love of self. As we take a closer look, this remark is equally to be put in parallel with a remark on the intellect. Just as the science that is granted to a detached man proceeds no longer through abstractions and representations, but through possession of ideas and essences, so he who suffers without being attached to his suffering has God bear his burden, making it light and gentle for him. To detach oneself from one's pain means to consider it not as one's own but as assumed by God himself. As much as some material good or cultural good, we can indeed jealously possess our sorrow. The parallelism takes the following form:

Knowledge attached to representations	Suffering with attachment which "is hard for you to bear"
all things are held together "essentially" in the intellect, in their ideas; knowledge by detachment	"you suffer for the love of God"; this "does not hurt and is not hard to bear"

In the case of suffering as in the case of knowledge, God assumes what man consents to abandon; God bestows on man happiness and knowledge which cannot be compared to the suffering and the "images" that he has left behind. Only such an interpretation according to the law of "leaving everything—receiving everything" as we have already applied to the analysis of knowledge justifies the quotation from the Gospel of Luke that occurs at the end of this passage. Eckhart teaches that it is not enough to receive suffering passively as a "virgin," free of all attach-

ment, but suffering must in turn be borne back into God. God is not
only a consoler; he is no longer the "why" of suffering, but its subject.
The condition of possibility for such a transfer is precisely the divine
nature of the will which, like that of the intellect, is realized to the very
degree that attachment disappears. A human being who is a "wife"
gives back to God the suffering that has befallen him. God then carries
it, and he fills man to the brim with joy and pleasure.

This last parallel confirms that with regard to the will (to which
Scholastic anthropology connects suffering), Eckhart quite simply repeats the least compromising expressions of his doctrine of the intellect.
His boldest affirmations are to be found in the context of his philosophy
of the intellect, from which he does not care to distinguish clearly the
type of operations proper to the will.

Finally, this parallelism shows that the sermons of Meister Eckhart
are not unregulated confidences made before a feminine audience with
the consequence that it would betray a lack of critical sense to analyze
them in detail. On the contrary, if the text published by the critical
edition is that which the preacher has indeed uttered, which seems
likely, then we should conclude that Meister Eckhart composed his
sermons with care. How could we otherwise explain those references
from one paragraph to another? Whatever truth there may be in the
hypothesis that contends that this sermon constitutes a later compilation, made by Eckhart himself, it is certain that we are dealing with an
elaborate text, carefully constructed, with occasional exclamations of
the type that we shall soon encounter: "If you could grasp this with my
heart, you would well understand what I am saying, for it is true, and
the truth says it itself."

[13–15] The Divine Destiny of the Ground of the Mind

I have sometimes said that there is a power in the mind, the only one that
is free. Sometimes I have said it is a guardian of the mind; sometimes I
have said that it is a light of the mind; sometimes I have said that it is
a spark. Here is what I say now: it is neither this nor that, and yet it is
a something. It is raised above this and that, higher than the sky is above
the earth. This is why I designate it now in a nobler way than I have ever
done before, though it resists nobleness and fashion, and surpasses them
by far. It is free of all names and devoid of all forms, entirely bare and
free, as void and free as God is in himself. It is perfect unity and simplicity
as God is unity and simplicity, so that in no way can one peer into it.

Eckhart's intellectualism, as we have established it, is not his last word on detachment. Starting with paragraph [13], he shows that identity with God occurs in the intellect only concomitantly with the identity of the ground: the original locus of oneness is neither in the intellect nor in any other faculty of the soul. Rather, the deification of man is always and already on the way to fulfillment, beyond all nameable faculties or regions. This new and final approach to detachment centers on the expression "ground of the mind," which is repeated from paragraph [7].[62]

Eckhart enumerates several designations which point, though in an inadequate manner, to this "most noble ground" in man. The first series of onomastic approaches consists of titles that are derived from a function of the intellect: "faculty in the spirit," "guardian of the spirit," "spark." These names will finally be negated.

"Power," *kraft*, is to be understood, as we have already seen, and as Thomas Aquinas taught it,[63] in the traditional meaning of a "faculty" of man. Eckhart apparently wants the image of the guardian, *huote*, to express a "watching," rather than a "protection": the ground of the mind is incessantly on the watch; it is the theater of a living exchange. The word "light," here as throughout the text, is ambiguous: are we to think of the light which faith in revelation brings to the believer, or of the simple, natural light of the intellect? Meister Eckhart, little inclined to distinctions which do not serve his purposes, would reject the question as irrelevant. If he amalgamates the philosophical, biblical, and psychological themes without any desire for a system, it is because all language is welcome that can serve as material for his unique plan, detachment. The "light" designates here neither the natural conformity of the spirit to truth nor the Christian revelation. Eckhart's thought is unitary, and it is repugnant to him to oppose any supernatural status to a natural status of intelligence. "Light" designates the divine invasion which solicits every spirit to let itself be.

A similar difficulty lies behind the word "spark," *vünkelin*. Most Gnostics, pagan or Christian, used it: man has fallen from his origin, but a little spark of divine fire in him still stirs the longing for a re-ascent. Gnostic myths teach an awakening: a vase of light was broken in ancient times, but each living being preserves in himself an imperishable spark which may become the agent for his return into the spiritual realm. Pseudo-Dionysius, on the other hand, concludes one of his treatises in the following way:

> I intensely hope that my book will make the sparks of divine fire, so to
> say, buried in you burst out of the earth.[64]

A third thread goes back to the Stoics. For them, just as the entire
cosmos had come out of a primitive blaze, so each human being was
formed, animated, and preserved by this πῦρ τεχνικόν. The knowledge
of the world originates in this kinship by fire.[65] Finally, "light" and
"spark" in Meister Eckhart may simply express the φῶς τοῦ νοῦ, the
light of the Aristotelian intellect. But whatever his source may be in this
domain, he makes only passing use of it. The term "spark" is an inadequate approximation of the ground of the mind, since it is a term relative
to the intellect.

"Here is what I say now: it is neither this nor that, and yet it is a
something." The designations which Eckhart finally decides are appropriate enough to adorn the ground of the mind refer beyond the intellect
to an unnameable unity. The discourse becomes negative: the ground
of the mind is raised above every mode, without form, void and free,
ledic und vrî. "It is perfect unity and simplicity as God is unity and
simplicity." The only attributes which we can have recourse to are the
very attributes of God, "one" and "simple," *ein und einvaltic,* which are
the negations of all attributes. "In no way can one peer into it." If it is
true that the divine ground of the mind, the One which is in the mind,
resides beyond the intellect, then *wîse,* "way" or "mode," denotes here
precisely the faculty of intelligence. The human spirit can only know
"this and that," *diz und daz,* composite and multiple things, but not
what is one and simple. The One cannot be known; it enters into no
relationship with the intellect. It escapes from all sight. This, then, is the
language in which Meister Eckhart proclaims the identity of the ground
of the mind and of the ground of God. All these negations constitute
a true henology of the *grunt.*

> In this same power of which I have spoken, in which God is verdant and
> flowering with his entire divinity, and the spirit in God—in this same
> power, I say, the Father begets his only Son as truly as in himself, since
> he truly lives in this power; and the spirit, in harmony with the Father,
> begets the sole Son and itself as this same Son, and it is this same Son,
> in this light, and it is the truth. If you could grasp this with my heart, you
> would understand well what I say, for it is true, and the truth says it itself.

One and simple, the ground of the mind is also immutable. The birth
of the Word cannot accomplish itself in this region within man, for that

would affect the ground with a movement. It is the spirit that begets the Son in man, a begetting which is produced without the ground of the mind being touched by it.

> Look and see: this little castle in the mind of which I am speaking and which is my intention, is so one and simple, elevated above every fashion, that the noble power of which I have spoken is not worthy to pry, were it only once for a moment, into this little castle; and also the other power of which I have spoken, in which God does not cease to glow and burn with all his riches and with all his delight, would not dare to ever cast a glance into it: this castle is so one and simple, an identical unity so highly elevated above every mode and every power, that no power nor any mode can ever look into it, not even God himself. In all truth and as truly as God lives! God himself will never peer into it, not even for an instant, and has never looked into it insofar as he possesses attributes and according to the propriety of his Persons. This is easily understood, for this identical unity is without mode and propriety. This is why, if God is ever to catch a glimpse of it, it will cost him all his divine names and the propriety of his Persons: he will have to leave all this outside, if he ever wishes to look inside. Rather, insofar as he is simple and one, without any mode or propriety, he is neither the Father, nor the Son, nor the Holy Spirit in this sense, and yet he is something that is neither this nor that.

> You see, insofar as he is one and simple, he penetrates into this unity that I call the little castle in the mind, but otherwise he will not enter into it in any way; it is only thus that he penetrates into it and is already within. With this part of itself the mind is equal to God and not otherwise. What I have told you is the truth; I give you truth itself as witness and my soul as pledge.

> May we so be a little castle in which Jesus ascends and is received and abides eternally with us the way that I have said: may God help us in this. Amen.

Neither the intellect nor the will attain to this castle in the mind: if it were otherwise, it would be subject to a mode and would not be simple.

The key word of these three paragraphs is "mode," *wise.* The theory of the absence of every mode in the intimacy of the mind culminates in the following: just as the "ground" in man is raised above the cognitive and volitional faculties, so the "ground" of the Godhead, in God, is exalted above the divine modes, namely Father, Son, and Spirit. God himself must rid himself of his modes if he wishes to be received in the castle in the mind. The One in the mind is of the same nature as the Godhead above the three Persons in God; in other words, it is above the

Father. God, inasmuch as he is considered with his attributes and in his Trinity, resides underneath the mind.[66]

We see that the statement of paragraph [7]: "[The mind] is fruitful out of the same ground from which the Father begets his eternal Word, and [it] begets together with him," did not denote the "castle" of which Eckhart speaks at the end of his sermon. The word *grunt* takes on different meanings. It now appears that "the most noble ground," which in paragraph [7] had to remain unexplained, designated the peak or the spark in the intellect.

The theory of the One in man is perhaps the most authentically Neoplatonic part of the sermon. Eckhart seems again to be inspired by Proclus. It suffices to check the Latin translation of Proclus, established by William of Moerbecke, for the main expressions relating to this henology of the mind are found there: "the One in the mind," "above understanding," "flower of the intellect."[67] Yet there is no doubt that in Proclus these terms refer to an intellectual power in man; to be sure, Proclus means the highest power, since it produces ἕνωσις, but it is still a principle of knowledge, ἐπιστήμη.

Moerbecke translates ἕνωσις by *unio*: this union Proclus describes as "knowledge above the intellect,"[68] the last degree of the trilogy of knowing: "understanding, intellect, the One of the mind."[69]

For Proclus the ultimate goal of man's progression is knowledge. The One in the mind designates the supreme cognitive faculty of man. According to the ancient maxim that "the like is known by the like," "it is by the One also that we know the supreme degree of Unity."[70]

Is the perspective of Meister Eckhart the same? The scandal that his doctrine of the castle in the mind aroused provoked an explanation on his part:

> In the nakedness of his essence which is above every name, [God] penetrates and falls into the naked essence of the mind which is itself also without a proper name and which is elevated above the intellect and the will, as the essence is above its faculties. This is the castle into which Jesus enters, in his being rather than in his acting, giving graciously to the mind the divine and deiform being. This regards the essence of being according to the words: "By the grace of God I am what I am." This is something moral; [with this sentence the Apostle Paul] teaches man to renounce everything and to bare himself, to become poor, not to have love for things of the earth; [he teaches] whoever wishes truly to be a disciple of Christ to love God without mode and without any property entailing a mode.[71]

"This is something moral." Summoned to explain himself, Meister Eckhart always returns to detachment. It is on this point that he most profoundly modifies the views of Proclus. From a philosophy of the intellect in the cosmos, he enunciates a call for a certain type of existence among things. Such is Eckhart's this-worldliness, which is opposed to the other-worldliness of the Neoplatonists. For Eckhart, the first and the last word of his preaching is a deontology of man exposed to risk: a risk for freedom in attachment and possession; a risk for deification in forgetfulness of the origin of the self and of the *grunt;* a risk for God himself, in a religion of names and modes. Such a deontology of the risk —"you will run the danger of detachment"—proceeds on the level of objects, it teaches an imperative for the use of what falls into our hands. It is removed from the Platonic doctrines of the elevation of the soul by cosmic contemplation. The noetics of the cosmos itself has changed, the "world" has become "our world": for the hearers of his sermons, this designates the monastery with its vigils, its exterior exercises, its prayers, and more generally the "images." The abandonment of what ties man to the world, i.e., to images, will be progressive. To engage in it, to become free as I was when I was not, this means to regain the original identity with the self, in the ground of the mind to which God gives himself in his being. Identity is gained only this way; identity with God is wandering. The deontology of risk and the way of detachment teach the wandering identity. Meister Eckhart remains "the old master to live and to read,"[72] whose teaching is substantiated by the concreteness of a new way to exist.

To illustrate the theory of the spiritual soul in Meister Eckhart that we have developed, a sermon devoted entirely to this question follows, in which Eckhart comments on the verse of the Gospel of John: "He who hates his soul in this world preserves it for eternal life."

SERMON,
"HE WHO HATES HIS SOUL
IN THIS WORLD"

(QUI ODIT ANIMAM SUAM IN HOC MUNDO, John 12:25)

I have spoken in Latin a word which our Lord speaks in his Gospel: "He who hates his soul in this world preserves it for eternal life."·

In these words pay attention to the purpose of our Lord when he says that one should hate one's soul. He who loves his soul in this mortal life, and as it is in this world, loses it in eternal life; but he who hates it as it is mortal and in this world, preserves it for eternal life.

There are two reasons why he says "soul." One master says: The word "soul" does not designate the ground and does not touch the nature of the soul. Therefore another master says: Whoever writes of movable things touches neither the nature nor the ground of the soul. He who wants to name the soul such as it is in itself, in its simplicity, in its clarity, and in its nakedness, will find no name to fit. They call it "soul," but that is no different than when we call someone "carpenter"; we call him so not as a human being, nor as Henry, nor properly according to his being, but we name him after what he does. Likewise, our Lord here means to say: he who loves the soul in its transparence, that is to say, in its simple nature, hates it and is its enemy in this earthly guise. He hates it, and he is sad and afflicted that it stands so far from the clear light that it is in itself.

Our masters say: The soul is called a fire because of the power, the heat, and the brightness it contains. Others say that it is a spark of heavenly nature. The third says that it is a light. The fourth says that it is a spirit. The fifth says that it is a number.

We can find nothing that is as pure and clear as a number. Therefore they mean to name the soul after something that is pure and
clear. Among the angels there is a number; we speak of one angel,
of two angels. There is also number in light. Hence one calls [the
soul] according to what is purest and most clear; yet this does not
touch the ground of the soul. God who is without name—he has
no name—is ineffable; and the soul in its ground is likewise
ineffable: just as ineffable as he.

There is another reason for him to say: "he hates." The word
"soul" refers to the soul as it resides in the dungeon of the body.
Thus he wants to say that the soul, with that part of its being
which it can make into an object of its thought, remains in its
dungeon. Wherever it has still some regard for these things of
here-below and where it draws something into itself through the
senses, the soul feels altogether constrained. Indeed, words are
unable to give a name to what lies beyond it.

There are three reasons why the soul should hate itself. First,
inasmuch as it is mine, I shall hate it. Inasmuch as it is mine,
indeed, it is not God's. The second [reason] is that my soul is not
totally established, planted, and reshaped in God. Augustine
says: He who wishes that God belong to him must first of all
belong to God. This is necessarily so. The third reason is: if the
soul finds a liking for itself insofar as it is a soul, and if it finds
a liking for God together with the soul, that is improper. It should
savor God for himself, for he is totally above it. For this reason
Christ says: "He who loves his soul loses it."

The soul should hate that part of itself which is in this world
or looks out into this world, and all that is in contact [with the
world] or which casts a glance on it. One master says: that part
of the soul which is most elevated and most clear is above the
world. Nothing but love alone draws the soul into this world.
Sometimes it has a natural love for the body. Sometimes it has
a voluntary love for the creature. One master says: the soul in its
nature has no more to do with all that is in this world than the
eye has to do with singing or the ear with color. This is why our
masters in natural sciences say that the body is in the soul rather
than the soul in the body. Just as the barrel contains the wine

rather than the wine the barrel, the soul contains in itself the body, rather than the body the soul. In its nature the soul is deprived of whatever it loves in this world. One master says: The nature and the natural perfection of the soul is that in itself it becomes an intelligible world, for in itself [in its ground] God has imprinted the first images of all things. Whoever claims that he has reached his [state of] nature must find all things formed in him in clarity and such as they are in God; not as they are in their own nature, but as they are in God. No spirit, no angel touches the ground of the soul nor the nature of the soul. By [this ground of itself] it reaches into the First; it reaches into the origin where God breaks forth with goodness into all creatures. In [this ground] it grasps all things, in God; not in their natural clarity, but in pure simplicity such as they are in God. God has made this entire world as if out of charcoal. The image which is of gold is more durable than that which is made out of charcoal. Likewise, all things are more clear and more noble in the soul than they are in this world. But the material from which God has drawn all things has less value still than does charcoal in relation to gold. If a man wishes to fashion a vase he takes for this a certain quantity of clay; this is the matter with which he works. Then he gives it form; this, he bears within himself. Also, the form within him is more perfect than the matter. Hence I want to say that all things are immeasurably nobler in the intelligible world which is the soul than they are in this world. The simple images of all things are in the soul in the same way as a design is hammered out and carved in gold. A master says: The soul has the possibility of receiving the images of all things imprinted in itself. Another one says: The soul will never attain [the state of] its pure nature without also finding the images of all things formed in itself, [that is to say] in the intelligible world which is incomprehensible. No thought reaches to it. Gregory says: When we speak of divine things, we have to stammer, because we have to express them in words.

Still a little word on the soul, and then nothing more. "Daughters of Jerusalem, do not be surprised that I am dark. The sun has tanned me, and the children of my mother have fought against me" (Cant. 1:5–6). She speaks of the children of the world. The soul says to them: What has warmed me and touches me coming from the sun, that is to say from the pleasures of the world, makes me dark and swarthy. Brown is not a perfect color; it holds clearness but also blackness. Everything that the soul thinks or works with its powers, as luminous as this may be, is nonetheless mixed. This is why she says: "The children of my mother have fought against me." The children, which are all the inferior powers of the soul, fight against it and abuse it. The heavenly Father is our true father, and Christianity is our mother. However beautiful and adorned Christianity can be and however useful it is by its works, all this still remains imperfect. This is why he says: "O you, the most beautiful among women, go out and depart" (Cant. 1:7). This world is like a woman, for it is weak. But why then does he say: "You, the most beautiful of women"? The angels are more beautiful, but they are raised far above the soul. This is why he says: "the most beautiful"—in its natural light—"go out and depart." Go out of this world and depart from all this towards which your soul still feels an inclination. And wherever the soul still touches upon something, let it hold it in hatred.

Pray your beloved Lord that we may hate our soul under the guise that makes it "our soul." In this way we shall keep it for eternal life. May God come to our help in this. Amen.[73]

Chapter
Two

SERMON,
"WOMAN, THE HOUR IS COMING"

(MULIER, VENIT HORA ET NUNC EST, QUANDO VERI ADORATORES
ADORABUNT PATREM IN SPIRITU ET VERITATE, John 4:23)

This is written in the Gospel of Saint John. Of the long story, I keep only one word. Our Lord says: "Woman, the time will come, and it is now, when the true adorers will adore the Father in spirit and truth, for such the Father seeks to adore him."

[1] Consider the opening words, when he says: "the time will come, and it is now." Whoever wishes to adore the Father has to commit himself with his desire and his trust into eternity. There is a higher part of the mind which keeps itself above time, and which ignores time as well as the body. All that happened a thousand years ago, the day of a thousand years ago, is no more remote in eternity than the moment in which I stand right now; again, the day which will come a thousand years from now, or in as many years as you can count, is no more distant in eternity than this very moment in which I stand presently.

[2] But he says that the "true adorers will adore the Father in spirit and truth." What then is truth? The truth is so noble that, even if God could turn his back on truth, I would cling to the truth, and would leave God. But indeed, God is the truth, and everything which is in time, everything created by God, is not the truth.

[3] Then he says: "These will adore the Father." Alas, how many are there who adore a shoe, a cow, or any other creature, and for whom this is their only concern. How foolish they are! As soon as you pray to God for the sake of creatures, you pray for your own damage; for as long as the creature is creature, it

carries in itself bitterness and harm, wrong and distress. So it is no wonder that these people obtain distress and bitterness. Why? —They have prayed for it!

[4] I have oft remarked: He who seeks God while seeking other things will never find God. But if someone really seeks nothing other than God, he finds God—and never quite alone, for all that God can offer he finds together with God. If you seek God, and if you seek him for your own advantage and for your own beatitude, then in truth you are not looking for God at all. This is why he says that the true adorers adore the *Father,* and rightly so.—Someone could ask a good man: "Why do you seek God?"—"Because he is God."—"Why do you seek the truth?"— "Because it is the truth."—"Why do you seek justice?"—"Because it is justice." Such people's attitude is the right one. All things that are in time have a why. Thus when someone asks a man: "Why are you eating?"—"In order to gain strength."— "Why are you sleeping?"—"For the same reason." And so with everything that is in time. But if someone asked a good man: "Why do you love God?"—"I do not know, because of God."— "Why do you love the truth?"—"Because of the truth."—"Why do you love justice?"—"Because of justice."—"Why do you love goodness?"—"Because of goodness."—"Why are you living?"— "My word, I do not know! But I am happy to be alive."

[5] A master says: Whoever has been touched but for a single moment by truth, by justice, and by goodness can no longer turn away from them, even for an instant and even if they entailed all the pains of hell. He says also: If a man is touched by these three —truth, justice, and goodness—he will no more be able to relinquish these three than God is able to relinquish his Godhead.

[6] A master says: The good has three branches. The first branch is usefulness, the second branch is delight, and the third branch is worthiness. This is why he says: "They adore the Father." Why does he say "the Father"? Look solely for God and you will find together with God all that he is capable of offering. This truth is certain, it is necessary, and it is attested. And even if it were not written, it would nonetheless be true. If God pos-

sessed still more, he could not hide it from you, he would have to reveal it to you, and he gives it to you. I have also oft remarked that he gives it to you, and he does so by virtue of birth.

[7] The masters say: The mind has two faces. The upper face beholds God incessantly, and the lower face looks a little towards the below and directs the senses. The upper face, however, which is the peak of the mind, stands in eternity. It has nothing to do with time; it is ignorant of time as well as of the body. As I have said now and again, in it is hidden something like the original outbreak of all goodness, something like a brilliant light which incessantly gleams, and something like a burning fire which burns incessantly. This fire is nothing other than the Holy Spirit.

[8] The masters say that from the higher part of the mind emanate two powers. The first is called will, the other intellect. But the highest perfection of these powers resides in the higher power, namely the intellect. This can never find rest. It aspires to God not as he is the Holy Spirit nor as he is the Son: it flees from the Son. Nor does it want God inasmuch as he is God. Why? Because, as such, he still carries a name. And even if there were a thousand gods, it would still break beyond: it wants him where he has no name. It wants something more noble, something better than God as having a name. What then does the intellect want? It does not know; it wants him as he is the Father. This is why Saint Philip says: "Lord, show us the Father and it is enough for us." It wants him as he is the marrow out of which goodness springs; it wants him as he is the nucleus from which goodness flows; it wants him as he is the root, the vein, from which goodness exudes. Only there is he the Father.

[9] This is what our Lord says: "No one knows the Father except the Son, and no one knows the Son except the Father." Perfectly: to know the Father we must be the Son. I have pronounced—when I don't know—three little maxims: take them as nuts, hot nutmeg, and thereafter drink. First: if we want to be the Son, we have to have a Father. No one, indeed, can say that he is a son unless he has a father; and no one is a father unless he has a son. If the father is dead, we say: "he was my father." If

the son is dead, we say: "he was my son." So the life of the son resides in the father, and the life of the father in the son. This is why no one can say: "I am a son," without having a father. But only such a man is truly a Son who carries out all works by love. Secondly, what constitutes man as Son most of all is equanimity. Is he sick? May he be as gladly sick as well, as gladly well as sick. Is his friend coming to die? He will renounce him, in the name of God. Is an eye plucked out of him? He will renounce it in the name of God. Thirdly, a son can bow his head to no one except the father. How noble is this faculty which stands above time, and which has no place! Elevated above time, indeed, it contains in itself all time; and it is itself the whole of time. Even if man possessed very little of what is so elevated above time, he would nevertheless very quickly grow rich. For what lies beyond the seas is not further removed from this power than what is present in this very moment. This is why he says: "These are they who seek the Father."

[10] See how dearly God loves us, how he implores us. God is impatient for the mind to turn away and scale off from the creatures. Also it is a sure truth and a necessary truth that God has such a need to seek us out—exactly as if all his Godhead depended on it, as in fact it does. God can no more dispense with us than we can dispense with him. Even if it were possible that we might turn away from God, God could never turn away from us. I say: I will not pray that he give me anything; no more than I will praise him for what he has bestowed on me. I will much rather pray that he make me worthy to receive. I will praise him for being of such a nature and of such an essence that he must give. He who would deprive God of this would deprive him of his proper being and his proper life. May the truth of which I have spoken help us become the Son in truth. Amen.[1]

ANALYSIS

We shall proceed a little differently in our analysis of the sermon "Woman, the Hour Is Coming," since it repeats, in more than one point, the teaching of the sermon "Jesus Entered." However, some elements of doctrine—"why," "creature," "truth," "justice," "goodness," and the "Father who must give"—appear here for the first time. Because of their decisive character for the understanding of Meister Eckhart, we shall explain them in the commentary below for themselves.

From these considerations we shall see that there is a logical progression in the thought of Eckhart which can be called the "Eckhartian Itinerancy." This itinerancy has a fourfold movement: starting with a theory of the creature *(Dissimilarity)*, this path of thought reveals a double relation *(Similarity* and *Identity)* of man to the transcendental qualities of being, i.e., to truth, justice, and goodness; finally, this path leads to the announcement of "living without why" and of "the Father who must give" *(Dehiscence)*. Dissimilarity, Similarity, Identity, and Dehiscence are the four types of relation between man and God that constitute the way upon which Eckhart invites his hearers. However, he does not describe an ascent through degrees, as in the Itinerary of Saint Bonaventure, by which the mind rises towards God. Rather, we should think of four determinations of existence in the here and now of the birth of the Son in the mind. Itinerancy is the comprehension of life which results from them. Further, this fourfold relationship to God evokes the four cardinal points of detachment in which childbirth takes place. We shall keep ourselves then from seeing in these four elements any progression other than logical: the idea of progress—childhood, adolescence, maturity, and old age—is absent. These elements are not the road itself that the detached man travels, but the air, the fire, the water, the earth, which he needs for each instant of walking.

In Meister Eckhart, many an inconspicuous expression yields a philosophical position which turns out to be as thoughtful as it is bold. The inconvenience of proceeding from an analysis of the argument to an explanation according to the order of reasons is evident: in this part of the chapter we shall touch on apparently diverging points of doctrine that seem to have no unity. However, the impression of a compendium, difficult to avoid, will be reestablished in the next part, the commentary.

The method of scriptural interpretation remains the same: in reference to a sentence of the gospel, Eckhart above all develops his own thought. For this purpose he uses some especially fitting biblical terms as a pretext—in this case the words "time," "truth," "Father."

[1–3] Time, the Body, Nothingness

Mulier, venit hora et nunc est, quando veri adoratores adorabunt patrem in spiritu et veritate.

This is written in the Gospel of Saint John. Of the long story, I keep only one word. Our Lord says: "Woman, the time will come, and it is now, when the true adorers will adore the Father in spirit and truth, for such the Father seeks to adore him."

[1] Consider the opening words, when he says: "the time will come, and it is now." Whoever wishes to adore the Father has to commit himself with his desire and his trust into eternity. There is a higher part of the mind which keeps itself above time, and which ignores time as well as the body. All that happened a thousand years ago, the day of a thousand years ago, is no more remote in eternity than the moment in which I stand right now; again, the day which will come a thousand years from now, or in as many years as you can count, is no more distant in eternity than this very moment in which I stand presently.

"The time will come, and it is now"; to speak of time is for Eckhart, here again, to speak of man. The time which is measured and counted, which "has a before and an after," is often opposed to "time without time," to the now of the birth of the Word in man. Time divides the human being into two zones: that by which he remains subject to duration and to the succession of physical things, and that where he possesses all things, in God, in an eternal instant. We have already met and commented on the expressions "power of the mind beyond time" and "higher part of the mind."

Speaking of time, then, is a manner of saying: eternity is now. The events of a thousand years ago, the events that will occur in a thousand years, and the events of today are collected into the instantaneity of the present by the divine spark in the mind. The key word of the first paragraph is "time"; it refers back to the created–uncreated constitution of man and to what we have called the "henology of the *grunt.*"

> But he says that the "true adorers will adore the Father in spirit and truth." What then is truth? The truth is so noble that, even if God could turn his back on truth, I would cling to the truth, and would leave God. But indeed, God is the truth, and everything which is in time, everything created by God, is not the truth.

The key word of this second paragraph is "truth." Its development is expeditious: God alone is true, everything created is not truth. Truth is so "noble" that it is preferable to God himself. If God could take leave from the truth, Eckhart would not hesitate to attach himself to the truth and to abandon God. "Noble" is here a technical term. Eckhart has devoted an entire treatise to the "noble man." The "nobleness" of the mind consists in its being of the same kind as God. God alone is the truth: if then his creation is not the truth, and if the "higher part of the mind" is uncreated and uncreatable, then to speak of God, to speak of the truth, and to speak of the summit of the mind will be to speak of things, not only very close in nature, but ultimately identical. God, the noble faculty of the mind, and the truth are mutually related. To these is opposed "what God has ever created," time and the body.

> Then he says: "These will adore the Father." Alas, how many are there who adore a shoe, a cow, or any other creature, and for whom this is their only concern. How foolish they are! As soon as you pray to God for the sake of creatures, you pray for your own damage; for as long as the creature is creature, it carries in itself bitterness and harm, wrong and distress. So it is no wonder that these people obtain distress and bitterness. Why?—They have prayed for it!

In this paragraph Eckhart now treats more specifically of the "creature," which is not the truth as it carries in itself "bitterness and harm, wrong and distress." At first sight, these epithets seem inspired by a depreciation of the entire empirical world. Do they not banish as evil whatever comes into contact with body and matter, with time and space? Does not Meister Eckhart preach, then, a retreat into the spiritual spark in the mind, which alone is worthy of consideration and of love? Such a "gnostic" dualism seems to suit Eckhart all the better as he declares: to pray to God with the hope of securing some visible advantage is to pray for one's own harm, so that "it is no wonder that these people obtain distress and bitterness. Why?—They have prayed for it!"

This text has a parallel in the Latin work. A passage from his commentary on the Book of Wisdom will help us to see if Eckhart is indeed to be ranked among the authors that extol a flight from all creatures.

> All that is created in itself is nothing. "He created all things that they may be," and being is preceded by nothing. He then who loves the creature, loves nothingness and becomes himself nothingness. Love indeed transforms the lover into the beloved.—He who prays for these perishable things prays for nothingness, he prays badly and for what is bad.[2]

The biblical text on which these lines comment says: "He has created everything, that it may be."[3] It is a traditional passage from which medieval writers would develop their theology of creation. It allowed them especially to raise questions about the end of the created work. The end of the act of creating is the being of creatures, replies Eckhart in accordance with the scriptural verse; this conforms entirely to classical theses. How then, if God creates all things that they may be, that they may possess being, can Eckhart conclude: "All that is created in itself is nothing"?

Eckhart considers the being of created things in its provenance—their being belongs first to God. Creatures receive being as a loan, not as their own. Their being resides in God, it is a gift; but he who gives can also take back. Their being is precarious, it comes to them from another. The created in itself is nothingness: what deserves attention in creatures is the origin of the gift, which is greater than its term. He alone attracts our love in creatures who has made them, and not "shoes or a cow. . . ." Hence, to keep one's look riveted on things is the source of harm: in themselves they are non-being, nothingness, for their being comes from elsewhere. Learn then to see the elsewhere! Learn to see the Creator in the creature.

This doctrine has nothing in common with the theories of a Zoroaster or a Mani. For Meister Eckhart there are not two principles, Good and Evil, that battle for dominance of the earth, but one alone. The unique, necessary, and sufficient determination of the creature is the gift by which being comes to it. The creature is not "bad," nor is it to be fled from, but it is "nothing in itself": it does not exist by itself. One sole and unique principle is deployed throughout the world: the superabundance of the divine being which becomes visible in the objects all around.

[4] Living without Why

I have oft remarked: He who seeks God while seeking other things will never find God. But if someone really seeks nothing other than God, he finds God—and never quite alone, for all that God can offer he finds together with God. If you seek God, and if you seek him for your own advantage and for your own beatitude, then in truth you are not looking for God at all. This is why he says that the true adorers adore the *Father*, and rightly so.—Someone could ask a good man: "Why do you seek God?"—"Because he is God."—"Why do you seek the truth?"—"Because it is the truth."—"Why do you seek justice?"—"Because it is justice." Such people's attitude is the right one. All things that are in time have a why. Thus when someone asks a man: "Why are you eating?"—"In order to gain strength."—"Why are you sleeping?"—"For the same reason." And so with everything that is in time. But if someone asked a good man: "Why do you love God?"—"I do not know, because of God."— "Why do you love the truth?"—"Because of the truth."—"Why do you love justice?"—"Because of justice."—"Why do you love goodness?"— "Because of goodness."—"Why are you living?"—"My word, I do not know! But I am happy to be alive."

This passage on the "why" is capital. From these questions and answers it follows that he alone finds God who seeks him without asking for "this or that": without seeking help for personal undertakings or favors for a better life. All such purposes have to fade, regardless of whether their intentions are an explanation of the world or a motivation of man's doings. God is not useful: he neither explains nor motivates anything; he asks to be searched for "without a why."

Eckhart refers back to another sermon: "I have said sometimes. . . ." We can presume that this reference is to the sermon "Every Excellent Gift." Here is the famous text:

Know this: as long as in one way or another you seek your own advantage, you will never find God, for you do not seek God exclusively. You are looking for something else besides God. You behave as if you transformed God into a candle, in order to find something; and when one has found what one looked for, one throws away the candle. You are acting likewise: what you seek together with God is nothingness, no matter what it may be: profit or recompense, interior satisfaction, or whatever else. You are looking for nothingness; this is why you find nothingness. If you find nothingness, it is because you seek nothingness. All creatures are mere nothingness. I do not say that they are small or anything at all: they are mere nothingness. What has no being is nothing. Creatures have no being, for their being depends on the presence of God. Were God to turn away from all creatures, be it for an instant, they would all fall into nothingness.[4]

The end of the passage confirms the creatures' neediness; they have no being; they are nothingness in themselves, for their being belongs to God. The first sentences are repeated almost literally in [4] of the sermon with which we are concerned: he alone will find God who seeks God alone. . . . What is subject to time and space does not suffice itself, its sufficient reason lies in God, the created has "a why." Men eat and drink "in order to" have strength, they act with a "why." When they seek for God for his usefulness, reducing him to the greatest dispenser of goods, they are still acting according to a "why" or an "in order to. . . ." To seek without a why would be to discover the primordial why of all things: God, who is the Truth of the true and who is the Life of the living.

Why things? Why the world? Why life? Why God? Why myself? We must unlearn to question in this fashion. What is, is—without a why. No longer asking a reason for whatever is, the inquirer finds its unique reason: the being of God; no longer looking for a why among the created, he discovers its unique why: the uncreated. Such an inquirer alone is the true God-seeker on earth; he searches without a why, he is no longer looking for anything.

The detached man seeks without seeking. He knows the why and wherefore of creatures: their being belongs to God, and through them, in them, he worships God. He is concerned with the things that make up his life as well as with his own life only insofar as God is transparent through them. He eats and he sleeps, and yet he does not know why he lives. He has ceased to search; yet he has found God, and with him the truth, justice, goodness, as well as all things in their first origin.[5] But what role do truth, justice, and goodness play here?

[5] General and Individual Perfections

A master says: Whoever has been touched but for a single moment by truth, by justice, and by goodness can no longer turn away from them, even for an instant and even if they entailed all the pains of hell. He says also: If a man is touched by these three—truth, justice, and goodness— he will no more be able to relinquish these three than God is able to relinquish his Godhead.

The dependency of all things on God, which has just been explained through the biblical category of creation, is now stated again through the philosophical categories of general or transcendental perfections. The creature, considered from the viewpoint of being, is nothingness: its being resides in God. Likewise, a just man, considered as just, is nothing: he is just only in Justice. A good man, as good, is nothing: he is good only in Goodness. A true man, as truthful, is nothing: he is true only in the Truth. The "individual perfections," justice, goodness, truth, limited properties belonging to created substances, are nothing. There are, properly speaking, only general perfections, from which the individual perfections draw their being.

Eckhart here separates himself from his master Thomas Aquinas. For Thomas the word "being" designates first the sensible substance: being is created, material, and it falls under the experience of the senses. Likewise, goodness, justice, truth are said first of good, just, true creatures. The Thomistic starting point is always experimental, created; that of Meister Eckhart is in God, uncreated.

In a significant text, in this regard, Thomas asks himself if goodness by essence belongs to God alone, or if other beings are good by essence.[6] He questions the mode of being of goodness, on the one hand, as an attribute of God, and, on the other hand, as a predicate of the sensible substance. A thing, he explains, is called good according to its perfection. Goodness pertains to "perfections" in general. To be good, true, just, is always a manner of being perfect in a given order. But, he says, there are three ways of envisaging the perfection of any reality whatsoever: either it is perfect by the very constitution of its being, or it is so thanks to some additional quality, or its perfection comes to it from an end to which it naturally aspires.

To be perfect according to these three viewpoints at the same time would mean to be perfect by essence. It is evident that, for Thomas Aquinas, God alone can be perfect in the constitution of his being, in the possession of his qualities, and in the enjoyment of his end. God's being is his essence; the qualities of God are God; the end of God is God himself. His perfection, says Thomas, thus joins together all modes: *perfectio omnimoda*. As to the creatures, they do not possess the identity of being and of essence: their constitution of being is always to be perfected; they accumulate superadded qualities: they must enrich themselves by accidental perfections; and they are far from enjoying their end: the perfection toward which they tend is always ahead of them, it requires from them a life impulse.

Everything that Thomas says of general perfections inasmuch as they pertain to God, Meister Eckhart subscribes to unreservedly. But here is the cleavage: the individual perfections for Eckhart are nothing. The Thomistic empiricism is totally foreign to Eckhart. For him, whatever a creature possesses comes to it as a loan; for Thomas, what a creature possesses is entirely its own, though acquired by gradually deficient appropriation. The difference is capital: for Meister Eckhart, the creature does not rule itself, it is not autonomous, its *nomos* is in God. Its qualities in truth are divine qualities become manifest in the world; there is for him strictly no perfection proper to things.

There is no room, in Eckhart's view of things, for the ontological constitution of creatures to attain greater perfection: they are nothing and will never then acquire anything. They cannot accumulate additional qualities: if nothingness is added to nothingness, the sum remains nothingness. Also, to speak of an end of creatures which solicits their impulse is forgetting that their end already possesses them. All that they are, their perfection, is in them, but belongs to God; they neither receive nor contain anything, but are rather received and contained in their perfections.

We shall not be surprised to see Eckhart's accusers startle and frown at this doctrine of created perfections. First, in their view, Eckhart put too much on the side of God, with regard to the ground of the mind, and now with regard to truth, goodness, and justice. They point out this statement of Eckhart:

> Goodness is neither created, nor made, nor begotten, but it is only productive, and it begets the good being.[7]

A good man is dependent upon Goodness as the creature is dependent upon the Creator. Goodness "makes" this man good, just as God "makes" the world. Because of this proportionality, whose middle term is "to make" or "to create," Goodness is creative as God is. It is God. Likewise for Eckhart, Truth is God, Justice is God.

> Just men take justice so seriously that if God were not just they would not care for God more than for a bean.[8]

The two statements of our sermon are now clear: "If God could turn his back on truth, I would cling to the truth and leave God" [2], and "if a man is touched by these three—truth, justice, and goodness—he will no more be able to relinquish these three than God is able to relinquish his Godhead" [5]. The good, just, true man can never be separated from goodness, justice, and truth: they are his nature. It is impossible for him to abdicate them, as it is impossible for God to abdicate his own nature, the Godhead. Both God and man are bound to their natures. This last opposition between God and the nature of God, the Godhead, *gotheit*, directly introduces the section that follows.

[6] "Motus" and "Breakthrough"

A master says: The good has three branches. The first branch is useful-ness, the second branch is delight, and the third branch is worthiness. This is why he says: "They adore the Father." Why does he say "the Father"? Look solely for God and you will find together with God all that he is capable of offering. This truth is certain, it is necessary, and it is attested. And even if it were not written, it would nonetheless be true. If God possessed still more, he could not hide it from you, he would have to reveal it to you, and he gives it to you. I have also oft remarked that he gives it to you, and he does so by virtue of birth.

A brief examination of the first sentence of this paragraph—"A mas-ter says: The good has three branches"—will provide the clue for the understanding of the paragraph as a whole. First, the division of the good into three "branches" parallels the distinction between God and Godhead: the same intuition is expressed but through two different models of thought. Second, "the master" referred to here by Meister Eckhart is again Thomas Aquinas, who in his *Summa Theologiae* explains the subdivisions of the good:

This division (into useful, worthy, and delightful goods) ... properly applies to goodness as such. For a thing is good if it is desirable and if movements of desire terminate in it . . . . Things that are desirable and that bring the movement to a relative end, being partway toward some other thing, we call "useful." That which is desirable and brings the movement of desire to a final end because it is the proper object of desire, we call "worthy," for worthy means desirable in itself. That which brings the movement of desire to an end and to its rest in the desired thing is "delightful."[9]

The diversity of goods is here understood as a function of the movement of desire, of the appetitive *motus*. For Thomas Aquinas, the useful good

is the least noble of the three as it is the means by which one obtains
something more elevated than this good itself. Such serviceable realities
are thoroughly "relative," since their goodness is exhausted in their
instrumental relationship to something other than themselves. For instance, the "drinking of bitter medicine"[10] is a relative good despite its
bad taste because it serves to restore health, a good more elevated than
sensual satisfaction. Whatever a man receives pleasure from he calls
delightful, even though such a good may do him harm. Alcohol may be
such a delightful good, but so is God himself: that is delightful in which
desire finds its rest. The worthy goods (the Latin word *honestum* is more
eloquent than its English equivalent, which suggests a moral quality
rather than a perfection of being) are things that have value in themselves.

Meister Eckhart expands upon this Thomistic distinction. According
to him, the sole "thing of value in itself" is the Godhead beyond God.
What Eckhart exactly intends by the real distinction between "God"
and "Godhead" remains to be seen. However, at this point it appears
that only the Godhead can offer man the place of repose where his quest
for a good, both delightful and worthy, comes to rest. Eckhart enumerates here the three types of good in order to make us feel the thrust of
desire, the "breakthrough" towards a haven. He says of this haven that
"God" does not offer it. The will, the faculty ordained to the good,
ascends through usefulness and delight into the very ground of God, in
which the Godhead offers both delight and worthiness. Desire thus
traces the path where man "breaks" into the very heart of God, which
is the Godhead.

The detached man has now found tranquility. God, insofar as he is
opposed to creatures, does not satisfy him, for his desire carries him
further to where there is neither any created relation nor any opposition.
Thematized according to the philosophy of the good, this passing
beyond distinctions is developed around the concept of *"motus"*: the
response of man to the solicitations of the good. One sole good solicits
us, the Godhead. "Breakthrough," *durchbruch,* which is an original expression in Meister Eckhart, is therefore quite simply a translation of the
appetitive *motus* of the Latin authors of the Dominican school to which
he belonged.

Thus God and the Godhead on the one hand, and the divisions of the
good on the other, are harmonized in the theory of the "breakthrough."

That Meister Eckhart has in mind here the "ground of God" or the "Godhead" beyond God, is confirmed in a twofold way: first by the expression "you will find together with God all that he is capable of offering"; then by the very Eckhartian twist "God has to." The first refers back to the theory of divine ideas,[11] the second, as will appear later, to that of an origin beyond God, which transcends all representation (cf. the section below entitled "Dehiscence").

If in this paragraph Meister Eckhart does indeed speak of the "Godhead" beyond the God who has a name, why does he call it "Father"? Why give this trinitarian title to the ineffable ground in which the breakthrough of desire comes to fulfillment? These questions are further complicated by the fact that in other sermons Eckhart clearly announces that the name "Father" cannot be applied to the divine ground. The sermon "Jesus Entered" insisted that we pass beyond all anthropomorphisms including Father, Son, and Spirit. The detached man seizes God inasmuch as he is "neither the Father, nor the Son, nor the Holy Spirit."[12] How are we to understand "Father" as it is used here?

It is the biblical text that constrains Eckhart to this title. One of the main manuscripts by which the sermon has been transmitted to us bears a variant, unfortunately isolated.[13] Here are the two versions:

Why does he say: "The Father"? If you seek God alone, you will find together with God all that he is capable of offering.	Why does he say: "the Father"? If you seek *the Father, that is God alone,* you will find together with him all that he is capable of offering.

In the gospel of the day Eckhart reads the word "Father"; at the same time he also intends to express, once again, his teaching on God beyond God, on the overcoming of divine modes and properties. Although "Father" designates such a mode or property, this particular day Eckhart feels free to call the Godhead "Father" so that Scripture and his thought are reconciled. The alternate version of the text gives evidence to his intention; "God alone" stands for the Godhead, so that we are to understand: If you seek the Father, that is, the Godhead, you will find together with him all that he is capable of offering. One encounters such malleability of expression in Meister Eckhart too frequently to be surprised by the liberties he takes.

[7–8] The Higher Part of the Mind and Its Faculties

The masters say: The mind has two faces. The upper face beholds God incessantly, and the lower face looks a little towards the below and directs the senses. The upper face, however, which is the peak of the mind, stands in eternity. It has nothing to do with time; it is ignorant of time as well as of the body. As I have said now and again, in it is hidden something like the original outbreak of all goodness, something like a brilliant light which incessantly gleams, and something like a burning fire which burns incessantly. This fire is nothing other than the Holy Spirit.

In this paragraph, Meister Eckhart briefly comments on a passage from Saint Augustine on the Trinity. The following seems to be the text to which he refers:

This is what we have said of the nature of the human mind, that both in the case when as a whole it contemplates the truth it is the image of God; and in the case when anything is divided from it, and diverted to the cognition of temporal things; nevertheless, on that side on which it beholds and consults truth, here also it is the image of God. But on that side whereby it is directed to the cognition of the lower things, it is not the image of God.[14]

Meister Eckhart replaces the terms "part" and "image" with the metaphor "face," which is also Augustinian. All these expressions designate something in the mind—not of the mind—neither created nor creatable. We may recall that this theory was the subject of a great deal of controversy at Cologne.[15] In the sermon incriminated then by the prosecution, Eckhart had held that in man's supreme faculty God begets both his Son and man as this Son himself. The present text establishes a parallel: man fosters the welling of the Holy Spirit in the core of his mind. In the ground of man's mind God works. His operations are the generation of the Son and the "outbreak," the "brilliance," and the "gleaming" of the Spirit.

Eckhart goes beyond the affirmation of the Spirit as the source of all goodness. In a typical movement of reduplication he asks: What is the source of the source? From where does its quality as source emanate? These questions are answered as the sermon reaches its pinnacle and describes the passage beyond the spiration of the Spirit.

The masters say that from the higher part of the mind emanate two powers. The first is called will, the other intellect. But the highest perfection of these powers resides in the higher power, namely the intellect. This can never find rest. It aspires to God not as he is the Holy Spirit nor as he is the Son: it flees from the Son. Nor does it want God inasmuch as he is God. Why? Because, as such, he still carries a name. And even if there were a thousand gods, it would still break beyond: it wants him where he has no name. It wants something more noble, something better than God as having a name. What then does the intellect want? It does not know; it wants him as he is the Father. This is why Saint Philip says: "Lord, show us the Father and it is enough for us." It wants him as he is the marrow out of which goodness springs; it wants him as he is the nucleus from which goodness flows; it wants him as he is the root, the vein, from which goodness exudes. Only there is he the Father.

Here the thought proceeds through a series of negations rather than affirmations: the passing beyond the Spirit, the fleeing of the Son, and the rejection of God objectified as "God." His unceasing quest leads the seeker beyond representation and design. Push ahead, says Eckhart, beyond the nameable, and reach the region of the unspeakable. To follow such a path to the end is to know no longer what one seeks or wants. The words that formerly marked out the road seem now to be erased. The last word to lose its meaning is the word "goodness." Only the allusive language of symbols remains: the mind now pursues the marrow, the core, the root, the vein which nourishes God as "God," and goodness as "goodness." The quest for God and his attributes has become radical; it has become a quest for the origin of God and for the origin of his attributes.

This sequence of thought sets out, again, with a doctrinal reminder. Eckhart establishes the superiority of the intellect and the will over the other faculties of the mind; to do so, a reference to the authority of the masters suffices. This sets up the next step: the breakthrough beyond all that has a name, he says, is the work of the intellect. In the preceding paragraph he praised the will, but here he praises the intellect: it is human knowledge that discovers the intimacy of the Godhead, not the will.[16] While the intelligence "can never find rest," the will rests in God, thus fulfilling its movement unlike the intellect. Now Eckhart has the habit of enlarging upon a point that he has hardly established. He not only passes from the Creator to the Godhead which terminates the movement of desire, but now the Godhead loses even this quality of bringing desire to rest, becoming merely the desert where the intellect strays without knowing why.

The negation of God as the Father, Son, and Spirit, and even of God "insofar as he is God" is quite explicit. In the sermon "Jesus Entered" we read that the castle in the mind will never know God "insofar as he possesses attributes and according to the propriety of his Persons." This served to negate the trinitary God of the revelation. Eckhart clearly states, then, that the intellect does not want God even insofar as he is "God." Thus the most general title, derived both from religious revelation and from philosophic reflection, is denied. In both cases, though, the argument is of an onomastic order: the negation bears on God inasmuch as he possesses a name.

What can be said of this "God" who has to be denied? The invitation to overcome a certain image of God is the acme of Meister Eckhart's thought. Let us briefly recall the path along which the sermon has guided us. Starting with a meditation on time, Eckhart refers to the body as the most manifest mark of the nonpossession of the self, and of the creature in general. Time, body, and creature form a complex of coordinated terms. This series of the created is opposed to the series of terms relating to the uncreated: the higher part of the mind, truth, goodness, justice, and God alone [1–4]. This is the first part of the mental itinerary. The viewpoint under which the two series are opposed is "creation."

The second part of the development [5–8], however, suggests the overcoming of the dichotomy just mentioned, between the created and the uncreated. God and Godhead [5], God and divine ideas [6], the Spirit and the source of his spiration above the Persons [7–8] indicate the three approaches by which Eckhart thinks out the abolition of this dichotomy. According to the first of these binary couples, God appears as distinct from his nature, the Godhead.[17] One usually speaks of God in opposition to the "world" or to "man": "God" is opposed to "non-God." In the Godhead all opposition is effaced.

The second couple, God and divine ideas, follows a similar path. The divine ideas, which are the sum of the images of everything creatable, preexist and subsist beyond "God." Their life, their "bubbling" or "boiling" (bullitio), precedes emanation, that is, the "ebullition" (ebullitio) outside the divine ground. In other words, it precedes the constitution of creatures and their distinction with God. Intradivine "bubbling" and productive "ebullition," therefore, symbolize from the viewpoint of created beings what "God" and "Godhead" symbolized from the viewpoint of God: namely the overcoming of the opposition between the creator and the creature.

Finally the third couple, the Spirit and the source of spiration, represents the crossing of the same threshold. The sending of the Spirit is a revealed article of faith; this sending causes the sanctification of men with the help of grace. In such a theological line of thought, the spiration of the Spirit appears as an eternal procession which prefigures its mission in history, prior to which there is nothing to be sent nor any person to be sanctified. To pass beyond the double sending of the Spirit, temporal and eternal, means again to pass beyond the opposition between God and non-God.

These schemes of thought exhibit three departures towards one and the same destruction. All oppositions are submitted to a radical challenge. The mind does not seek God insofar as he is God; it does not seek God insofar as he is the complement of non-God; it does not seek God insofar as he can be opposed to the created. It is not satisfied with anything that can be named. The identity of the name presupposes and consecrates the nonidentity of him who names. Whatever bears a name can be juxtaposed or be compared with something that has another name. The proper name of God, insofar as he is "comparable," is Creator. Man "compares" creatures with their Creator and exclaims: all that you have made is marvellous! In such an exclamation, God is not sought in his proper place but from where he is not, that is, from the whole of his work. Seeking God outside his proper place is not seeking God at all. It is making him into the "candle" which enlightens the multiplicity of things that draw their being from their distinction from God. A man attracted by God must break through beyond the creator-God.

On the road to the God beyond "God," the intellect no longer recognizes itself. "What, then, does it want? It does not know." But what can it not be ignorant of? What can it know? It can know that things exist around its path; it can know the marvels of creation, and it can discover that these have been made. But such knowing proceeds from distinction, thus remaining tied to creation: there are no marvels that lead the intellect beyond the creator-God. Its knowing is made by division and composition of concepts. The God beyond the creator-God transcends all division and composition; he gives himself to ignorance. This is the God whom Meister Eckhart calls "Father." In the context, this name is now only an additional symbol for the unknowable Godhead, so that speech will not have to be broken off.

Thus the end of the paragraph, concerning goodness, becomes more understandable. For the entire theological tradition which is inspired by the Neoplatonists, and especially Pseudo-Dionysius—an author whom

Meister Eckhart quotes as readily as Augustine and Thomas Aquinas—
the goodness of God is the supreme principle of all exterior production.[18] It is the divine perfection by virtue of which God creates. Goodness is the proper name of the creator-God. God is good because he
makes all things admirably. But if the thought in this paragraph is to
penetrate beyond the creator, the goodness of God will have to be
denied. "God" is good, the "Godhead" is not good. This is why the
intellect wants God "as he is the marrow out of which goodness springs;
it wants him as he is the nucleus from which goodness flows; it wants
him as he is the root, the vein, from which goodness exudes."

It is characteristic of the Neoplatonism of Meister Eckhart that, for
him, passing beyond the creator-God and passing beyond the three
Persons of the Trinity constitute one and the same passage towards the
ineffable. Not that the Son and the Spirit are for him created Persons.
But in both of God's operations, the procession of the Persons and the
creation of beings, God gives himself a name: Father, Son, Spirit, or
Creator. Eckhart refuses to distinguish between the operations of God,
for their multiplicity draws away from the unspeakable ground. What
appears as a double divine operation, the emanation of the Persons and
that of the created, is one single and unique act of production in God.
In the sermon "Jesus Entered" he tied together into a single phrase "the
modes and the Persons" (the "modes" referring to the attributes of God,
such as his creative goodness). Now he says: "the intellect flees from the
Son," and "the intellect wants the origin of goodness." The first expression speaks of the overcoming of the trinitary God, the second of the
overcoming of the creator-God.

[9] Birth of the Son and Equanimity

This is what our Lord says: "No one knows the Father except the Son, and
no one knows the Son except the Father." Perfectly: to know the Father
we must be the Son. I have pronounced—when I don't know—three little
maxims: take them as nuts, hot nutmeg, and thereafter drink. First: if we
want to be the Son, we have to have a Father. No one, indeed, can say
that he is a son unless he has a father; and no one is a father unless he
has a son. If the father is dead, we say "he was my father." If the son is
dead, we say: "he was my son." So the life of the son resides in the father,
and the life of the father in the son. This is why no one can say: "I am
a son," without having a father. But only such a man is truly a Son who

carries out all works by love. Secondly, what constitutes a man as Son most of all is equanimity. Is he sick? May he be as gladly sick as well, as gladly well as sick. Is his friend coming to die? He will renounce him in the name of God. Is an eye plucked out of him? He will renounce it in the name of God. Thirdly, a son can bow his head to no one except the father. How noble is this faculty which stands above time, and which has no place! Elevated above time, indeed, it contains in itself all time; and it is itself the whole of time. Even if man possessed very little of what is so elevated above time, he would nevertheless very quickly grow rich. For what lies beyond the seas is not further removed from this power than what is present in this very moment. This is why he says: "These are they who seek the Father."

The "breakthrough" constitutes the center of our text. The following describes the breakthrough's consequences for man, which are three in number, metaphorically described by Eckhart as "hot nutmeg."

The first of these consequences is the begetting of the Son. A man who has experienced the silence of the Godhead begets the Son in the unity of operation with God.[19] In this sermon "Father" stands for "Godhead." "The life of the son resides in the father, and the life of the father resides in the son": the detached man brings forth the Son in the ground of God, and concomitantly God brings forth the Son in the ground of the mind. The two operations are but one single and the same bringing forth; one single and the same event, which may be described as the energetic identity beyond procession and creation. The condition of this birth is called at times "detachment," at times "breakthrough," at times, as here, "love." A detached man "breaks through" beyond the Creator and "carries out all works by love." The joining together of these three determinations allows for a better grasp of what Meister Eckhart means by the birth of the Son in us: essentially a new relationship, under the sign of liberty understood as dispossession, with things and beings.

The second consequence is what Meister Eckhart here calls *gelîcheit*, in modern German *Gleichmut*.[20] During the time of Eckhart, this word meant in ordinary usage "likeness," "homogeneity," "parable"; to the mystics, it is a technical moral term which can be translated by "impassibility," "equality," or, best, "equanimity." As the intention of this text can easily be misunderstood, we shall briefly recall the three schools, in the history of ideas, where this concept of impassibility has come to be prominent long before Eckhart. Such a reminder will enable us to examine the extent to which Meister Eckhart remained faithful to his predecessors in this matter.

Gelîcheit is the German equivalent of the Greek word ἀπάθεια, apathy. This concept has entered into the western linguistic and philosophical tradition in several Latin expressions: sometimes as *insensibilitas,* sometimes as *imperturbatio,* but most often as *impassibilitas.*[21] Apathy originally designates the ascetic ideal of the Stoa, but it is also present in the Neoplatonists. Finally this ideal was adopted by certain Greek Fathers of the Church.

In the Stoa, apathy describes the state of a man, wise or spiritual, who has delivered himself from his passions (the idea of despoiling, of privation is expressed in the grammatical form of the words themselves: im-passibility, a-pathy), and who has reached a perfect inner freedom. Such a state of mind is learned; this ideal demands a training:

> Begin with little things. Is your oil spilled? Is your wine stolen? Say: this is the price for apathy.[22]

The apprenticeship of Stoic equanimity begins with and is verified by minute contradictions. The most ephemeral passions are the worst enemies of serenity, for even though they are apparently without influence on the deeper equilibrium of man, they nevertheless corrode it. The Stoa teaches that the spirit grows heavy as a result of the most fleeting movements of the "concupiscible" and of the "irascible." Such transient irritations constitute the privileged moment in which resignation can and ought to convert into liberty. The petty price that buys apathy, for instance restraining your temper when your oil is spilled, is in fact so high that it produces and at the same time manifests a transformation of the entire human being.

Plotinus teaches that divine resemblance is acquired through the mastery of the passions. Likeness to God is the goal of man's progressive transformation. Detach yourself from the sensible, from the lower reason, and from all that is not the One; act only according to the intellect, and you will resemble God. Perfect detachment and perfect obedience to the νοῦς are the two faces of one and the same moral perfection, apathy.

> As the soul is evil by being interfused with the body and by coming to share the body's states and to think the body's thoughts, so it would be good, it would be possessed of virtue, if it threw off the body's moods and devoted itself to its own act—the state of intellection and wisdom—and never allowed the passions of the body to affect it. . . . Such a disposition

in the soul, become thus intellective and immune to passion (ἀπαθής), it would not be wrong to call likeness to God.[23]

Stoics and Neoplatonists, however, do not put the accents in the same way: Stoic apathy leads towards perfect mastery of the impulses and the free possession of the self. Plotinian apathy has as its goal the return of the soul towards the νοῦς and of the νοῦς towards the One that is its origin and the end of the assimilation.

The "apathy" which some Fathers of the Church recommend, despite the fundamental differences between Christian and pagan thought, recalls on many points the teaching of the Greek and Latin sages. The Fathers' usage of this word indicates an ascetic way towards "gnosis," that is, the knowledge of the revealed mysteries. However, once this doctrine is integrated into Christian initiation, it largely transcends its original form.[24] We shall quote but one text from Evagrius the Pontian, one of the main defenders of this school. For him, freeing oneself from passions is only a first step within Christian asceticism. Apathy has to lead to mystagogy, and then to the contemplation, without mediation, of the divine light. Evagrius writes:

> To perceive in oneself the place of God, the soul must be raised above all thoughts concerned with things. It will not succeed in this if it does not rid itself of the passions which, through thought, tie it to sensible things. It will rid itself of passions by means of the virtues, and of simple thoughts by means of spiritual knowledge. It will leave this knowledge in turn when that light appears which, at the hour of prayer, forms the place of God.[25]

The introduction into Christian spirituality of themes and methods adopted from non-Christian origins, as we have in Evagrius, provoked strong confrontations. Some Greek Fathers show an unreserved admiration[26] for the Stoics, integrating into their own systems the doctrine of apathy. Others, however, were less bold about the possibility of a perfect abandonment of all sensations and of all thoughts. They were more concerned about their brothers' progression, and although they recommend apathy as an ideal, they grant that it may be impossible to attain. Still they consider this ideal precious in daily life, where one should remain unimpressed "like a diamond-wall."[27]

In the West, especially as a result of the Anti-Pelagian controversies, this doctrine of apathy was always combatted. The two champions of this combat were Jerome[28] and Augustine.[29] Thomas Aquinas endeavored to bring about a kind of equilibrium between the two positions. According to Thomas, disordered affects such as the "irascible" and the "concupiscible" may without doubt be called passions insofar as they escape the control of reason. This was, he explains, the position of the Stoics, whose way of thinking resulted in an irreducible opposition between virtues and passions. Thomas, for his part, prefers to call "passions" all the impulses of sensibility, whether they are directed towards some moral good or not. Such impulses and such affects constitute the matter of the virtues and therefore have to be subjected to reason in order to receive the virtuous form. Only when this imposition of form upon matter is completed will the passions be called ordered. Hence the moral man does not eliminate them at all; rather, he pursues them as the very substance of his acting.

Contrary to the Stoic doctrine, then, the more perfect a moral virtue is, the more it will harmonize the passions, and the more repercussions it will have even over the most elementary sensitive forces of man. The classical debate with the Stoics, says Thomas, is mainly a quarrel of words. By "passions," in the broad sense, he understands impulses and passibility, which are the matter of moral acting. They have to be integrated into a behavior subordinate to the will and enlightened by reason. Thomas therefore rejects apathy, understood as a liquidation of the passionate forces, in the name of a broader theory of the roles of will and reason.

Thus equanimity in the non-Christian and Christian traditions takes on different meanings. Sometimes it designates the way to happiness through the conquest of an imperturbable inner equilibrium, as with the Stoics; sometimes it describes the preparation for contemplating the One, as in Plotinus; sometimes it is a name for the initiation into the knowledge of revealed divine mysteries, as in Clement and Origen, or it establishes the place of divine indwelling, as in Evagrius; again, it may reflect the pride of man, who believes he can dispense with the grace of God, which was the doctrine that Jerome and Augustine chastized in their polemic against Pelagius. Finally, in the more modestly anthropological analysis of Thomas, it denotes an improper understanding of the role of the passions in moral life. Yet, despite their great differences, there is one common denominator for all its defenders: apathy is an ascetic attitude with the purpose of acquiring a higher, spiritual good promised to man.

Meister Eckhart evokes equanimity in a very precise context. The word *gelîcheit* comes to his lips when he speaks of the begetting of the Son and of man's ensuing intimacy with the Godhead without name. Like love, equanimity is a quality of the detached man, who in the present moment does not belong any longer to creatures but "to God alone." This man recognizes creatures as creatures, that is, as having their being in God whom they manifest. Equanimity is the consequence of detachment with relation to the created as created. It is a condition of nothing; nor does it lead anywhere; it is rather a result. It is a sign which makes visible the appropriation of God:

> If you are sick and you pray to God for health, then your health is dearer to you than God, and he is not your God: he is the God of heaven and earth, but he is not your God.[30]

Equanimity, a consequence of the "breakthrough," unveils, according to Eckhart, what the ground of the mind is like: it is of divine nature. Equanimity points to this nature. It is not an ascetic behavior but a manifestation. It is the conduct by which a deified being manifests his belonging to God. It does not precede deification as a condition, but follows from it as the consequence in which the profound destiny of man becomes notable.

The detached man "is as gladly sick as well, as gladly well as sick." He can accept a friend's death or his own eyes being plucked out without revolt. His attitude of equanimity is a sign that he has been born Son of God. "Like a lamb led to the slaughter, he does not open his mouth";[31] "Pilate said to him: do you not hear all that they are attesting against you? But he did not give him a single answer, which quite astonished the governor."[32] The muteness of the victim is a sign: he knows he is the Son of God.

We can take this a step further: *gelîcheit*, "equality," "similitude," "resemblance," mean that the mind remains "equal," like an untroubled lake, in the midst of good and evil. This is the literal meaning of the English "equanimity," which implies that the soul holds all things as "equal," as equivalent. Whatever may happen is all the same to the mind. Good and evil are of the same value to it. *Gelîcheit* combines these two aspects: a detached man in all circumstances remains equal to himself, and for such a man all things are equal. Where and how is such an equality of man and things possible? Man and things, Eckhart says, are equal in God. The place of the equality of the mind's temper is God himself, for in God there is no longer any distinction between great and small:

The highest angel, the mind, and the gnat have an equal model in God.[33]

In their model, or their original image, all things are equal. In the sermon "Woman, the Hour Is Coming," the manifestative function of *gelicheit* —manifestative of equality—appears in the exclamation "in the name of God!" This little sentence is not a rhetorical ornament. In the context it has to be understood as the summary of Eckhart's theory of equanimity: all things are the same to me in God. It is to be taken not in the apathetic sense of moral indifference, but in the apophatic sense of an ideal indistinction. The importance of this theory is attested by the fact that Eckhart upheld it even before the Inquisition.[34]

The third consequence of the breakthrough is that "the Son can bow his head to no one but the Father." He "can" not: this recalls by symmetry that God "must." This impossibility and this "must" are repeated in the paragraph that follows.

[10] "God Must"

See how dearly God loves us, how he implores us. God is impatient for the mind to turn away and scale off from the creatures. Also it is a sure truth and a necessary truth that God has such a need to seek us out— exactly as if all his Godhead depended on it, as in fact it does. God can no more dispense with us than we can dispense with him. Even if it were possible that we might turn away from God, God could never turn away from us. I say: I will not pray that he give me anything; no more than I will praise him for what he has bestowed on me. I will much rather pray that he make me worthy to receive. I will praise him for being of such a nature and of such an essence that he must give. He who would deprive God of this would deprive him of his proper being and his proper life. May the truth of which I have spoken help us become the Son in truth. Amen.

God "implores us," he "needs to seek us out," he "must give." These texts speak of a compulsion in God, of a necessity. This theme has already presented itself earlier in our sermon. Eckhart's position can and should surprise us. Surely, all is not scandalous in this teaching. For this reason it has to be asked which is the exact point at variance with the traditional views. Necessity is the contrary of freedom. That which is free is called "its own cause," and that which is necessary is called "what cannot not be."[35] This traditional metaphysical approach borrows its categories from the philosophy of the natural world: causality, generation and corruption, becoming. Thomistic theodicy poses the problem of God's freedom in the terms of causality. In such a context Eckhart's declaration that God needs us must raise some questions that disturb metaphysical security: Does Eckhart's proposition impair the freedom of God as cause of himself, and does it attribute to him an action which cannot not be? On the other hand, are Eckhart's categories, in this matter, of a causal type like those of Thomas Aquinas?

Generally speaking, is there something in God that cannot not be? Thomas Aquinas answers in the affirmative: there are certain things which God cannot not will.

> The divine will has a necessary relation to the divine goodness, since that is its proper object. Hence God wills his own goodness necessarily. But he wills things other than himself insofar as they are ordered to his own goodness as their end. That God wills things other than himself is not absolutely necessary. Yet it is necessary by supposition; for supposing that he wills a thing, God cannot not will it, as his will cannot change.[36]

The key to this passage is "goodness." God's goodness is the only reason for his actions. In both realms, natural reflection on the creation and supernatural listening to the revelation, he shows himself as Goodness. Philosophically as well as theologically it is impossible for God not to be good. God has freely manifested himself so, but having shown himself as good, he "must" remain good. God has freely willed this necessity: if he could miss his goodness, he would not be God. He then wishes it absolutely, or essentially, naturally: it is his essence and his nature to be good. But he wills the created, by which he sets this natural quality into operation, only with a necessity "by supposition." This means the following: if one supposes that God wills, then it must be assumed that what he wills is ordered towards Goodness, as a means to its end. God orders the objects which are other than himself towards himself as to their end. He wills them therefore with relative necessity, namely relative to his own goodness.

Thomas would say then: God needs to seek us out, it is true; however, this is not an absolute, but a relative necessity; it follows upon the fact that he has created us. The necessity with which God loves us is linked to his free initiative of creating.

The cleavage between Thomas and Eckhart, then, may be described in the following way: both of them would agree with the proposition "God must love us" (although Thomas is less fond than Eckhart of using such striking expressions). But Thomas would add: ". . . because in loving his creature, he loves himself"; in other words, creation is the praise of love which God gives to himself through all things. Eckhart, in return, would continue the proposition, saying: ". . . because the uncreated ground in man loves God with that love by which God loves himself." The uncreated in man is the "end" of divine love, just as God himself is the end of divine love: God gives glory to the mind, and he gives glory to himself through one and the same act of love.

> God . . . implores us. God is impatient for the mind to turn away and scale off from the creatures.

The glory of God is that man "breaks through" beyond the Creator. Then the Son is born in the paternal heart, and man finds his God, the Godhead. The glory of God is man deified: a man such as this God "must" love. His love for him "cannot not be" since he gives to this man the very love with which he loves his own nature, that is, the Godhead.

> God has such a need to seek us out—exactly as if all his Godhead depended on it, as in fact it does.

For Thomas, the necessity that binds God to man is a thoroughly relative necessity—"by supposition" and thus entirely concomitant with his creative initiative. God cannot be unfaithful to his love as Creator. This necessity is established according to the philosophical schemes of causality and of the first principle: "God the Creator is necessarily good" is equivalent to "the first cause is not subject to change." Meister Eckhart, although his expressions recall some of Thomas's, affirms the exact contrary of him. The necessity that binds God to man is absolute, a necessity of nature. It transcends the relationship of Creator to creature and refers to the energetic identity in the birth of the Son. If we follow Meister Eckhart's thought to the bottom, we find that there is no God without man. God is placed in dependence on man, to the point of receiving his being and his life from him:

I will praise him for being of such a nature and of such an essence that he must give. He who would deprive God of this would deprive him of his proper being and his proper life.

Detachment not only reveals man's condition and the condition of the ground, but also God's own condition: God is not; God is nothing as long as man lacks the breakthrough to the Godhead. If you do not consent to detachment, God will miss his Godhead, and man will miss himself.

COMMENTARY

Intensities of Releasement

To make Meister Eckhart's thought come to life for us today, the exegesis of his texts is hardly enough. The interpretation has to show which are the concrete steps that lead man's existence towards God and finally beyond God. Exegesis isolates the elements of Eckhart's thought according to the letter of the argument, interpretation restores it according to the order of reasons. Eckhart announces a simple message; his doctrine has nothing esoteric or extraordinary about it. It concerns what is most ordinary in an existence. It deals with experiences that the majority of men have. It responds to elementary questions in the apprenticeship of life: What about my original liberty, and how can it be regained? How can I come back to myself? Where can I find joy that does not tarnish? The answer to such questions will result from a reconstruction of the main themes enunciated in the sermon "Woman, the Hour Is Coming." Thus Meister Eckhart's teaching will appear in its unity.

The single thought around which this message is articulated is expressed in verbs that speak of deliverance: "to rid oneself of something," "to become free," "to be a virgin," "to let be." These verbs indicate a road, most often called *abegescheidenheit*. This word becomes a technical term for Meister Eckhart and his disciples and today is entered as such in dictionaries.

Abegescheidenheit, in modern German *Abgeschiedenheit*, is formed of the prefix *ab-* which designates a separation (*abetuon*: to rid oneself of something; *abekêre*: turning away, apostasy) and of the verb *scheiden* or *gescheiden*. In its transitive form, this verb means "to isolate," "to split," "to separate," and in its intransitive form "to depart," "to die." The word *abegescheidenheit*, "detachment" or "renunciation," and the verbs of deliverance evoke, in the allusive thought of Meister Eckhart, a mind that is on the way to dispossession from all exteriority which might spoil its serenity.[37]

To understand such an itinerary of existence instructs man about more than himself. Speaking of man engaged on the way of detachment means also to be speaking of God; and of God Meister Eckhart does not speak otherwise than through his praise of the detached man. All that is essential about man and God would have been said if only it were possible to retrace the steps of detachment. Detachment draws the horizon within which God encounters man. The difficulty in interpreting Meister Eckhart stems from the necessity of reproducing in ourselves the disposition that allows such an encounter to occur. This disposition can be more or less intense. Eckhart seems to imply a fourfold gradation: Dissimilarity, Similarity, Identity, and "Dehiscence." These four titles serve as road signs marking the way of *abegescheidenheit* that leads to the origin. As existence moves ahead on this road, all ascetic imperatives vanish. Thus detachment turns progressively into releasement, *gelâzenheit,* which, as has been said, is a broader concept. The lower intensities of releasement require an effort of the will; the higher intensities of releasement exclude every voluntary determination. To speak of intensities in this context is quite paradoxical; it does not mean that Eckhart's experience results from a performance or from contractions of the will; quite the opposite is true. We have seen that he does not even care to develop a "philosophy of the will." The intensities of releasement result from the actualization of the center, or ground, in man.

Under Dissimilarity, God and man appear as radically foreign to one another. With Similarity, the latter discovers himself to be a reflection of the former. Identity brings to the fore the unique nobleness of the ground of man. Finally, "Dehiscence," the last road sign, points in the direction of an itinerancy where there is no longer God or man, but only the desert.[38] *Abegescheidenheit* is the intrinsic folly of this rational course. The origin, whose signs it unravels, conceals itself from all human experience except such folly.

Dissimilarity

All creatures are mere nothingness. I do not say that they are small or anything at all: they are mere nothingness.[39]

Here the dissimilarity between God and man is declared to be absolute—just as absolute as the difference between "yes" and "no." God is, while man, inasmuch as he is created, is not. "Creature" designates a being that incessantly receives itself from elsewhere; it has received existence, life, and intelligence from another. It does not possess itself, the other is its being, in itself it is nothing.

> What does not possess being is nothingness. But no creature has being, for its being depends on the presence of God. Were God to withdraw for an instant from all creatures, they would be annihilated.[40]

From the condition of creature, Eckhart concludes that the created is nothingness. Earlier he spoke in images: "As long as the creature is creature, it carries within itself bitterness and harm, wrong and distress." This is a metaphorical way of stating the nothingness of creaturehood. A short inquiry into Eckhart's vocabulary of being will reveal how we are to understand "nothingness."

Eckhart uses three groups of words for "being." The word *wesen* is the most remarkable because of its semantic broadness. Generally it is used to translate, in the form of a verb, the *ens commune* of the Scholastics. Thus it designates the being of beings. But it is much wider in extent and overlaps with "essence." We therefore translate *wesen* either by "essence" or, according to the context, by "essential coming forth." *Wesen* is the word for the totality of what shows itself, from the point of view of its coming forth. The being of beings is thought of as coming continually to the light. Being is thought of as the daybreak over beings.

Conversely, *unwesene* is reserved by Meister Eckhart for that essential coming forth which, at the same time, retreats into concealment, that is, into the darkness in which the acting of the mind is united to the acting of God.

> The mind acts in *unwesene,* and it follows God who acts in the *unwesene.*[41]

In a certain sense, *unwesene* could be translated by "nothingness"; but as it expresses the abolition of the positivity of being, it points, so to speak, not beneath but beyond being, as the $\dot{v}\pi\dot{\epsilon}\rho\text{-}\breve{o}\nu$ of the Neoplatonists. In the *unwesene* of the Godhead, the activity of the ground of the mind is identical with the actuality of God. *Unwesene,* then, does not apply to creatures. The opposition between being and nothingness in creatures is expressed in a different terminology.

The Middle High German word for "nothing" is *niht.* It is composed of the particle of negation *ne-* and of *iht,* "something" or "anything whatsoever." "The creature is nothing." What exactly is it that Eckhart wants to negate in the created? *Iht* is denied; the creature is not "a something." *Iht* designates the existing in general: the creature endowed with a borrowed being, the *entitas* of the *ens* or the *ousia* of the *on. Iht* speaks of the fact that a being is. It denotes that which qualifies thought to represent to itself a being as a being. One is reminded of what Martin Heidegger calls *Seiendheit,* a word which has been translated by "being-ness."[42] *Niht* is the negation of the fact of being. The creature in general cannot be represented as being; its *iht* resides in God, not in itself.[43] (The opposition *iht–niht* has an equivalent in modern Dutch, *iets–niets,* but not in modern German.) The individual being is called *ihtes iht,* "this individual being" or "this something." Here the terminology is most incisive. The corresponding negation, *nihtes niht* is properly translated by "non-being." It expresses the negation of the individual fact of being. The individual being is not; it does not possess *ihtes iht.*

The opposition between *iht* and *niht* gives the conceptual tool with which Meister Eckhart grasps the domain of the created. "All creatures are *ein lûter niht*": this applies to the created in general. As for *nihtes niht,* it designates that "nothingness" which is the individual creature. Such a creature is *ein lûter nihtes niht.* In all strictness, the individual creature is not. Its being is in God. Its being does not properly belong to itself. This applies to any particular image, to any object or work, and most of all to man himself insofar as he is created: all this inhibits detachment and is *nihtes niht,* nothing.[44]

The third family of words derives more directly from the verb "to be." They are the words *sîn,* to be, and *isticheit,* which is constructed out of *ist,* it "is," and designates primarily God's being. Meister Eckhart sometimes connects it with *wesen* and calls God the *weseliche isticheit.*[45] *Wesen,* too, is then mainly found in the context of divine union. Now the union is no longer considered apophatically as a veiling darkness, but cataphatically as an identity in the primordial being. We translate *isticheit* by "primordial being." *Sîn* and *isticheit* have often the same extension and comprehension:

> God's being is my being and God's primordial being is my primordial being.[46]

"The creature is mere nothingness." *Iht* comes to a thing as God incessantly lavishes being upon his creature. Let God's prodigality of *iht* cease for an instant, and the universal presence of the cosmos will immediately vanish.

All creatures are with God, and God grants them their essential coming
forth together with his presence.[47]

Outside of God there is nothing but only nothingness.[48]

Finally, in some texts "nothing" takes on a moral meaning: sin is
nothing. But by temperament as well as by conviction, Eckhart is not
a moralist. These passages are found in his scholarly works, in Latin, and
are less significant. Even here, Eckhart proposes a "metaphysics" rather
than a morals of sin.[49]

From the viewpoint of the history of doctrines, this entire theme of
nothingness and dissimilarity can easily be traced back to the Bible and
to Augustine. When Eckhart speaks of *unglicheit,* the country of dissimilarity,[50] he claims either the authority of the *regio dissimilitudinis* in
Augustine,[51] or that of the "foreign land" in the psalms.[52]

Meister Eckhart's vocabulary of being shows the creature existing
"with God." Being-with expresses a distance resulting from birth in the
world. Before I came to be, I was, on the contrary, "in God." But when
I came to be, nothingness appeared in me. To "be with" means to be
removed, separated. Everything that is not "in" God is far from God;
and everything that is "in" God is God. What is "with" God is nothingness: it is nothing in itself, since it exists only by the grace of another
—in *fluxu et fieri,* says the commentary on the Book of Wisdom.[53]

The dissimilarity in me between being and nothingness is due to the
mode of the divine presence, a presence not intrinsic, as in my preexistence, but extrinsic. I am no longer my being, I receive it; what I am as
a creature is nothingness.

At the opposite of the zone of divine indwelling, as described in the
sermon "Jesus Entered," there is thus a region in man where he is only
a creature, that is, nothingness: consequently, where there is no truth.
It is by virtue of this latter region that he belongs to the world. It is from
here also that the difference between God and man becomes thinkable.
The boldness of Eckhart's position clearly appears when one has understood that this difference introduces identity and otherness into man
himself: identity with God in the core of the mind, and otherness in the
faculties or powers and in the body. Man is the locus of union and
disunion, the Difference between identity and difference. In the
"ground," man lives in God and God in him; but in his creaturehood,
man is of the world. Disunion is rooted in the dissimilarity, in the

being-with by which man is "close to," therefore removed from God. The difference between God and not-God is a cleft that splits man thoroughly. Only out of this cleft can God, man, and the world be thematized. At this point, it should not surprise us any longer that Eckhart actually abolishes the methodological distinction between theology, anthropology, and cosmology. All these three sciences would have to develop the same opposition between "in-God" and "with-God" which is entrusted to man alone. He is at the same time the being-there and the being-elsewhere of the origin; he is among all beings the one that is alike-unlike the origin.

> When the Father engendered all creatures, he brought me forth. I emanated together with all creatures and yet I remain within, in the Father.[54]

"Created" and yet "in the Father": these two determinations do not intend to isolate two entities in man, one divine, the other human. Man is not composed of being and nothingness, that is, of a duality similar to the ancient duality of soul and body or of a subsisting form and matter. His composition is rather accomplished by antecedent and consequent, quite as an adolescent is composed of childhood and adulthood. Detachment evolves under the imminence of being, in provenance from nothingness. Man on the way of detachment opens a double horizon: the *being* of God's Son in the bosom of the Father ahead of him, and the *nothingness* of the creature behind him. Between these stretches Meister Eckhart's path.

This is the ontological meaning of preaching, the literary form chosen by Meister Eckhart. It is not accidental that he was a preacher. He invites his listeners to return from the forgetfulness of *iht*, the created being that depends on God, and to be mindful of the *wesene*, the coming-forth of the ground of the mind, which has been present from all eternity in the Godhead. His preaching urges our freedom to commit itself upon a path which, from the being of provenance or from the creatures' nothingness, leads to the being of imminence or to the Godhead's nothingness. Being as coming forth is encountered first of all in the preached word itself.

This dispersion of man is his strangeness. Everything created is nothingness;[55] temporal things are nothing. Provided that man return to his primitive simplicity, that he come back from dissimilarity and from the temporal things among which he is erring, provided that he make himself like nothing nor anyone (*entglichet*), only then will he be like God and will he inhabit the unity beyond all difference.[56] Joy here is not pleasure, it is arid: you will not find it among creatures.

Throughout such an understanding of nothingness, a great unitary dream betrays itself: that all things be one. This wish crystallizes around two poles, the new birth in God and the ancient dissemination of the self among objects, images, and works. The awakening arises from a meditation on the being of creatures. Their being is not their own. The secret of creatures is that in themselves they are nothing. Inclining oneself towards creatures results in being commingled with them in nothingness. *Abegescheidenheit* is an urging which demands of man that he "let nothingness be."[57] He who dismisses this urge, even if he believes that he is alive, is already dead. While he shuts himself off from this demand, he annihilates his true self.

These exhortations are not metaphors. Their background is a very elaborate ontology, which is also very personal. In order to honor the central place that Meister Eckhart's thought ascribes to the way of detachment, we call it a peregrinal ontology: a λόγος on being, whose λέγειν—collecting under the light of the original unity what is alike-unlike—cannot be experienced otherwise than on the way from dispersion and nothingness to full actualization of the ground of the mind. Yves Congar writes: "Everything falls into place, as if there were a proper ontology of the spiritual rapport, which has its unity, its certitude, but which is beyond natural ontology, so that it is antinomic and paradoxical for the latter. It is the 'who loses wins' of the Gospel."[58] This other or "proper" ontology has been very judiciously called a "functional"[59] ontology. Our last chapter will return in more detail to the way in which Eckhart understands being.

Repeating an ancient play on words on *mundus*, "world," and *mundum*, "pure," Eckhart interprets the verse of the first Letter of John, "God sent his only Son into the world" (1 John 4:9), translating it as "God sends his Son into the pure heart." The sending of the Son fulfills the one who has turned away from nothingness:

> "He sent him into the world": in one of its usages *mundum* means "pure." Notice that no place is more proper for God than a pure heart and a pure mind; there the Father begets his Son such as he begets him in eternity, neither more nor less. What then is a pure heart? That heart is pure which is separated and detached from all creatures, for all creatures soil, since

they are one nothingness. Nothingness is decay, and it soils the mind. All creatures are mere nothingness; neither angels nor creatures are anything. They soil because they are made out of nothingness. They are, and always have been, nothing. What is repugnant to every creature and causes it aversion is nothingness. If I placed a glowing coal on my hand it would hurt me. This comes solely from nothingness. If we were liberated from nothingness, we should be free from blemish.[60]

Here the intention behind the doctrine of nothingness, based on the doctrine of dissimilarity, shows forth: indicate a pause when equability before things may arise. What is created, in things, their being insofar as it is theirs, is nothing; nothingness burns and soils the freedom of detachment. Contact with the burning coal is painful because its glowing gives something to the hand that it is naturally deprived of. It is this lack of conformity with the fire that the hand actually suffers from. The pain is one of privation. If on the contrary our skin possessed the very attributes of the live coals, if it were itself fire, all negation and privation, and hence all pain, would disappear. Our body would encounter in the coal its own nature, and this would be highly agreeable. It is likewise for all creatures: their being belongs to God; this privation corrodes man, on whom they inflict their lack.

Every itching for possession, the enemy of serenity, has its origin in the creature as creature. It should be pointed out, however, that such a doctrine must not be reduced to a bewildered discrediting of the things that envelop our existence. Rather, it aims at an education of seeing:

He who knew nothing other than creatures would have no need for thinking of sermons, for each creature is full of God and is a book.[61]

If one renounces creatures inasmuch as they are creatures, one's eyes will be opened to God, who is hidden in them. Meister Eckhart, "a monk appreciated for his administrative qualities,"[62] did not feel that things deserved no attention at all; however, he considered that only He from whom things hold their being is worthy of interest in them. Every creature is to the credit of the Creator and not to its own credit. Here again, the thrust of the argument is not "indicative," but "imperative."

The "indicative" thought treats of substances, and by stressing their independence and sufficiency of being it assigns to man his place within the universal order. Indicative thought ponders what is given, therefore it is *old* by nature. "Imperative" thought, on the other hand, even though it can call on a tradition as ancient as Socrates, is essentially *new* since it addresses the hearer who has become ready to turn around on his road. This is the protreptic meaning of Eckhart's statement that "the being of the world is to receive being." The being of the world is radically dependent, insufficient; thus the union with the One requires a negation (detachment) of the negation (creature).

Meister Eckhart's instruction is the same throughout his teaching: turn your attention towards what *is* truly and exclusively, towards the source and estuary from which detached life comes and where it goes. Source and estuary are the same. Eckhart never tires of recalling the trace of the same in us which gives us being and which attracts us:

> There is something above the created being of the soul and inaccessible to creatures which are nothingness. . . . Many a priest stumbles here! This something is foreign and a desert, rather unnamed than named and rather unknown than known. If you could annihilate yourself but for an instant or even less than an instant, all that it is in itself would be yours. But as long as in some way your mind is on yourself or on any object, you know no more of God than my mouth knows about color or my eye about taste: so little do you know and discern of what God is.[63]

Man's complexity manifests the absolute in two ways: in man's created-ness the absolute is attested to by privation, and in his uncreatedness by superabundance. Eckhart experiences createdness morally as the region of attention to oneself and to things, ontologically as nothingness and exclusion from God, and epistemologically as ignorance. And this is how he experiences uncreatedness: morally as turning one's eyes away from individual images, ontologically as fulfilled being and inclu-sion in God, and epistemologically as learned ignorance. Created man in the deified man, because he is radically unlike God, bears the marks of God's absence. The manifestation of the origin proceeds simulta-neously by the "no" of nothingness in us and the "yes" of the trace.

Thus Michel Henry can write that "the internal structure of the absolute is thought of by Eckhart through the exclusion from it of all otherness. The 'world' and all the 'images,' according to Eckhart, are precisely what is rejected outside the absolute; they are what must be excluded from it." Eckhart's reflections on nothingness picture created man as veiling his face before the manifestation of the absolute in deified man, and as denying the ground of the mind. But this denial is only another revelation of the trace. "To understand the identity between the inclusion of man in God and the exclusion from him of all creatures is to understand Eckhart."[64]

Similarity

Eckhart observes that when a burning straw is brought close to a tree trunk, the wood, at first, refuses to catch fire. The dissimilarity is too great. But an ember buried in the ashes and smoldering overnight will not long resist the flame; crackling will soon fill the fireplace. *Gelicheit* is established, not in the moral sense,[65] but in being.

> God's endeavor is to give himself to us entirely. Just as fire seeks to draw the wood into itself and itself into the wood, it first finds the wood unlike itself. It takes a little time. Fire begins by warming it, then heating it, and then it smokes and crackles because the two are so unlike each other. The hotter the wood becomes, the more still and quiet it grows. The more it is likened to the fire, the more peaceful it is, until it becomes entirely flame. That the wood be transformed into fire, all dissimilarity must be chased out of it.[66]

We recognize in this text the strategy of detachment: from dissimilarity to similarity, and from similarity to union. The sermon "Jesus Entered" invoked the axiom in this regard: "the likeness of the like alone is the basis of union." The comparison with the fire which, by assimilation, attracts the ignitable to the perfection of the ignited, suggests a slow growth: in order for the blaze to absorb the wood, "it takes a little time." The wood is reborn "son" of the blaze, by *gelicheit*. When the absorption is completed, it will be distinct from the fire by its very indistinction, as the Son is alike–unlike the Father. The wood will be the perfect image of the fire:

> Nothing is so much alike and unlike at the same time . . . as God and the creature. What is there indeed so unlike and like each other as these whose unlikeness is their very likeness, whose indistinction is distinction itself? . . . Being distinct by indistinction, they resemble by dissimilarity. The more they are unlike, the more they are alike.[67]

The like and the unlike are resolved by flames and incandescences. Assimilation spreads the glory of that to which we are likened: because of the nature of its constituents, dissimilarity overcomes itself into similarity, and likeness shines into unlikeness. Beyond the similar, a union announces itself which, here again, will turn out to be nothingness: it will arise when all flames are extinguished. On the threshold of the union, the fire collapses, man is *ingebildet* or *übergebildet* into the indistinct.

Gelicheit, likeness or similarity, means more than equality. It gathers two beings under the same becoming, such as fire and wood in combustion, while equality is nondialectical and exhausts itself in comparisons. Between the child and the father there is a likeness based on common ancestry and destiny. Between the father and his business associate, there is equality—for instance, before the law. Equality refers only to the present. Similarity, on the other hand, points upstream: it recalls the source or the origin; it also points downstream: it intimates the assimilation, that is, the ocean where all is one. Similarity is not static, it constantly gives a new departure. It is an exodus. But as it evolves in the imminence of union, it is also already a repose. As an exodus, it anticipates the not-yet of the One; as a repose, it dwells in it already. As exodus, it is the abandonment of all differences, it is ordered *(aufgegeben);* as a repose, it is the discovery of a unity, and it is given *(gegeben).*

In some sermons, Eckhart expands his theory of assimilation into a theology of the image of God: "Outside of likeness, one cannot speak of an image."[68]

> An image is not of itself; nor is it for itself. It has its origin in that of which it is the image. To that it belongs properly with all that it is. It does not belong to what is foreign to this origin, nor does it owe anything to this. An image receives its being immediately from that of which it is an image. It has one being with it and it is the same being.[69]

The repose in which a detached man already lives means that "with all that he is" he belongs to Him whom he reflects as an image. With Him he "has one being and is the same being." As to the not-yet that separates similarity from perfect identity, Eckhart says:

> You often ask how you should live. Note this carefully. See what has just been said of the image: in exactly the same way you should live. You should be in him and for him, and not in yourself and for yourself.[70]

Such an understanding of similarity begins a dialectical process in which the being in and for God consumes the being in itself and for itself. Only a hermeneutic of the One will spawn such an ignited vision of existence. Just as fire "makes everything run towards its first simplicity,"[71] so detachment incinerates the old man, that is, the created man in man, who does not carry the imprint of the image of God. The conquest of resemblance with the origin passes through the abandonment of all created likeness. When man is *ungelîch*, unlike the created and totally *entglîchet*, no longer resembling anything, then he will be like God.

Eckhart's speculation on the being of images echoes the patristic ponderings on the same subject. Imagine a man standing before a mirror. Properly speaking, where does the image that absorbs his attention reside? Does its being inhere in the body from which it emanates, or rather in the reflection which he contemplates? "The image is in me, of me, towards me," answers Eckhart.[72] Were I to move back a step, the image would no longer be.

> Every image has two properties. The first is that it receives its being immediately from that of which it is an image, without interference of the will. Its outgoing is indeed natural, and it thrusts itself out of nature like a branch from the tree. When an image is cast on a mirror, our face will be reflected in it whether it likes it or not. . . . The second property of the image lies in its resemblance.[73]

The first point accords with the conclusion on created being: the image has no proper being, being comes to it from another, it does not exist originarily. The image exists only in its "outgoing" *(ûzganc)*. The second point explains from where it extracts its being: it is nothing else but that very dependence we call reflection. Eckhart applies these considerations to the relationship between man and God. Man, as an image of God, remains "with" him of whom he is the image, distinct from him and not "in" him. In its outgoing, the image stays at the periphery of the origin.

Now Eckhart develops the idea of "being-with" according to two models of thought: "justice" and the "word." Either model corroborates the theory that derives being from resemblance, although the model of justice is by far the one most developed by Eckhart.

> He who understands my teaching about justice and the just man understands everything I say.[74]

According to this first model, the just man lives "with justice."[75] The just man *qua* just does not possess being, he receives the being-just from justice. His being is exhausted in this dependence. According to this model, the constitutive principle, justice, and the constituted derivate, the just man, maintain a relation of actual similarity: each time and insofar as the just act is accomplished, the just man "is" just. Receiving his being from justice, he is assimilated to it as wood is assimilated to fire, or as the ground of the mind is assimilated to the ground of God. He acts not "in justice" but "out of" or "with" it, that is, by virtue of it. The appropriation of the reflection of justice determines his action; he is what justice is. Were he to commit injustice, the similarity would be broken. He would become alien to justice, that is, dissimilar. A just man, then, inasmuch as he is just, has no proper being, his origin is not in him. Devoid of justice in himself, he is summoned to turn towards justice and to receive from it his being as an image.

> Whoever loves justice remains so firmly established in it that what he loves becomes his own essence. No thing can distract him from this, and he heeds nothing else.[76]

The just man no longer looks for support elsewhere; nor does he let his acts be determined by external precepts. If he strove for conformity with exterior laws, his acting would simply be legal. The just man who acts out of intimate assimilation with justice "is" just in the same way that the reflection of a beautiful face is beautiful: totally by another and yet totally in itself. As just, as an image, a man engaged on the way to detachment is assimilated towards his origin. Near his origin, "with" it, he finds rest, and in its solicitations he recognizes the call to perpetual exodus: from dissimilarity, he passes to similarity.

According to the second model, the word, Eckhart will say that man should be an "adverb," *bîwort,* to the Word or Verb of God.

> I have in mind the little word *quasi* which means "like"; children in school call it an adverb. This is what I intend in all my sermons. The most appropriate things that one can say of God are "Word" and "Truth." God called himself a "Word." Saint John says: "In the beginning was the Word," meaning by this that we should be an adverb to this same Verb.[77]

A detached human being is destined to become an ad-Verb. Eckhart's thought proceeds along the following lines. A man speaks. Through the numerous words of his discourse, it is possible that one single utterance makes itself heard and stands out to whoever knows how to listen. To the hearer, words may then seem suddenly so transparent that he is able to declare: "Now I know exactly what you mean." From the flow of many statements, he is able to assimilate the single intention that they all purport. We speak of what someone "means," although he pronounces perhaps many sentences and periphrases. The numerous words "mean" one single utterance. A single thought or sense makes itself understood in all the vocables. We do not only follow word after word, but we "get the idea," we comprehend one single utterance which is necessarily broken up into many words.

It may also happen that this single utterance appears as the focus where the sheaves of thought and feeling converge. It is around this type of utterance that biographers build their reports. Such a focus is a Word of existence: a forever unpronounceable single Word in which a life is comprehended. From the struggles of a man an utterance emerges that shows and conceals itself as the impetus behind the many pieces of information coming from him and transmitted to us. The gospels can be read in this way, and so can the sermons of Meister Eckhart.

This *wort*, Word of existence, has to become a *biwort*, adverb for the Verb. God has not begotten man "like" his image, but he has made him "in" or towards his image: *ad imaginem*, ad-Verb. The assimilation always remains to be perfected. The secret of the mind, understood as an image, is *ad:* it is unlike all things, yet like God. Eckhart perhaps draws too radical a distinction between the mind as an image of God and creation in general; conversely, he does not distinguish the mind enough from the divine Persons. Like the Son and the Spirit, the mind is defined by its *ad,* which establishes it near to God. Just as Christ is with the Father, the detached man should be with Christ, in turn engendering the unique Word which he becomes himself. Then the assimilation will be perfect. In the sermon on Justice, Eckhart illustrates this teaching by the proximity of Eve to Adam:

> The just live eternally "with God," directly with God, neither below nor above. They accomplish all their works with God, and God accomplishes his own with them. Saint John says: "The Word was with God." It was totally alike and next to him, neither below nor above but alike. When God created man, he drew woman from the rib of man, so that woman was alike to man. He made her neither from the head nor from the feet, so that she would be neither above nor below man, but that she would be equal to him. Likewise the just mind is to be equal with God and next to him: exactly alike, neither inferior nor superior to him.[78]

The Word is with God *(bî gote),* Eve was with Adam, the just man is with Justice: likewise the man devoid of all created images is with God and is the image of God.

From similarity springs praise:

> What praises God? It is likeness. Thus everything in the mind which is like God praises God. What in any way is unlike God does not praise God. In the same way an image praises the artist who has imprinted upon it all the art that he has in his heart, thus making it entirely like himself. This similarity of the image praises its master without words.[79]

Before passing to the third stage of the itinerary of detachment, it will be instructive to read a sermon in which Meister Eckhart dwells further on this entire theory of the image. This text marks the step from similarity to identity as it stresses that we should not be content with resembling the eternal Word, but that we should be one with it: "You should not only be like the Son, but you should be the Son himself." It also develops the condition of such an identity: "Always remain equable."

SERMON,
"LIKE A VASE OF
MASSIVE GOLD"

(QUASI VAS AURI SOLIDUM ORNATUM OMNI LAPIDE PRETIOSO,
Ecclus. 50:9)

I have quoted a statement in Latin that is to be found in today's epistle. It can be applied to Saint Augustine and to every good and saintly mind: they resemble a massive and solid golden vessel, adorned with all precious stones. The nobility of the saints is such that they can never be characterized by one single comparison; this is why we symbolize them by the trees, the sun, and the moon. Thus Saint Augustine is here compared to a vase of firm and stable gold set with all kinds of precious stones. Indeed, this can truthfully be said of every good and saintly mind, which has let all things be and keeps them where they are eternal. He who lets things be as they are by accident, possesses them as pure being, that is, as they are eternally.

Every vessel has two aspects: it receives and holds. However, spiritual vases differ from physical ones. Wine is in the barrel, but the barrel is not in the wine, no more than the wine [penetrates] into the barrel, that is, into the staves. Indeed, if it were in the staves, one would not be able to drink it. Not so with the spiritual vase! Here everything that fills the vase penetrates into it, and the vase is in it, and it is the vase itself. Everything with which the spiritual vase is filled is of its own nature. It is God's nature to give himself to every good mind, and it is the mind's nature to receive God: this must be said of what is most noble in the mind. In this [nobleness], the mind bears the image of God and is like God. There can be no image without similarity, but there can very well be similarity without an image. Two eggs are equally white,

99

and yet one is not the image of the other. Indeed, for one thing to be the image of another, it must spring from the other's nature, it must be born of it, and it must be like it.

Every image has two properties. The first is that it receives its being from that of which it is an image. This reception is produced without mediation, above the will, for the outgoing of the image is natural: it emanates from nature like the branch from the tree. When a face is placed before a mirror, the face will necessarily be reflected, whether it wills it or not. Yet its nature is not reflected in the image sent back by the mirror, but only the mouth and the nose and the eyes and the overall shape of the face are reflected in the mirror. So here is what God has reserved for himself alone: that in everything into which he casts his image, he reproduces at once his total nature and all that he is and can accomplish. The will here plays no part at all. The image, indeed, gives the will a purpose. The will follows the image as the image constitutes the first emanation of the [divine] nature. The image assimilates all that nature and being can achieve. The nature reproduces itself totally in the image, and yet it remains entirely in itself. The masters, in this matter, locate the image not in the Holy Spirit, but in the middle Person, because the Son represents the first emanation of the [divine] nature. This is why he is properly called the "image of the Father" and not the Holy Spirit who is only an efflorescence from the Father and the Son, though he has one single nature with them both. Yet, the will does not mediate between the image and the nature; even more, neither knowledge, nor science, nor wisdom can act here as intermediaries, for the divine image breaks forth from the fruitfulness of nature without any mediation. If there is, however, a mediation of wisdom here, it is the image itself [that is, the Son]. This is the reason why, in the Godhead, the Son is called the Wisdom of the Father.

You should know that the simple divine image that is impressed on the mind in its innermost nature is received without mediation. What is most intimate and most noble in the [divine] nature reproduces itself quite properly in the image of the mind, and without the mediation of either will or wisdom. As I just said, if wisdom mediates anything here, it is the image itself. God is immediately in the image and the image is immediately in God. Yet, the presence of God in the image is much nobler than the presence of the image in God. The image possesses God not as Creator, but as an intelligible being. What is most noble in the [divine] nature reproduces itself quite properly in the image. This is a natural image of God, which God has naturally imprinted on all minds. More than this I cannot attribute to the image [of God in the mind]. If I ascribed a little more to it, it would turn out to be God himself. But that is not so, for then God would not be God.

The second property of the image you should recognize in its likeness. Note two points in particular. Firstly, the image is not of itself; secondly, it is not for itself. Its way is the same as that of an image received in the eye: it neither originates in the eye nor has its being in the eye. It depends and bears solely on that of which it is the image. Therefore it is neither of itself nor for itself. It properly proceeds from that of which it is the image and belongs to it totally. From this it takes its being, and it is its selfsame being.

Now, listen to me carefully. When you properly understand the nature of an image you will recognize it by four elements, or perhaps there will be more. An image is not of itself, nor is it for itself. It rather springs from the thing whose reflection it is and belongs to it with all its being. It owes nothing to a thing other than that whose image it is; nothing else is at its origin. An image takes its being immediately from that of which it is the image and has one sole being with it, and it is that same being. Saying this, I have not spoken of matters to be professed only in school; they can, on the contrary, be just as well preached for instruction from the pulpit.

You often ask how you should live. Listen carefully to what I am going to say, and learn from it. What has been said of the image's way of being—exactly that should be your way of life. You should be of Him and for Him, and you should not be of yourself nor for yourself. You should not belong to anyone. When I came to this convent yesterday, I saw sage and other plants on a tomb, and I thought to myself: here lies someone's dear friend, that is why this parcel of ground is so dear to him. If someone has a friend whom he truly loves, he will also love everything that belongs to him; likewise, what is repugnant to his friend, he will not love. Take for example a dog, which is only an animal without intelligence. He is so faithful to his master that he hates everything that can harm his master, while to his master's friends he extends friendliness without regard for wealth or poverty. Much more, if there were a poor blind man with great affection for the dog's master, the dog would love him more than a king or an emperor who would dislike his master. The truth is that, if the dog could be unfaithful to his master with one half of his being, he would have to hate himself with the other half.

But now some people complain that they feel no inward awe or devotion or sweetness, nor any special consolation from God. These people are indeed still mistaken. One can bear with them, but their attitude is not the best. I say in truth: as long as something other than the eternal Word reproduces its image in you, even if it is some exterior aspect of the eternal Word, however good that may be, it is altogether wrong. Therefore the only man thoroughly just is he who has annihilated all created things; who without looking anywhere else stands in a straight line turned towards the eternal Word; who reproduces his image in this Word, and who in return receives the imprint of justice. A man such as this receives where the Son receives. Indeed, he is the Son himself. Scripture says: "No one knows the Father except the Son" (Matt. 11:27). Hence, if you wish to know God, you should not only be like the Son, but you should be the Son himself.

But there are people who want to see God with the same eyes with which they look at a cow, and they want to love God in the same way as they love a cow. You love it for the milk and the cheese and for your own profit. So do all people who love God for the sake of outward riches or inward consolation. But they do not love God correctly, for they merely love their own advantage.

It is the plain truth that whatever you strive after other than God himself can never be so good as to not obstruct your way to the supreme truth.

As I said before, just as Saint Augustine can be symbolized by a golden vase that is closed at the bottom and open at the top, so you yourself should be. If you want to keep yourself near Saint Augustine and in the holiness of all the saints, then close your heart to all that is created, and open it to receive God as he is in himself. This is why men are compared to the highest powers, as their heads are always bare. Women, on the other hand, are compared to the lowest powers, as they always have their heads covered. The higher powers are raised above time and space, and they originate immediately from the being of the mind. They are compared to men because they are always uncovered. This is also why their work is eternal. A master says that as soon as the lower powers of the mind are touched by time and space, they lose their virginal purity. They can never be so thoroughly cleansed and so finely sifted that they may reach into the higher powers. However they receive the imprint of an image comparable [to that in the higher powers].

You shall be constant and firm, that is, you shall remain equable in love and sorrow, in luck and misfortune. You shall be set with all precious stones, that is, all virtues shall be enclosed in you and emanate from you essentially. You shall step across and beyond all virtues and accept virtue only in that primordial ground where it is one with the divine nature. And the more you are united to the divine nature, over and beyond the angels, the more perfection they must receive from you. May we become One, so help us God. Amen.[80]

COMMENTARY

CONTINUED

Identity

Dissimilarity and Similarity have to be overcome, that is, both cancelled and preserved, into Identity:

> Scripture says that we have to become like God (1 John 3:2). "Like," the word is bad and deceptive. If I liken myself to someone else, and if I find someone who is like me, then this man behaves as if he were I, although he is not and deceives people about it. Many things look like gold, but since they are not, they lie. In the same way all things pretend to be like God; but they are lying, since they are not like him. God can no more suffer likeness than he can suffer not being God. Likeness is something that does not occur in God; what does occur in the Godhead and in eternity is oneness. But likeness is not oneness [*glîcheit enist niht ein*]. Whenever I am one with something, I am not like it. There is nothing alien in oneness. In eternity there is only oneness, but not likeness.[81]

Eckhart illustrates his conception of identity through the example of fire: when everything combustible has been absorbed, fire passes beyond dissimilarity and similarity. It blazes, becoming "entirely one single and unique flame,"[82] "heat and conflagration,"[83] which "always seeks the One."[84] It does not seek likeness, which is created, but the One: *ein unglich*.[85] Combustion, carried out by the fire and undergone by the wood, results in identity. Eckhart calls this identity *ein im gewürke*, identical in operation. Such identity or oneness terminates the cataphasis of detachment. The apophasis, further on, will lead us beyond this concatenation by fire.

> Acting and becoming are one. God and I are one in this work: he acts and I become. Fire transforms all things it touches into its own nature. The wood does not change the fire into itself, but the fire changes the wood into itself. In the same way we are transformed into God so that we may know him as he is.[86]

Fire and light are frequent metaphors for oneness in Meister Eckhart. In the context of the sermon "Jesus Entered" we have evoked the example of vision. Just as light projected on a colored surface becomes one with it and shines in identical clarity with it, so in perfect availability to the will of God I become one with the Father. From this unity emanates an identical incandescence, the Son.

Appeal could also be made to the example of music. The hearer of such melodious beauty is "all ears." If he does not know how to reproduce inwardly, simultaneously, identically, that which his ears hear, if by distraction or incapacity he omits to accompany in himself the sounds that the senses perceive, then he does not know how to listen. Properly speaking, perfect listening implies that the distinction between the soloist, on one side, and the listener, on the other, is no longer true. Through the unique event of the song that enraptures us, one identical being accomplishes itself. Thus the fundamental determination of existence is "operative identity" or, in homage to Aristotle, "energetic identity."[87] According to Eckhart, human existence seeks to fulfill itself in identity. This trait appears particularly in the most decisive acts of life: in the foundation of a family or of a community, in a dialogue that actualizes two "words of existence," or again in the acceptance of destiny. These events always unite those whom they affect. They are destined for man. It is not someone's will that has favored the course of things, but the course of things that favors us. We say: "It" so happened, "there were" circumstances, "there is" being. Hidden under the anonymity of these neuter forms is a power that gathers men to their fate. When anonymity befalls us, it delegates destiny to us. Such a mittance, *geschick*, is not a matter of the will and asceticism. One has to be very released, *gelassen*, to respond properly to what destiny sends. Eckhart suggests an example to explain this: consider what happens in conversation. Through your words a clearance of understanding opens up which points towards the word of existence murmured in all that you say or do. But the event of such an opening is the work of neither you nor me. The "we" is not the achievement of the "I" or of the "you"; rather it comes to be of its own accord. When it occurs there "is" nothing else besides itself. In such moments two existences are determined as identical: identical in the *gewürke*, that is, in the event. The Greek verb συμβάλλειν, origin of the word "symbol," literally means "to throw together." The anonymity of what imparts itself to you and me unites us in the same operation, that is, it "throws together." The operative or energetic identity is thus "symbolic identity."

Symbolic identity is opposed to the identity of substances. This latter identity is the one that metaphysics and its offspring, pantheism, deal with. It is quite clear that Eckhart had overcome representation of substances. Because he preached out of another form of thought, he was condemned as a heretic. Metaphysical representation admits of no other identity than that of substances with themselves: the ontic identity of a thing that remains itself. In objection to our interpretation of symbolic identity as the rise of the "we" in the event of a dialogue or of the harmony between the soloist and his hearer, representational thought would reply: substances are *"simpliciter diversa,"* otherness remains the first and inescapable fact in any relation. To Eckhart's teaching of the simultaneous begetting of the Word it has been objecting for six centuries that God and man are ontologically distinct beings.

From the foregoing it results that there are two conflicting ways or orders of understanding identity: that of being as a process and that of being as substance. We have already hit upon this conflict. In a "verbal" understanding of being, one will emphasize symbolic identity, while in a "nominal" understanding of being, one will speak of substantial or ontic identity. Meister Eckhart's understanding of being is "verbal" and that of identity, "symbolic." This term should not be opposed as "metaphorical" to "real," or as "formal" to "material." "Symbol" and "symbolic" are used here exclusively in their etymological meaning, which covers the same semantic scope as Eckhart's *gewürke*. This vocabulary reflects Eckhart's fundamentally innovative philosophical position: prior to the distinction into substances, he says, the acting of God and the becoming of man join both God and man into an identical event. Being-other appears only as a consequence of being-identical: God manifests his otherness only to reflection. But reflection withdraws from the immediacy of the event. Distance and difference are not original. Eckhart says: they are "created." They become objects of thought once identity has already been experienced. Strict and simple difference, without primitive identity, cannot be thought.

Such, at least, is the mind of Meister Eckhart: ontic differences presuppose and point towards symbolic identity. Texts in this sense abound:

> I have sometimes spoken of a light which is in the mind, uncreated and uncreatable. Of this light I treat ordinarily in my sermons; it seizes God

without mediation, uncovered and void as he is in himself. This is to be understood according to the actuality of the begetting that penetrates into God.[88]

As long as any difference pertaining to created things gets response in the mind, it thereby feels chagrin. I repeat what I have already said on many occasions: as far as the mind's natural and created being goes, there is no truth. I say that there is something which is beyond the created nature of the mind. Many priests, however, do not grasp that there is something so closely related to God and so identical with him. . . . A man who is thus borne above all light dwells in unity.[89]

Living in the light beyond light, man no longer lives "with" God but "in" him:

God is not found in distinction. When the mind reaches the original image [of which it is a reflection] and finds itself alone in it, then it finds God. Finding itself and finding God is one single process, outside of time. As far as it penetrates into him, it is identical with God, . . . not included, nor united, but more: identical.[90]

Identical is the event as God begets me as himself and begets himself as me. He begets me as his essential being and as his nature. There is one life and one essential being and one work there.[91]

The ground of the mind and the ground of God are one sole essential being.[92]

Eckhart wants so much to insist on this energetic identity between God and man that he does not hesitate to accumulate adjectives against all customary usage: *ein einic ein ungeschieden*,[93] one unique unity without difference.

To the realm of differences and substances these texts oppose another realm, that of identity and of event. Remembering the theory of the uncreated in created man, we may now add: man is the locus of the Difference where identity meets differences. He is the Difference itself, the conflict of the One and the multiple. However, he is not the differences, since he is not lost in the multiple. His fate is to live on the border of the Difference, to be the borderline of the created and the uncreated. In this context, what is the role Eckhart ascribes to detachment? He sometimes seems to suggest that detachment makes man cross the border, that the Difference can be reduced to identity. The destructive side of detachment appears as the reduction of the Difference to identity.

This is the power of "symbolic" thought: the *symballein* aims at burning away whatever reminds man of his createdness.

In his program of exclusion of differences and of the multiple, how does Eckhart determine the identity which supports and demands this putting to death of the scattered self? The difficulty lies for us, as for the judges of the Inquisition, in avoiding the error of representing it as the ontic identity of a universal megasubstance with itself.

It is only possible to speak of the exclusion of mediations in identity if identity is thought of as a *geschehen*,[94] a happening. For such thinking a few customary categories of representation turn out to be inadequate, in particular the opposition between transcendence and immanence: identity as transcendence would infringe on the Eckhartian principle of exclusion of all mediations from God; identity as immanence would rehabilitate the being of creatures and would thus weaken the onto-phanic project of detachment. It is on the identity of the totality, the *symballein* of God, man, and the world, that we find some of the most astonishing statements that Meister Eckhart has left us.

> God gives to all things equally, and as they flow from God, they are all equal. Indeed, angels and men and creatures are equal in their primitive emanation, by which they flow from God. Someone who would get hold of things in their primitive emanation would get hold of them as they are all equal. If they are thus equal in time, they are still more so in eternity, in God. If we take a fly, in God, it is more noble in God than the highest angel is in itself. This is how all things are equal in God and are God himself.[95]

The last sentence expresses a kind of axiom dear to Eckhart which is found in different forms in his sermons:

> All that is in God is God.[96]
>
> In God, no creature is more noble than the other.[97]
>
> In God, there is nothing but God.[98]
>
> What is in the first, is the first.[99]
>
> What is in the One is the One.[100]

These propositions can be read with reference to the theory of the preexistence of all things in God, or the theory of divine ideas. But to be content with such a Neoplatonist reading of Meister Eckhart would mean to auscultate the letter of his sermons, unmindful of releasement. With the affirmation that all things are identical in God and with God, the third partner is introduced into the universal *symballein*; after releasement has playfully brought together man and God, the part of the world is played. Releasement is now a thought about the world. God, man, and the world are joined in the free play of identity where "God is altogether our own and where all things are our own in him."[101] With this free interplay detachment itself fades away. There is nothing left for man to detach himself from. He is perfectly released. The effort of detachment has overcome itself into pure releasement. As releasement loses all voluntary or ascetic connotations, the totality comes to presence. Their primitive flow from the origin renders all things, God, man, and the world, present to one another. Releasement accounts for the restorative new birth of all things to identity. The symbolic identity is thus more primitive and, as it is uncreated, more real than substantial identity. Likewise releasement is more primitive, uncreated, than detachment, whose function is to regulate man's dealings with things, that is, created substances.

The identity of the totality is here neither transcendence made immanence (metaphysical identity) nor universal ontic homogeneity (pantheistic identity), but playful presence (symbolic identity). God, man, and the world are joined together by the play of this identity. The mind devoid of all *eigenschaft* is the "there" of their threefold intercourse. He who renounces himself entirely and reinstates the ancient void of images, by his serenity, sets the threefold free and grounds their identity on play.[102] Man is the field where the threefold appears, unendingly dislocated as long as he turns himself towards nothingness, but reunited in their first identity when he commits himself to *gelâzenheit*.

The true nobility of the ground of the mind lies in that a released man becomes the locus where the energetic identity of God, of himself, and of the world, produces itself. According to the cipher of unity, the universe is genuinely "universe," that is, a turning towards the One, only in a released man. "What is in the One is the One." According to the cipher of truth, releasement leads beings back to their primitive emanation; through the released spirit, they enter into their primitive truth. "What is in the Truth is the Truth." Or again, according to the cipher of "God," in a released man, things reside in their perfections, which are no longer individual but common; they are identical to

God, they are God, for "everything which is common, as common, is God."[103]

The identity of the totality by the free play of the threefold in releasement is sometimes expressed in terms borrowed from the theology of the mystical Body.[104]

> When God created all creatures, they were so petty and so narrow that he could not move in them. Then he created the mind so equal to him and so much in his image that he could give himself to the mind. Whatever he gives to the mind other than himself it does not heed. God must give himself and become my own just as he is his own. Otherwise nothing is given to me at all and nothing satisfies me. He who is to receive God so completely must have abandoned himself completely and must have departed from himself. Such a man receives from God all that God possesses, he receives it as his own just as God possesses it as his own as well as Our Lady and all those who are in heaven: all this belongs to such a man, in the same way and as his own.[105]

In the interplay of identity in the threefold, the totality is mine and I belong to the totality. When children get together to play, each one is for all and all are for each one. Identity grants itself through play; it requires the continuous abandonment of both human and divine *eigenschaft*, property.

> I wondered recently if I should accept or desire anything from God. I shall consider this carefully, for if I accepted something from God, I would be inferior to God like a serf, and he, in giving, would be like a lord. But in eternal life, such should not be our relation.[106]

Eternal life means that man may live again, here and now, out of his ground, and that releasement may accomplish itself, so that God, man, and the world play their identity. In the beatitude promised for today, this interplay swallows up every difference or otherness.[107] This blessed identity is already in me, not in germ, but in totality, exactly in the same way as God is in me: not according to his effigy, but in totality.

The difficulty in reading Meister Eckhart arises because such a bold cataphatism is mixed, as we shall see without delay, with a no less bold apophatism. Classing Meister Eckhart exclusively among the defenders of either the first or the second of these intellectual attitudes results in missing the very core of his thought. On this matter, it is undoubtedly prudent to speak of the "dialectic" of Meister Eckhart.[108]

Dehiscence

When autumn comes, the time of dehiscence, fruits come to maturity and their capsules burst open to let the grains sow themselves in the soil. Whence and why the threefold? Whence and why identity? What is it that bursts open and gives free passage to God, man, and the world? What is it that their dehiscence manifests? Where do these three emanate from? And what primordial unity does their interplay suggest? What does symbolic identity symbolize?

Following the thread of the texts, we have uncovered a trail in man which is not made by his own hands and which leads to the ground of the mind. But who has originally traced out the trail? Where does the way of *gelâzenheit* lead? Is the interplay the final word on releasement? Whom or what does the interplay extol? Who calls the interplay together? Can we think of something still more original than God, man, and the world, and of which these three are only the threefold trace? All these questions, however, ask the same thing: what is the ultimate intensity of releasement, or what is the origin?

The question concerning the origin, raised from the experience of releasement, crystallizes around a supposition: could the identity of "imminence" which calls us ahead towards a playful existence not also be the region of our "provenance" behind us, the playful incipiency of that existence? If identity is the *télos*, the whereto of the way of releasement, should it not also be its *arché*, its wherefrom? How are we to articulate the supposition that these two faces of the origin, provenance and imminence, or identity as wherefrom and identity as whereto, are one? Does the same original *logos* speak perhaps in archeology and teleology? We want to question releasement in order to know the origin.

It is in the name of the strictness of releasement that Meister Eckhart criticizes the pretension of the supreme being, "God," to the rank of the origin. The supreme being has still a "why," namely all other beings. We speak of God as the highest reason behind life. We speak even of his will and his intention. But intentionality and purpose have no place in releasement. To think of God divinely is to render his ebullience aimless.

The identity of the three is effected by the free unfolding of an existence that has left everything and that therefore lets everything be. This effecting and this unfolding, Meister Eckhart says, can be compared to the pace of a stallion launched at full speed over spacious grassland: its nature will urge it to expend itself in galloping and leaping as much as its strength will allow. In this way it finds its happiness.[109] We could ask: why does it run? It runs in order to run, without a why. Likewise the identity of the threefold accomplishes itself for its own sake, without a why.

> "Why do you love God?"—"I do not know, because of God."—"Why do you love the truth?"—"Because of the truth."—"Why do you love justice?"—"Because of justice."—"Why do you love goodness?"—"Because of goodness."—"Why do you live?"—"My word! I do not know! But I am happy to live."[110]

The last of these questions actually remains unanswered. Instead of an answer, a response is given. An answer exhibits some knowledge, but a response involves the entire human being. To the question, "Why do you live?" one can only correspond in living without a why (quite as to the question, "What is Philosophy?" one cannot produce a reply in propositions, but must correspond by a way of living). God is, man lives, things subsist and perish—all this without a why. Eckhart expresses this in multiple ways. His meditation on the why is an unveiling. God, man, and the world unveil themselves in their first "dehiscence" (ûzbruch, Ausbruch or ûzvluz, Ausfluss) from their origin, without a why.

What is the sense of a quest which seeks an origin beyond God? The metaphysician will object that beyond God, the highest being, no origin can be thought. But are the new birth and releasement thinkable as long as the excellence of God is objectified in this way? If God is represented as the duplicate beyond or within man, that is, as the Perfect above our imperfection, the divine birth can only be represented by sacrificing either identity to difference (God as the partner of the soul, Pietism) or difference to identity (God as the oceanic substance which swallows up the soul, Pantheism). Meister Eckhart, however, maintains both identity and difference. He attempts to think the origin prior to the manifestation of the threefold. To do so, he turns towards man as that being who needs only to come back to himself for the question of the origin to be raised. There is no path other than releasement that can overcome the representation of God as the highest being. The apprenticeship of releasement points beyond the threefold to the source of their common egress. It points towards a formless totality, without a why, in which the identity of imminence or man's whereto recovers the identity of provenance or man's wherefrom. It was this very concept of a totality at the beginning and at the end of releasement, unfolding itself without a why, that was to enchant Friedrich Hegel five centuries later.[111]

Living *sunder warumbe*, without a why:[112] whoever has abandoned himself entirely and "lets" himself live, is not motivated by any exterior inducement, not even by God. Loving and serving the Lord in order to deserve the title of a servant of the Lord, this, Eckhart says, is loving him as one loves a cow, namely with an ulterior motive, in this case the milk and the cheese that the cow brings.[113] A life devoted to others, even dedicated to God, is not yet the detached life as Meister Eckhart teaches it. A person will be released only when he ceases devoting and dedicating himself to "this and that." Let God be, stop seeking him, abandon God, and then you will find him. Only he who does not seek will find.[114] There is no higher attestation of God than this diffidence.

Leaving things, leaving God, living without a why: these teachings of Meister Eckhart surely sound subversive.[115] Why the world? Why God? Why man? Why identity? They are, Meister Eckhart answers, without a "why."

> Those who seek something with their works, those who act for a why, are serfs and mercenaries.[116]

For traditional metaphysics the thought of a threefold interplay that enacts itself for no reason is sheer folly. But Eckhart charges that the intellectual quest for unshakable foundations keeps itself aloof from any original disclosure as it is attached to the "why," to the raison d'être of things. One imagines what happens to Scholastic constructions when unexpectedly a preacher comes who unveils the nothingness of foundations; the Scholastic mind is seized with dizziness. The God whom this other way of thinking annihilates in his function of foundation is indeed the God of western Christianity. If you seek God for the sake of a foundation, Eckhart says, if you look for God even for the sake of God himself, then

> you behave as though you transformed God into a candle in order to find something with it; and when one has found what one looks for, one throws away the candle.[117]

However, to "look for nothing" is neither subversion nor absurdity. Meister Eckhart only draws the ultimate consequence of letting-be. What is, let it be. Everything could as well not be, but since it is, let it be. God, man, and the world could not be, but since they are, let them be.

As the *arché*, the origin as wherefrom (represented by the words "since they are"), is without a why, so, too, the *télos*, the origin as whereto, (represented by the words "let them be") is without a why. For Eckhart, such thought leads man into the desert, which is prior to God, man, and the world.

> I have spoken of a power in the mind. In its first manifestation, it does not apprehend God. It does not apprehend him insofar as he is good, nor insofar as he is the truth. It penetrates into the ground, it pursues and burrows, and it apprehends God in his oneness and in his desert (*einoede*); it apprehends God in his wilderness (*wüstunge*) and in his own ground.[118]

The outcome of the soul's breakthrough is the disappearance of God: *got entwirt*.[119] The sermon "Woman, the Hour Is Coming" said that the intellect is not satisfied with God inasmuch as he is God. Releasement makes man reach for the origin, but for such a man there is no longer any God. "God" is the opposite of the creature, but if there are no created men to invoke him, God must vanish as God. There is then nothing other than the unknowable desert prior to the threefold. In the origin, everything is origin.

The interplay of the threefold appears no longer in disconcerting multiplicity, but God, man, and the world show themselves arising from one single gift which precedes them. Play is not yet entirely without a why, since playing requires the affirmation of self. Receiving a gift, on the other hand, is totally gratuitous. A gift spreads serenity. At the apogee of releasement God, man, and the world show themselves granted gratuitously.

Eckhart has at his command a rich vocabulary to express what we have translated as "origin." We have already encountered the word Godhead, *gotheit*.

God and Godhead are as distinct as heaven and earth.[120]

The distinction between God and Godhead is that between antecedent and consequent. God acts, but to the Godhead every operation is foreign. Operation is of the order of consequences. The desert is not fertile in anything: likewise the Godhead is arid, it does not create anything.

In the desert everything begins only: but God disappears. The desert is the vast solitude, there is no place for two in the desert. The opposition between a Creator and a creature vanishes. In the desert, entreaties are of no avail, there is no opposite of man towards whom he might raise his hands. In the desert, the wind and the sand wipe out the traces of the caravans: the steps of God disappear together with those of man and the world.

The desert is full of seeds, but they do not sprout there. The Godhead is a house, Eckhart says, full of people but from which no one as of yet has gone out. Let the dwellers go out into the street and they will be hailed: "God," "Eckhart". . . .

God becomes; where all creatures enunciate God, there God becomes. When I still stood in the ground, the soil, the river, and the source of the Godhead, no one asked me where I was going or what I was doing. There was no one there to question me. But when I went out by dehiscence, all creatures cried out: "God." If someone were to ask me: "Brother Eckhart, when did you leave home?" this would indicate that I must previously have been inside. It is thus that all creatures speak of God. And why do they not speak of the Godhead? Everything that is in the Godhead is one, and of this nothing can be said.[121]

Whoever speaks of God intends to speak of his most sublime counterpart, that is, of a being opposable to other beings. He invokes him as the one who saves, the one who judges . . ., always as the Other. But to speak of the Godhead is to think of God prior to all opposition, in his "silent darkness" and in his "concealed intimacy,"[122] in his "abysmal,"[123] "limpid,"[124] "hidden,"[125] origin. One may say that the distinction between God and Godhead concerns two aspects—exterior and interior, active and inactive, knowable and unknowable—of the same origin. But since "God" signifies for us primarily the Other whom man reflects and whom he invokes, loves, or "puts to death,"[126] it is preferable to speak of the Godhead, in which there is neither reflection nor invocation, neither love nor death. This word "Godhead" designates the exclusion from the origin of all relations, be it the external relation of creation or the internal relation of the Trinity.

To think of the origin as Godhead is to refuse to represent it as an afterworld transcending the created world, it is to attempt the abrogation of any representational transcendence. The Godhead is the destruction of all metaphysical configuration, whether outside or inside God.

Vladimir Lossky notes that the distinction between God and Godhead
—which, by the way, occurs only in Eckhart's German works—stands
for the distinction between "God" as the efficient principle of creation
and "God" as the final principle of assimilation, the goal of all spiritual
creatures.[127] This acceptation, however, does not entirely do justice to
Eckhart. The most famous texts, especially the sermon "Blessed Are the
Poor," refer to the Godhead precisely as *ursache* (cause), stressing at the
same time the Godhead's total passivity with regard to the created.
"Ursache" must therefore not be translated by "final cause," but more
generally by "first cause." The term refers to the fullness of ideas of
which the sermon "Jesus Entered" has already spoken: " 'Virgin' designates a human who is devoid of all foreign images and who is as void
as he was when he was not yet," that is, when he still dwelt within the
Godhead.

> When I still stood in my first cause, I had no God, I was cause of my-
> self. . . . But when by free will I went out and received my created being,
> then I had a God. Indeed, before there were creatures, God was not yet
> God, but he was what he was.[128]

He was what he was: the origin is radically unknowable. The expression
"I was cause of myself" is very strong: according to the traditional
teaching God alone is *causa sui.* Here it is applied to man. It has to be
understood according to the axiom of identity: in the first cause, everything is first cause. The sermon "Blessed Are the Poor" continues:

> This is why I pray to God to rid me of God, for my essential being (*min
> wesenlich wesen*) is above God insofar as we comprehend God as the
> principle of creatures. Indeed, in God's own being, where God is raised
> above all being and all distinctions, I was myself, I willed myself, and
> knew myself to create this man [that I am]. Therefore I am cause of myself
> according to my being which is eternal, but not according to my becoming
> which is temporal. Therefore also I am unborn, and according to my
> unborn being I can never die. According to my unborn being I have always
> been, I am now, and shall eternally remain. What I am by my [temporal]
> birth is to die and be annihilated, for it is mortal; therefore with time it
> must pass away. In my [eternal] birth all things were born, and I was cause
> of myself as well as of all things. If I had willed it, neither I nor any things
> would be. And if I myself were not, God would not be either: that God
> is God, of this I am a cause. If I were not, God would not be God. There
> is, however, no need to understand this.[129]

I do not reflect God, I do not reproduce him, I declare him.

Even the comforting thought of being "adverb" to the Word, *bîwort*, now becomes meaningless. For that matter, so do all relational and representational attributes. In the breakthrough beyond the Word, nay, beyond God, the theology of the evangelist John is also overcome. John says of the Word that he is πρὸς τὸν θεόν, "turned towards God"; he also has the Word say: "There where I am, I wish that you be too."[130] Thus John sees the Christian "with God," "turned towards God" like the Word. But Eckhart sees him giving birth to God, beyond even the begetter of the Word.

God, then, undergoes the same fate as things; that is, they both perish. The Godhead, on the other hand, is not a something. Every "thing" has to disappear with time, for it belongs to the day. "Thing" designates beings in their determinate existence. Between the "things" that are God and the mind there is a reciprocity of determination, and this reciprocity makes them be. The reciprocity of determination is their being. God disappears together with all things. Concerning this understanding of "thing" Martin Heidegger writes:

> "Thing" denotes anything whatsoever that is in any way. Accordingly Meister Eckhart uses the word *dinc* (thing) for God as well as for the soul. God is for him the "highest and uppermost" thing. The soul is "a great thing." This master of thinking in no way means to say that God and the soul are something like a rock: a material object. *Dinc* (thing) is here the cautious and abstemious name for something that is at all.[131]

Dinc and *sache* indicate that which is in general, but which according to Eckhart was not always. God and man were not always. *Ursache* adverts to what is primordial and from where any *sache* receives its being. *Sache*, when it is not simply a synonym for *ursache*, designates the multiplicity of beings, whereas *ursache* points towards the unique unfolding of being throughout beings and whose determinations make them be. The ground of the mind is *ursache*; inversely God, face to face with man, is not *ursache*, but *sache*. In the divine destiny of the ground of the mind, where I differ in nothing from the Godhead, I am *ursache*, cause of God.

If one paid attention only to the letter of some expressions used by Eckhart, one would not hesitate to discern at the core of his teachings the philosophical content of atheism: God owes his existence to man who is above God. The intention that speaks through such formulations in Meister Eckhart is nevertheless diametrically opposed to that of modern agnostic humanism. Contemporary atheistic thought, for all its unsuccessful quest for assurance in an ultimate foundation, despairs of the God-foundation and ultimately rejects him. Atheistic despair is the counterpart of the increasing urge for security in our civilization. But Eckhart frustrates the scaffolding of guarantees, theistic as well as atheistic, when he declares: whoever looks for assurance will find nothing; only he who is not attached to any *sache,* any firm support, will find the *ursache* where all guarantees vanish.

Meister Eckhart, according to a "descending" schema, considers man as proceeding from his origin in the Godhead. Indeed, at times his thought supports a materially atheistic reading, but it is formally "theocentric." The premise of atheistic thought is the search for assurance. It declares that man can be sure only of himself. Eckhart's premise, on the other hand, is the refusal of all assurance, which leads him to exalt not man, but the unknowable ground of God.

That Eckhart's expressions bear the germs of atheism when wrenched out of their context is apparent in the sermon "Woman, the Hour Is Coming," where Eckhart says of God that "he must give." The idea that God "must" love man, *got muoz,* is frequent in his writings.[132]

> I will never thank God that he loves me, for he cannot do otherwise, whether he wishes it or not; his nature forces him to it. I will rather thank him that in his goodness he cannot cease loving me.[133]

"God loves us"—this describes a relation of exteriority between subjects that are capable of love. "I thank God because he loves me," then, expresses the love one person shows to another person in testimony of reciprocity. Representational thinking declares: "God loves me." On the other hand, "God must love me" intends to abolish the representable relationship of exteriority: reciprocity falls, and every relation between persons or subjects passes away. We are borne not by God's love, but by his having-to-love, that is, by his nature. God's nature is that he loves; God is love.

The intrinsic necessity which a being obeys lies in its nature. If God necessarily bears us in his love, then he bears us in his nature or his Godhead. "God must" is a way for Eckhart to intimate the origin. "God must love us": in a love so lavished, God vanishes. "God" is the name for someone who loves me because he freely chooses to do so. But by his nature, God loves me beyond all choosing and willing. He introduces me to that realm where he ceases to be God, namely, into the desert of his primordial unfolding, *wesen*, which is impersonal. Only then am I loved necessarily, and yet no one is there to love me.

Paradoxically, man will respond by violence to the necessary gift of God. "I will rather thank him that he must love me": such a thanksgiving consists in commanding him and constraining him. "Detachment forces God towards me," says Eckhart: *Daz abegescheidenheit twinge got zuo mir.*[134] "His nature constrains God to love," "I constrain God to love," these two propositions express the same thing, that is, the unspeakable origin where the Godhead and I are one, where I am the nature of God. This coercion does not signify any absurd trial of strength or a disposition of the human "subject" over the divine "subject"; on the contrary, it signifies the free unfolding of that which, through the ciphers "God" and "I," disposes of us. The necessity on the part of God as well as the violence on the part of man extol a gift from the same—better, the Same.

Several Middle High German parlances used for this origin of dehiscence denote the idea of a "first" or a "first beginning": *erste begin,*[135] *erste anefanc,*[136] *erstekeit.*[137] Again, this is not to be understood as referring to the first in a series of effects, since Eckhart designates not only the origin of provenance, the beginning of beings, but also the origin of imminence, their end. When the mind flows back into its nature, when it rises above its personal being, above even God, it penetrates into *erstekeit,* the source of identity which in its ground it had never left, and it recovers a joy that it had never lost. The First, the Godhead, is source as well as ocean: always in back of and always ahead of detachment.[138]

The word most often used in this context is *ursprunc.* Literally it means "primitive (*ur-*) springing" (from the verb *springen,* to spring). Another Middle High German form, today obsolete, was *ursprinc,* effervescence, efflorescence. The idea is always that of a kind of eruption.[139] In Eckhart's Latin works the equivalent expressions are *bullitio* and *ebullitio.* There is, however, a sharp distinction between these two terms: the first refers to the boiling within the Godhead before the created appears; it refers to the Life before life, in which I already was before I came to be. The second, *ebullitio,* indicates the boiling-over of the archetypes from the Godhead, that is, the emanation of all created things from their primitive ground.

> "Life" means a kind of seething in which a thing ferments and first pours itself into itself, all that it is into all that it is, before spilling over and pouring itself outside.[140]

Before things come to appear, they are "teeming" with a respiration without a why in the bosom of the Godhead. If we call the act of expiration, by which created things are diffused outside, their "origin," then the tranquil intradivine respiration that precedes creation will have to be called a "preoriginary" origin. This is meant by the word *ursprunc:* an actuality prior to God in which life diffuses "all that it is into all that it is." The preoriginary origin is animated throughout by one single and identical breath. Everything that breathes in the origin is the origin.

Properly speaking, however, the preoriginary origin *is* not. If it were, its being would make it opposable to other beings; it would have to be the God of the metaphysical tradition. For Eckhart *ursprunc* (ἀρχή) is not the beginning of being; rather it is nothingness and anarchy. The *ursprunc* is nothingness. Previously we have said: creatures are nothingness.

> All things have been drawn from nothingness; this is why their true origin (*ursprunc*) is nothingness.[141]

The departure as well as the arrival of detachment is nothingness. From foliation to dehiscence, the fruit of detachment "nihilates." The *ursprunc* as anarchy breaks the fetters of individuation and rids me of all attachments and links, even of God. Through such riddance I become as free as I was when I was universal nothingness in the Godhead.

> When this will turns for an instant away from itself, and returns to its first origin (*in sînen êrsten ursprunc*), then the will recovers its proper free fashion, and it is free.[142]

In its preoriginary origin the will sets itself loose from any principle; it is anarchic. Nothing precedes it; therefore it has nothing to obey, except itself. Detachment, at this stage, ignores or suspends any reference to determinate being. Man is perfectly released. He exists himself as the preoriginary origin, he is the origin of the origin, and no one can lay restrictions upon his freedom, not even God. The order of commanding and obeying is reversed:

The humble man does not solicit (*bitten*) anything [from God], but he can indeed command (*gebieten*) him.[143]

An existence that dwells in nothingness is one in which everything just begins. It abides in the origin of the Creator. In this preoriginary origin, says Meister Eckhart, only silence maintains itself.[144]

At the outset of his odyssey of detachment, man did not expect that much. His path appeared as one of voluntary poverty, but now it has led him into a region beyond God where he no longer recognizes himself. He feels as if he had reached that point of wandering that Japanese Zen masters depict by a canvas totally covered with black:[145] God, man, and the world are no more, there is only the unspeakable intradivine "ebullience," without a purpose and in which nothing lasts. But his wandering exploration of the origin has changed him. He has become playful. He asks no more for meanings and goals. As the preoriginary origin opens the play, it grants itself by "allusion," *ad-ludere*. Earlier, God, man, and the world had appeared reconciled by the play of the symbolic identity of the three. Wandering identity, or dehiscence, goes a step further. The three subsist no longer, they allude to a oneness that preserves the manifold in the unity of provenance and imminence.

A man who has experienced this "allusion," Meister Eckhart says, goes back to the businesses of the world: the stable or some other trade. He is no longer eager to hold God; he knows that eagerness, even mystical, makes one forgetful. Eagerness wants to get hold of God as though to envelop his head in a cloak and put him away under a bench.[146]

A detached man has unlearned to objectify God in an extrinsic relation; in his learned ignorance[147] he has abolished all relation and otherness; he no longer knows the singular; he has experienced the failure of God represented as opposite to man. His joy comes from afar, from the unfathomable ground of the Godhead.

To close this chapter on the four intensities of releasement, a sermon dealing specifically with "nothingness" and with "God, the fruit of nothingness" follows. Eckhart, commenting on Saint Paul's sudden blindness on the road to Damascus—"he saw nothing"—explains the different meanings of *niht*.

SERMON,
"SAUL ROSE FROM THE
GROUND"

(SURREXIT AUTEM SAULUS DE TERRA APERTISQUE OCULIS NIHIL
VIDEBAT, Acts 9:8)

This phrase that I have quoted in Latin is written in Saint Luke's Acts and concerns Saint Paul. Its meaning is: "Paul rose from the ground and with open eyes he saw nothing."

It seems to me that this little phrase has a fourfold meaning. First, when he rose up from the ground, with his eyes open he saw nothing, and this nothingness was God. Indeed he saw God, and that is what he calls a nothingness. Second, when he rose up, he saw nothing but God. Third, in all things, he saw nothing but God. Fourth, when he saw God, he saw all things as nothingness.

Previously he had reported how a light came suddenly from heaven and threw him to the ground. Notice that he says: a light came from heaven. Our best masters say that in itself heaven is filled with light, but that nevertheless it does not shine. The sun, too, is full of light in itself, but it also shines. Likewise the stars possess light, although it comes to them from elsewhere. Our teachers say that fire does not give any light in the simple and natural clarity of its highest state. There its nature is too pure for any eye in any way to see. It is so subtle and so unlike the eye that, were it here below within our view, the sight of our eyes could not reach it. On other things, though, when it is absorbed by a piece of wood or coal, we see it very well.

By the light of heaven, we understand the light that is God. No one can reach it by his sense organ. This is why Saint Paul says: "God dwells in a light to which no one can attain" (1 Tim. 6:16). He says: "God is a light to which there is no access." There

122

is no access to God. No man still on the ascent, still growing in grace and in light, has ever yet come into God. God's light does not grow, but it is by growth that we attain him. Not that we attain God in the process of growing. If God is at all to be seen, it must be in a light that is God himself. A master says: In God there is no more nor less, neither this nor that. As long as we are still in the ascent we do not attain into him.

Further he says: "A light from heaven bathed him." He means to say that everything belonging to his mind was embraced. A master says that in this light all the powers of the soul surpass themselves and are elevated: the exterior senses, by which we see and hear, as well as the inner ones which we call thoughts. How vast and unfathomable these [thoughts] are is a marvel: I can indeed think as easily of things beyond the sea as of what is close to me. Above the thoughts goes the intellect in its pursuit. It goes about and seeks; it is on the watch, here and there, gathering and losing. But above this intellect that seeks, there is another intellect which is not a seeker. It stands in its pure and simple being which is inundated by that light. And I say that in this light all the powers of the soul are superelevated. The senses soar up into the thoughts. Of these thoughts no one, except God and the mind, knows how high and unfathomable they are. Our masters say—and the question is difficult—that even the angels know nothing of our thoughts as long as the thoughts do not break out and soar up into the intellect that seeks, and as long as the intellect that seeks does not soar up into that intellect which seeks no more and which is a pure light in itself. This light embraces all the powers of the soul. Accordingly he says: "The light of heaven bathed him."

A master says: things from which others emanate receive nothing from lower things. God overflows into all creatures, and yet he remains untouched by all. He has no need of them. God lends nature the power to act and first of all it produces the heart. Some teachers conclude therefore that the soul is located entirely in the heart and flows from there into the other members, giving them life. This is not so. The soul is in each member, whole.

However, it is true that its chief work is in the heart. The heart is placed in the center so that it is protected on all sides. Likewise heaven receives no alien influence and suffers no intrusion. It contains on the contrary all things in itself. It touches all things and remains itself untouched. Even fire, however sublime it may be in its point, does not touch heaven.

In the encircling light he was thrown to earth, his eyes were unsealed and he saw with open eyes all things as nothingness. And when he saw all things as nothingness, he saw God.

Now pay attention. In the Book of Love the soul speaks the following words: "In my bed, all through the night, I sought him whom my soul loves, and I found him not" (Cant. 3:1). She sought him in her bed, which means: if anyone remains attached or bound to anything below God, then his bed is too narrow. Everything God can create is too narrow. The soul says: "I sought him all night long." There is no night without light, but its light is hidden. The sun shines even during the night, albeit it is hidden. By day it shines and covers all other lights. So it is with the light of God, it covers all other lights. What we look for among creatures is night. Here is my advice: whatever we expect from creatures is all shadow and night. Even the light of the highest angel, exalted though it be, does not touch the soul. All that is not the first light is darkness and night. Hence she does not find God. "I rose and sought him all about, I ran far and near. The watchmen, the angels, found me and I asked if they had seen him whom my soul loves? And they kept silent." Perhaps they could not name him. "Then, having passed by a little, I found whom I sought." The little, the trifle, which hindered her on her quest so that she did not find him, has been my theme at other times. He to whom all perishable things are not petty and like nothing, will never find God. She says therefore: "Having passed by a little, I found whom I sought." When God informs the soul and pours himself into it, if you comprehend him then as a light or as a being or as goodness—as long as you still know anything of him, it is not God. Look, one has to go beyond the little, one has to subtract all attributes and know God as One. This is why she says: "Having passed by a little, I found him whom my soul loves."

We often say: "he whom my soul loves." But she, why does she say: "he whom my soul loves?" He is indeed far above the soul. Thus she did not name her love. There are four reasons why she did not name him. The first reason is that God is nameless. Were she to give him a name, one would have to imagine [a content] to it. But since God is above all names, no one will be able to pronounce God. The second reason why she did not name him, is this: when the soul dissolves entirely by love into God, it knows about nothing any longer except love. It believes that everyone knows him as itself does. It is surprised when someone knows still another thing rather than God alone. The third reason is that it does not have enough time to name him. It cannot turn away long enough from love. It can pronounce no other word than love. The fourth reason is that [the soul] supposes perhaps that he has no other name than "love." Saying "love," it pronounces at the same time all names. This is why she says: "I rose and ran far and near, and having passed a little, I found him whom my soul loves."

"Paul rose from the ground and with open eyes he saw nothing." I cannot see what is One. He saw nothing, that is to say, God. God is nothingness, and yet God is a something. What is something is also nothing. What God is, he is totally. Therefore the illuminated Dionysius, wherever he writes about God, says: he is super-being, he is super-life, he is super-light. He does not attribute to him any of these [qualities], but he intimates through them that he is an—I do not know what—that lies far beyond them. If you visualize anything or if anything enters your mind, that is not God; indeed he is neither this nor that. Whoever says that God is here or there, do not trust him. The light that is God shines in the darkness. God is a true light. To see it one must be blind and one must divest God of everything that there is. A master says: to speak of God in any simile is to speak of him in an impure mode. But whoever speaks of God through nothingness speaks of him to the point. When the mind penetrates into the One, entering in pure dereliction of itself, it finds God as in a nothingness. A man had a dream, a daydream: it seemed to him that he was big with nothingness as a woman is with a child. In this nothingness God was born. He was the fruit of nothingness. God was born in nothingness. This is why he says: "He rose from the ground and with open eyes he saw nothing." He saw God where all creatures are nothing. He saw all creatures as a nothingness, for he [God] has all creatures' being in himself. He is a being that has in itself all being.

He means still another thing by saying "he saw nothing." According to our masters, to know something of exterior things is to be invaded by it, or, at the very least, to have received an impression of it. To obtain a representation of a thing, for example of a rock, I do not draw into myself what is grossest about it; abstraction leaves that outside. It is found in the ground of my mind in its highest and noblest form, as nothing other than a [mental] image. Something alien falls into my mind with everything it learns about the outside. But what I know of creatures in God introduces [into my mind] nothing but God alone, for in God there is only God. When I know all creatures in God, I know them as nothingness. He saw God, in whom all creatures are nothingness.

There is a third reason why he saw nothing: the nothingness was God. A master says that all creatures are in God as in nothingness, for he has in himself the being of all creatures. He is a being that has all being in itself. [Another] master says: Everything inferior to God, however close it may be to him, contains also something alien. [Another] master says that the angel knows himself as well as God without mediation; but with anything else that he may know, an outside element comes into him; an impression, however small, enters into him. If we are to know God, it must be without mediation. Nothing foreign can be mixed with it. If we know God in that light, [our knowledge] must be sufficient in itself, it must be enclosed in itself and it must be free from the intrusion of any created thing. Only then do we have immediate knowledge of the eternal life.

"When he saw nothing, he saw God." The light that is God flows out and darkens every other light. In the light in which Paul had his vision, he saw God and nothing else. This is why Job says: "He commands the sun not to shine, he puts a seal on the stars" (Job 9:7). Because he was bathed in this light, he saw nothing else. Everything belonging to his mind was anxious about and concerned with the light that is God, to such an extent that he could perceive nothing else. There is a lesson in this for us: if we care about God, then the exterior cares will hardly matter.

The fourth reason why he saw nothing is that the light which is God has no mixture. No mixture falls into it from outside. It was a sign that he saw the true light which is nothingness. With the "light," he means only that with his eyes open he saw nothing. Seeing nothing, he saw divine nothingness. Saint Augustine says: When he saw nothingness, he saw God. Saint Paul says: He who sees nothing other and who is blind sees God. This is why Saint Augustine says: God is a true light, a support for the mind, and he is nearer to the mind than the mind is to itself. From this it follows that when the mind turns away from all things that become, God shines and radiates in it.

When the mind experiences love or anguish it knows where these come from. But when the mind ceases to egress towards outside things, it has come home and lives in its simple and pure light. Then it has neither love nor anguish nor fear. Knowledge is a groundwork and a foundation of all being. As to love, it has no hold except in knowledge. When the mind is blind and sees nothing else, it sees God. This is necessarily so. A master says: the eye in its supreme purity, in which it is deprived of all color, sees all colors. But it should not be colorless only in its [essence]: rather it must be colorless in the body also, if we are to see colors. Colors are seen by what is deprived of color, even if this were down at one's feet. God is a being who bears in himself all being. If God is to make himself known to the mind, it has to be blind. Therefore he says: "He saw the nothingness" from whose light all light emanates and from whose being all being comes. The bride says in the Book of Love: "I passed by a little, and I found

him whom my soul loves." The "little" beyond which she passed
was all creatures. If one does not reject these, then one never finds
God. She also suggests that no matter how transparent, how
subtle, a means may be by which I know God, it must go. Indeed,
even if I took the light that is really God, but only as it touches
my mind, that would still be improper. Rather I must take it
where it breaks out. I could not properly see the light that is
projected on a wall unless I turned my gaze to the source from
which it breaks out. Even then, as I take it from where it breaks
out, I must still rid myself of this outbreak: I must take it as it
sustains itself in itself. Even then, I say, it is still not correct: I
ought to take it neither as it touches us, nor as it breaks out, nor
as it sustains itself, for all these are mere modes. But one must
take God as the mode without mode and as being without being,
for he has no mode. This is why Saint Bernard says: Whoever,
God, wishes to know you, must measure you without measure.

Let us pray to our Lord that we may reach that knowledge that
is without mode and without measure. So help us God. Amen.[148]

Chapter
Three

SERMON,
"SEE WHAT LOVE"

(VIDETE QUALEM CARITATEM DEDIT NOBIS PATER, UT FILII DEI
NOMINEMUR ET SIMUS, I John 3:1)

[1] It should be understood that to know God and to be known by God, to see God and to be seen by God, are one according to the reality of things. In knowing and seeing God, we know and see that he makes us see and know. And just as the air which is illumined is nothing other than illumination—it illumines indeed because it is illuminated—likewise we know because we are known and because He makes us know Him. This is why Christ says: "You will see me again," that is, I make you see, and by this you know me. He continues: "and your heart will rejoice," namely in the vision and in the knowledge of me; "and no one can take your joy away from you."

[2] Saint John says: "See what love the Father has given us: we are called Sons of God and we are." He does not only say, "we are called," but also, "we are." Correspondingly I say, just as man cannot be wise outside of wisdom, he cannot be the Son outside of the Son of God's being and without having the identical being that the Son of God himself possesses, quite as there can be no being-wise outside of wisdom. Hence, if you are to be the Son of God, you will never be it unless you possess that same being of God which the Son of God has. At present, though, this is hidden from us. The text goes on to say: "Beloved, we are Sons of God." How are we to understand this? The explanation follows: "and we shall be like him," which means, we shall be exactly what he is, the same being and the same sensibility and intelligence; entirely the same as he will be when "we shall see him as he is God." This is why I say: God could never make me

131

be the Son of God without my having the being of the Son of God, just as God could not make me be wise without my having wisdom's being. How then are we children of God? We do not know yet: "that is not yet revealed to us." We only know what he himself says about it: "We shall be like him." There are certain things in our minds which hide this likeness from us and veil this knowledge.

[3] The mind encloses something within itself, a spark of the intellectual power, which is never quenched. This spark is the higher part of the spirit; in it is located the image of the mind. Yet, in our minds there is also a knowledge directed towards external things, namely, the knowledge through the senses and through reason. This knowledge proceeds by representation of images and by concepts, and it conceals from us that other way of knowing.

[4] How then are we "Sons of God"? By having one and the same being with him. In order to know that we are the Son of God, we have to be able to distinguish between outer and inner knowledge. The inner knowledge is of an intellectual kind and is grounded in the being of our mind. Yet, it does not coincide with the being of the mind. It only takes root there; it is something of the life of the mind. When we say that this knowledge is something of the life of the mind, we are referring to its intelligible life. It is in this life that man is begotten as the Son of God and that he is born to eternal life. Also this knowledge is without time and without space, without any here and any now. In this life all things are one, they are all together all in all, and all united to all.

[5] This may be compared to the body, all the parts of which are united in such a way that the eye belongs also to the foot, and the foot to the eye. If the foot could speak, it would say that the eye, though it is located in the head, is as much its own as if it were located in the foot, and the eye in turn would say the same thing. In the same way I consider that all the grace which is in Mary belongs equally and even more properly to the angel; it is just as much his, although it is in Mary, as if it were in him or in the saints. Indeed, all that is in Mary belongs also to the saint

and is even more his own. He relishes the grace that is in Mary more than if it were in him.

[6] But this interpretation is still too crude and too physical, as it is taken from a sensuous comparison. I will now present to you another meaning, still more transparent and spiritual. I say: In the kingdom of the heavens all is in all, all is one and all is ours. The bliss that Our Lady possesses is all mine—when I am there —and in no way as flowing and emanating from Mary, but dwelling in me as my proper good, not as derived from elsewhere. And thus I say: what someone possesses in the beyond, another possesses equally—not as acquired from him or taken from him, but as dwelling in himself, so that the grace which is in the one is fully also in the other, exactly as one's own grace.

[7] In the same way the spirit is in the Spirit. This is why I say: I cannot be the Son of God unless I possess that same being that belongs to the Son of God. It is the possession of this identical being that likens us to him and makes us see him in his divinity. But what we shall be hereafter is not yet manifested. Therefore I say that in the sense of which I have spoken there will be no similarity and no difference, but rather, without any difference, we shall be the identical being and the identical substance and nature that he is himself. But "this is not yet revealed." It will be manifest only when "we shall see him as he is, God."

[8] God makes us know himself, and he makes us know himself by his act of knowing, and his being is his knowledge. For him to make me know and for me to know are one and the same thing. Hence his knowledge is mine, quite as it is one and the same in the master who teaches and in the disciple who is taught. Since his knowledge is mine, and since his substance is his knowledge, his nature, and his being, it follows that his being, his substance, and his nature are mine. Thus since his substance, his being, and his nature are mine, I am the Son of God. "See, brothers, what love God has given us: We are called the Son of God and we are."

[9] Notice by what we are the Son of God: by having that same being that the Son has. How then are we the Son of God,

or how does one know that one is the Son of God, since God
resembles no one? For this is assuredly true. Indeed, Isaiah says:
"To what have you compared him, or what image do you give
him?" (Isa. 40:18). Since, then, it is of the nature of God not to
be like anyone, we are compelled to conclude that we are nothing,
so that we may be transported into the identical being that he is
himself. When this is achieved, when I cease projecting myself
into any image, when no image is represented any longer in me,
and when I cast out of myself and eject whatever is in me, then
I am ready to be transported into the naked being of God, the
pure being of the Spirit. All likeness has to be expelled from it.
Then I am translated into God and I become one with him—one
sole substance, one being, and one nature: the Son of God. And
after this has been accomplished, nothing is hidden anymore in
God which has not become manifest or mine. Then I become wise
and powerful. I become all things, as he is, and I am one and the
same being with him. Then Zion becomes truly a seer, a "true
Israel," that is, "a God-seeing man." Indeed, nothing is hidden
from him in the Godhead. Thus man is led into God. But in order
that nothing remain hidden from me in God, that all be revealed
to me, no likeness nor any image may endure. Indeed, no image
will disclose the Godhead or God's being to us. If some image or
similitude remained in you, you would never become one with
God. Therefore in order for you to be one with God, no image
must be represented in you, and you must not represent yourself
in any. This means that nothing should stay concealed in you that
does not become unconcealed and ejected. Pay attention now to
where our inadequacy comes from. It comes from nothingness.
Consequently, what pertains to nothingness in man must be
eradicated, for as long as there is such inadequacy about you, you
are not the Son of God. What man complains about and suffers
comes always from his inadequacy. Therefore, in order that man
become the Son of God, all this has to be exterminated and
expelled. Complaints and sufferings will then be no more. Man
is neither stone nor wood, for all this is inadequate and nothing.

We shall never be like him so long as this nothingness is not expelled. Only then may we be all in all, as God is all in all.

[10] There are two births of man: one is into the world, and the other out of the world, that is, spiritually into God. Do you want to know if your child is born and if it is denuded, that is, if you have become the Son of God? As long as you have sorrow in your heart, for whatever reason, be it for sin, your child is not yet born. Does your heart ache? You are not yet mother. You are still on the way to give birth, you are near birth. Do not fall prey to doubt while you are afflicted for yourself or for your friend: if the child is not yet born, it is nevertheless close to being born. It is born perfectly when man no longer feels any torment in his heart for anything whatsoever. Then he has the being and the nature and the substance and the wisdom and the joy and all that God has. Then the very being of God's Son becomes ours, it comes into us, and we attain the identical being of God. Christ says: "He who wants to follow me, let him deny himself and take up his cross and come after me" (Mark 8:34). This means: throw all anxiety out of your heart, so that in your heart there be nothing but constant joy. Then the child is born. When the child is so born in me, even if I had to see with my own eyes my father and all my friends killed, my heart would not be moved by it. If however my heart were moved by it, the child would not yet be born in me, but it would perhaps be close to birth. I say: God and the angels have so great a joy by every single action of a good man that no other joy could resemble it. This is why I say: When it happens that the child is born in you, you have so great a joy by all good deeds done in this world that your joy reaches the greatest evenness; it never alters. Therefore he says: "No one can take your joy away from you." And when I am correctly translated into the divine being, God becomes mine as well as everything he has. This is why he says: "I am God, your Lord" (Exod. 20:2). I have rightful joy only when neither sufferings nor torments can ravish it from me. Then I am translated into the divine being where no suffering has a place. We see indeed that in God there

is neither wrath nor grief, but only love and joy. Even if sometimes he seems to be wrathful against the sinner, this is not wrath
but love, for it proceeds from a great divine love. Those whom
he loves he punishes, for he is love itself, which is the Holy Spirit.
Thus the wrath of God comes from love, for he is wrathful
without bitterness. If you reach a state where you feel neither
suffering nor vexation from whatever may happen, so that suffering is not suffering for you and that all things are sheer joy for
you, then the child is truly born.

[11] Exert yourself so that the child be not only in the process
of being born, but that it be already born, just as in God the Son
is always born and in the process of being born.

May God help us that this be our destiny. Amen.

ANALYSIS

The sermon "See What Love"[1] is constructed quite clearly; in three dialectical steps, it sets forth Meister Eckhart's understanding of being. These three steps are: paragraph [1], which under the guise of an Aristotelian thesis posits the problematic; paragraph [2], which opposes a thesis of Platonic inspiration; and paragraphs [5-8], which properly contain the Eckhartian doctrine of being. This third passage, the central part of the sermon, is prepared by a gnoseological theory found in paragraphs [3] and [4]; it is followed by the exposition of two consequences: the double acceptance of "nothingness" in paragraph [9], and the doctrine of equanimity in paragraph [10]. The conclusion, paragraph [11], sums up in a single phrase Eckhart's dialectic of being, which is the subject matter proper of this text.

[1] Union by Knowledge

See what love the Father has given us: we are called Sons of God and we are.

It should be understood that to know God and to be known by God, to see God and to be seen by God, are one according to the reality of things. In knowing and seeing God, we know and see that he makes us see and know. And just as the air which is illumined is nothing other than illumination—it illumines indeed because it is illuminated—likewise we know because we are known and because He makes us know Him. This is why Christ says: "You will see me again," that is, I make you see, and by this, you know me. He continues: "and your heart will rejoice," namely in the vision and in the knowledge of me; "and no one can take your joy away from you."

As he often does, Eckhart here proceeds thetically. His starting point is the thesis that knowing God and being known by God, or seeing God and being seen by him, are one and the same thing. This thesis brings together several elements: it speaks of God, and then of what God knows and sees, that is, things created; it also speaks of those who know

137

and see God, namely man; finally, it affirms a oneness or unity. God and man are not considered as two separate beings, one facing the other, but in their act: knowing, seeing. This act, Eckhart says, is indistinguishably human and divine, it is one and the same act for both man and God.

The unity of act between the subject knowing and the object known is a familiar[2] Aristotelian doctrine amply orchestrated by Thomas Aquinas, which Eckhart's argument here recalls. His inquiry is into the foundation of our knowledge of God. We can know God, he says, only because God knows us. The uncreated act of knowing and seeing is constitutive of the created act of knowing and seeing. This relation of constitution or foundation is known to us by the very act of knowing God. "In knowing and seeing God, we know and see that he makes us see and know."

How are we to think of one identical act and at the same time of a threefold actuality? Why does the intelligible unity between man and God require three terms? What is the purpose of distinguishing our act of knowing God from the divine act of knowing us by means of a third term, our act of knowing this relation of foundation? To see, to know, is to establish a relation. This relation is an act, precisely the act of vision or intellection. It connects the subject that sees and knows with the term that is seen and known. Such an approach to unity between man and God uses the Aristotelian scheme of a relation "as knowledge to a thing known, a term being called relative because another is relative to it."[3] Of these terms, "relative not by themselves," Aristotle says that the being of the knower and of the knowable resides differently in their relation. Thought is relative to what it thinks, but what is thus represented by thought is not relative to thought itself. The reciprocity between thought that represents and things represented is predicamental, not essential. In this way it differs from the reciprocity between concepts such as simple and double, which are "relative by themselves." This type of predicamental relation is an application of the relations between substance and accidents to the domain of substances. Such a relation between substances unites extremes by ordering them ($\pi\rho\delta\varsigma$ $\tau\iota$) to one another. In this act of nonessential ordering subject, foundation, and term are one. In the relations between substances, for instance, knowledge, the subject and the term subsist by themselves; their relation is accidental. This is why the foundation, the reference of one to the other, is really distinct from the two. But since it is also inherent in the two, since it is a certain reality in the subject as well as in the term, it establishes a reciprocity between the two. Distinction and reciprocity characterize this Aristotelian metaphysics of relation. Further below in the sermon, Meister Eckhart will see in this an insufficiency for his understanding of identity. To be relative to, πρός τι, is to be the other without being other. But Eckhart considers that in its ground the mind is precisely "other," that man at his bottom is divine. The concept of distinction will then have to be changed into its contrary, identity; and predicamental reciprocity will be changed into man's freedom, which "forces" God, thus abolishing any distance.

Distinction and reciprocity eminently affect the relation constituted by vision or knowledge. The subject, the intelligence in act, is really distinct from the term, truth in act, but the subject is united to the term in the actual intellection which serves as foundation for this relation. The phrase of our text "to see and to be seen" refers to this kind of reciprocity. Between the actuality of intelligence and the intelligible in act a real distinction appears which is analogous to the distinction between substance and accident. The same relation prevails between the actuality of knowing truth and the truth known in act. The inherence of the subject in the term establishes the same kind of accidental presence: it is afferent to a predicamental unity, and thus entirely ephemeral.

The Medievals have applied the Aristotelian category of relation to the domain of knowledge between man and God. The relation of creation, according to Thomas Aquinas, brings together two substances, the Creator and the created. It is of accidental order, even if it is the most perfect of accidents, since this relation puts man into communication with God. It is a predicamental relation, even though it is grounded in the very being of the created[4] and even though through it God "governs" and "conserves" the world. For Thomas Aquinas a transcendental or substantial relation between man and God cannot exist. This strict position results from Aquinas's desire to attribute to the created substance as much autonomy as possible. Man is really "relative to God," but he is so extrinsically and not intrinsically, *secundum dici*, not *secundum esse*. If the Creator were the subject of such a transcendental relation *ad extra*, he would depend in some way on the created: the act of creating would be for him a necessity. The relation of creation is therefore "real" only when seen from the perspective of man's being. Knowledge establishes a relation of union in act between man and God which is real when understood from the side of man, but only "of reason" when understood from God's side. This relation is rooted in the being of created substances which, through distinction and reciprocity, it orders towards the term while at the same time it preserves their autonomy.

Meister Eckhart is faithful to this received teaching when he ascribes the reality of the relation only to the created: "He makes us see and know." On this point he would simply repeat Thomas Aquinas almost literally.[5] Eckhart nonetheless considers this entire metaphysics of the relation unsuitable for giving an account of the intimate union between God and man. The πρός τι of the created to its cause allows for rigorous language, but it leads away from the direct experience of union. By definition the theory of relation never transcends the realm of accidents. It remains embedded in the irreducible otherness between man and God. This limit is the one drawn by the *suppositum,* the pure and univocal position of a fully constituted finite being. It is the abyss between substances, ontologically separated from one another, that the metaphysics of relation cannot bridge. It does not reach the "ground" of man and God. It warrants a unitary discourse only in the accidental domain of vision or of knowledge. The metaphysics of relation is not applicable to the being-Son whose perfect appropriation is the theme of this sermon.

Meister Eckhart therefore turns towards Neoplatonism in his quest for a language that would suit his intuition of identity. From this shift in vocabulary he expects a language that would overcome the exteriority of man "before" God and would allow us to see man introduced "into" God. However, Eckhart by no means rejects Aristotle out of hand. From the analysis of relation, he retains the elements concerning being. He will finally say that we *are* one with God just as, in the act of knowing, the intellect is one with what it knows. But this oneness will no longer have to be developed according to the modes of substantial distinction and of predicamental reciprocity. "The air illumines because it *is* illuminated"; but the air is no longer considered as a substance: it "*is* nothing other than illumination."

[2] Union by Participation

Saint John says: "See what love the Father has given us: we are called Sons of God and we are." He does not only say, "we are called," but also, "we are." Correspondingly I say, just as man cannot be wise outside of wisdom, he cannot be the Son outside of the Son of God's being and without having the identical being that the Son of God himself possesses, quite as there can be no being-wise outside of wisdom. Hence, if you are to be the Son of God, you will never be it unless you possess that same being of God which the Son of God has. At present, though, this is hidden from us. The text goes on to say: "Beloved, we are Sons of God." How are we to understand this? The explanation follows: "and we shall be like him," which means, we shall be exactly what he is, the same being and the same sensibility and intelligence; entirely the same as he will be when "we shall see him as he is God." This is why I say: God could never make me be the Son of God without my having the being of the Son of God, just as God could not make me be wise without my having wisdom's being. How then are we children of God? We do not know yet: "that is not yet revealed to us." We only know what he himself says about it: "We shall be like him." There are certain things in our minds which hide this likeness from us and veil this knowledge.

The Neoplatonic vocabulary permits Eckhart to go further in his search for identity: the wise man participates in the universal perfection of wisdom; in fact he is truly and identically Wisdom. The man who possesses the being of the Son participates in the universal perfection of being-Son, he is truly and identically the Son. When one sole and same attribute thus pertains to a plurality of terms, one can indeed speak of an identity of the participated in the participants.

In this model of thought, the disputed question of the universals is the key to the understanding of union. Which is real by priority, the universal or the singular, the general perfection or the particular being? The question is an ancient one. In the Middle Ages those who felt indebted both to Plato and Aristotle answered it by explaining how the being of things is real precisely insofar as it is one in the multiple. They tried to reconcile the one and the multiple by the bond of participation. Since Plato,[6] the attraction of such a solution has stemmed from the epistemological armature that it gives to the intuition that ideas are more real than the sense-reality, and that they are actually one with the first being.

According to Anselm, concepts are progressively more real as their extension approaches universality. Following the Neoplatonic degrees of reality, the intensity of being grows as the mind ascends towards God, who is the universal and real being in fullness. This was the state of the question when Thomas Aquinas asked himself if universals are known by us prior to singulars. His answer is twofold. On the one hand, he says, knowledge of the universal indeed precedes any knowledge of the singular. But this precedence is thoroughly relative as we have to distinguish, on the other hand, the universal *post rem* and universal *ante rem*. He attributes the first of these two usages to Aristotle: the intellect abstracts the intelligible universal from the sensible particular; and the second to Plato: the subsistence of the universal founds and maintains any particular being. Thomas attempts to harmonize these two tendencies by his own version of the theory of forms in which they become the principles of knowledge in the human mind and the principles of creation in the divine mind. From our point of view, *quoad nos,* the universal forms exist primarily in particular finite beings, but from God's point of view they exist first of all in the knowledge that he has of his creation.

Meister Eckhart's own argument rests on a parallelism: "Just as man cannot be wise outside of wisdom, he cannot be the Son outside of the Son of God's being." At first sight, Eckhart seems to side with the Neoplatonic realism of universals: only Wisdom itself is real, and the wise man is real only by participation; only the Son of God is real, and man born again is real only by participation in the being-Son; only the universal is real, the particular is nothingness. The impression of Platonism seems to be confirmed: the unique Wisdom, indivisible, indistinct, numerically one, makes all wise men wise. Likewise, the sole being of filiation, the being of Christ, makes all adoptive sons be the Son of God. From the viewpoint of the union which interests us: all wise men, as such, are one; all those in whom the Son is reborn are one. Meister Eckhart, thus interpreted according to the Platonic schema of participation of universals, thinks nothing less than oneness of man and God. The perfection accorded to man (Wisdom, Sonship) is really that of God and not another perfection. Otherness is cancelled. Wisdom is not different in itself and in the wise man. If there were any such differences, one would have to accept an irreducible multiplicity of ways of being wise. According to the same schema the being-Son is not different in the Son himself and in us; we are the Son of God by virtue of the "self-same being of the Son." Between the Son who is reborn and man who receives this birth, there is only one sole being of filiation.[7]

But is this concept of identity any different from that of accidental identity through knowledge or sight? Does the Neoplatonic vocabulary of participation constitute a real step beyond the Aristotelian vocabulary of the metaphysics of relation? The shift lies in the notion of total appropriation. We appropriate, Eckhart says, "the identical being of the

Son of God." If we are not mistaken in reading this affirmation in a Neoplatonic light, then identity takes on a new meaning. It is no longer the energetic identity between two entities subject to one and the same predicamental or extrinsic determination, but it is the identity by deficient similarity of a universal which is participated in totally, although not without admixture, by a singular. The counterpart of this total appropriation is the realism of universals: the identity is that of a "form" or of a "quality"—to be wise, to be the Son—but this universal form remains at the same time totally distinct from the finite being that participates in it through formal limitation. The infinite quality is thus subjected to the limits of an unequal perfection. The appropriation is total, but finite. Identity then affects only the attribute in question (to be wise, to be the Son), but not its degree of being. The so-called participation by deficient similarity or by formal limitation is defined precisely by this inequality of perfection. It is the element of limitation and inequality that Meister Eckhart intends to bypass. We shall be, he says, exactly "what He is: the same being and the same sensibility and intelligence; entirely the same as he will be when 'we shall see him as he is God.' "

Eckhart goes still further. He sees in God the universal par excellence: everything universal, inasmuch as it is universal, he says, is God. Here again he follows Anselm, with the exception that for Eckhart the universal as such exists only in the ground of the mind, and thus in supreme individuality. Eckhart pushes to extremes the Aristotelian teaching according to which universal forms exist only in particular beings. In the ground of the mind the universal is particularized (I possess intelligible forms), and the particular is universalized (I am detached from sensible forms). In fact this thrust leads Meister Eckhart to abolish both universal and particular in the ground of the mind. The identity of a shared quality is a false identity. The effect of participation is that a perfection is no longer the same, but other. Participation depends on that formal hierarchy which Eckhart intends to destroy. Participation sanctions the gradual loss of intensity through the degrees of being. The issue that is the basis of Eckhart's thinking is the opposite of such gradual loss: it is rather the identity of the ground of the mind and the ground of God. This identity happens in the supreme intensity of being; thus it tolerates no representation of a hierarchy of degrees. This is why the Neoplatonic doctrine of formal participation that we have sketched must in turn be overcome.

Further below in this sermon, when he speaks of grace, Meister Eckhart expounds a theory of perfect appropriation freed from the restrictions imposed by both the Aristotelian and the Neoplatonic traditions.
Participant and participated will then come together in one and the same
being. He will base himself on the two theories of being, Aristotelian
and Platonic, which underlie these two first paragraphs. The way of
their overcoming has already been indicated by the example of the
energetic presence of light in its transparent milieu, the air. Light is
"participated" by the air, but there is only one sole being: illumination.
A new understanding of being will thus have to be worked out in order
to overcome the radical distinction between substances (paragraph [1])
as well as the no less radical distinction between universal perfections
in themselves and as participated (paragraph [2]).

[3] Exterior Knowledge and Interior Knowledge

The mind encloses something within itself, a spark of the intellectual
power, which is never quenched. This spark is the higher part of the spirit;
in it is located the image of the mind. Yet, in our minds there is also a
knowledge directed towards external things, namely the knowledge
through the senses and through reason. This knowledge proceeds by
representation of images and by concepts, and it conceals from us that
other way of knowing.

"There are certain things in our minds that hide this likeness (with
God) from us and veil this knowledge." This sentence which closes the
preceding development introduces and at the same time summarizes the
two following paragraphs.

The sermon "Jesus Entered" speaks of "the spark," the principle of
interior knowledge.[8] In the present paragraph Eckhart is content with
enumerating, as a reminder, the fundamental aspects which guide him
in this matter. On the one hand, the "spark" is "something" that is
related to the power of intellection: it is of an intellectual nature, "in"
the mind and not "of" the mind, and yet it is not itself a faculty. On
the other hand, it is "never extinguished": this spark is beyond time, in
eternity. Finally the spark, the "higher" part of the human being, bears
in itself the image of God. "In this spark, as the higher part of *gemüete,*
is located the image of the mind," which is to say: "the image of God
that the mind is," or, again, since Eckhart stresses the locus of this
resemblance: "the image of God in the mind."[9]

The word *gemüete* or *gemuote,* rare in Eckhart, episodic in Tauler, but very frequent in Suso, has been called by de Gandillac "the cross of translators." It appears here for the first time. Dictionaries have recourse to a paraphrase: "the totality of thoughts and sentiments," says Lexer. Some have translated it by "deep-seated will" or again by "heart," "heart of the mind"; others have proposed "habitual tendency." In the fourteenth century, when the first texts of Thomas Aquinas become accessible in Middle High German, *gemüete* is found wherever the Latin author says *mens.* The Thomist notion of *mens* has of course an Augustinian flavor; it is remarkable precisely because of its psychological breadth. The word designates not another faculty along with the intellect and the will, but their common root insofar as it actuates man's "return" upon the image of God in himself, which requires a certain conduct in life as well as in reflection. The *gemüete* of the later Rhenish mystics largely agrees with this Thomist concept of *mens:* a fundamental disposition to know and to love, and the spiritual vestige of the divine life in man. The only English word that expresses a similar semantic richness—psychological, moral, and metaphysical—is "spirit." Thus we translate: "In this spark, as the higher part of the spirit, is located the image of the mind."

The *gemüete* contains in itself the whole of the spiritual activities, from the ramifications buried in the sensible up to the peak that touches the One. Meister Eckhart distinguishes, as we know, the divaricate capillaries of the *gemüete* turned towards the multiple from its unified and unalloyed summit or core. In this he adopts the ancient theory of the two faces of the mind. The *verstantnisse* or *verstentnisse,* reason, corresponds to the *ratio inferior;* the *vernunst* or *vernunft,* the intellect, to the *ratio superior* of the Scholastics.[10] This division of the mind into exterior knowledge by abstraction and interior knowledge by intuition is commonly accepted by most of the predecessors and contemporaries of Meister Eckhart. The difficult question which separates Augustinians and Thomists in this matter, the knowledge of the soul by itself and especially the role of the phantasms in it, does not seem to have retained the attention of Eckhart. The interior eye that sees God without images or any mediation knows a universal in the ground of the mind: the common perfection of humankind. A detached man possesses simultaneously, in a unique act of intellection, God, things, and himself. When detachment reaches the ground of his mind, he has abandoned knowledge by representation, and he possesses knowledge through ideas. But how is this double passage to the mind's extremes, the one and the multiple, possible? The answer to this question will reveal the nonintellectual "basis" of the intellect, where the union takes place. Another question subsidiary to this is, on what condition can the place of such an experience be understood as really distinct from the intellective faculties? The difficulty consists indeed in thinking of the *vünkelin*, spark, as naturally different from the activities of the *gemüete*, particularly, all mental activities. The spark is not a faculty, but "in" a faculty. Yet, how is the expression "spark of the intellectual power" to be reconciled with the henological affirmations? The One in the mind is elevated above the intellect and the will, as heaven is elevated above the earth. If Eckhart's intention is essentially the union and the birth of the Son in us, why should he link the spark, here and elsewhere, to the cognitive faculty of man? Why this intellectualism in Meister Eckhart? One might be tempted to settle this debate with an argument from authority: the doctrine of the spark in the mind goes back to Augustine and the Stoics, and the *apex mentis* and its equivalents are of an intelligible nature.[11] Yet still other authors known to Meister Eckhart have taught him a different, transintellectual, vision of the mind. In Proclus the ἕν is a hypostasis really distinct from that of the νοῦς.

The answer is to be sought in the intellect "destined to become all things." The mystique of union is intellectualist because the Aristotelian νοῦς has the privilege of becoming all things. To be purely νοῦς would be to become purely and simply the universality of the forms of being.

In his commentary on the book of Genesis, Eckhart elucidates the biblical term of "image of God" with the help of the Aristotelian concept of "pure intellect."[12] The tenet that states that the intellect "is what it is by virtue of becoming all things"[13] establishes also the likeness between the spark and God:

> The intellectual nature resembles as such God himself. . . . The reason for this is that the intellect as such is open to become all things and not this or that specifically determined being. . . . Therefore Avicenna says: "The perfection of the soul endowed with reason is to become the intellectual world and to have inscribed in it the form of all."[14]

Following the tradition of Aristotle and his Arabic commentators, Eckhart recognizes an unlimited power in the mind: the intellect becomes the totality of the world, for the "form" of all things can be impressed on it. No thing is excluded from such potential appearance before the intellect. Hence expressions such as "similitude with all being," "universality of beings," "absolute being," all of which are taken over from the Aristotelian school and are used to describe the proper object of the human intellect.[15]

If we look at the context in which Eckhart uses those traditional expressions, the advantage they offer to his concept of union becomes evident. The intellect is capable of receiving the universe; this is why and how it is naturally like God. Man's similarity with God consists in his openness to the totality of what is; tradition attaches the label of intellect to this capacity of total openness. Eckhart's anthropology connects the "spark" with the intellect, because the intellect is naturally connected with the universe.

This connection between the speculations on the image of God in man and the philosophy of the $\psi v \chi \acute{\eta}$ is reflected in our sermon: "In this spark, as the higher part of the spirit, is located the image of [God in] the mind." The same connection is stated in the commentary on Genesis: man is "the image of God," because he is *capax divinae essentiae,* capable of receiving the divine essence.[16] Man's resemblance is due to his boundless openness to all that there is. He is godlike because his mind is all forms, and not inversely. Eckhartian intellectualism is the theoretical link that explains how the ground of the mind belongs entirely to the universe and to God. It does not entail any exaltation of the faculty of arguing, or of discursive reason. Rather it indicates a real and instantaneous gathering together of God, man, and the world. Connecting the "spark" with the faculty of knowing is for Eckhart the means towards a more appropriate language within his vision of man: the dimensions of the mind are the very dimensions of God, because the finite intellect and the infinite intellect are naturally directed to universality. Eckhart distinguishes himself from his predecessors and contemporaries when he tells his audience: in the present, and not only in eternal life, you possess the totality of the forms in the ground of your mind—not virtually but actually. It remains to be seen how this syncretism of a Neoplatonic realism of universals and an Aristotelian theory of the mind's potentialities can be justified by an ontology.

The henological vocabulary did not permit Eckhart to get to the very bottom of his doctrine of the spark. For a medieval author, "intellect" is the term that best evokes man's affinity with the totality of beings;

that is why Aristotle's treatise *On the Soul* is so dear to the mystics. The receptive νοῦς is the key term that allows Eckhart to build a doctrine from the experience of the proximity between man and all that surrounds and faces him. But this word does not abolish the otherness of being; hence Eckhart's recourse to the νοῦς as hypostasis or to the subsisting Wisdom whose perfection the wise appropriate. The hesitation in our sermon between the identity of act (Aristotelian noetics) and the identity of perfection (Platonic participation) will be resolved only in birth, where there will no longer be an encounter with surrounding things, and thus otherness will be abolished. The terminology of the spark is not Eckhart's last word.

[4] Interior Knowledge and the Mind's Being

How then are we "Sons of God"? By having one and the same being with him. In order to know that we are Sons of God, we have to be able to distinguish between outer and inner knowledge. The inner knowledge is of an intellectual kind and is grounded in the being of our mind. Yet, it does not coincide with the being of the mind. It only takes root there, and it is something of the life of the mind. When we say that this knowledge is something of the life of the mind, we are referring to its intelligible life. It is in this life that man is begotten as the Son of God and that he is born to eternal life. Also this knowledge is without time and without space, without any here and any now. In this life all things are one, they are all together all in all, and all united to all.

The opposition between interior knowledge and exterior knowledge, in this fourth paragraph, does not exactly cover the opposition between the intellect and the other faculties. This new distinction prepares the way for Eckhart's doctrine of the being of the mind.

Beforehand he repeats the conclusions already obtained: first, as we possess the identical being of the Son (identity of act and identity of perfection), we are the Son of God; second, the locus of identification is the "spark" within that higher faculty of the mind, the intellect, by which we also know this identity. At the peak of the *gemüete* the intellect looks within; thus it is opposed to reason, which is turned towards the outside. The third point yet to be developed argues that the intellect is "rooted" in the mind's being, from which it is, however, distinct. The orientation of the research remains the same: the quest for identity retains the positive aspect of the "spark," that is, its correlation with totality—"in this life, all things are one, they are all together all in all, and all united to all"; but it will have to go beyond the division which separates the knower from the known. "The mind's being" is now the title that must satisfy these conditions.

Meister Eckhart proceeds in five steps, easily summarized: a) the intellect is grounded in the mind's being; b) the mind's being and the intellect are really distinct from one another; c) the mind's being is also called the life of the mind: "the inner knowledge ... is not the mind's being, it only takes root there, and it is something of the life of the mind"; d) the life of the mind is intelligible; e) we are born Son of God in this life. This demonstration accomplished, Eckhart returns to the interior intellectual faculty by which we know this childbearing. He repeats its two characteristics, which are habitual with him: the freedom from time and space and the simultaneous possession of the divine ideas.

The triad "being–life–intelligence" is not new. A text of Proclus, in whom it holds a special place, will show, however, to what extent Eckhart's use of this triad differs from the ancient representation of hypostases:

> All things which participate intelligence are preceded by the unparticipated Intelligence, those which participate life by Life, and those which participate being by Being; and of these three unparticipated principles Being is prior to Life and Life to Intelligence.[17]

The proposition in Proclus that immediately precedes this quotation relates the three "series" of being, life, and intelligence to a first principle in each order which is their nonparticipated cause, dependent only on the One. The proposition that follows enumerates the participated qualities, constitutive of the effects: $\pi\acute{\epsilon}\rho\alpha\varsigma$ and $\ddot{\alpha}\pi\epsilon\iota\rho\sigma\nu$, the limit and the infinite for the effects of the $\ddot{\sigma}\nu$, movement for those of $\zeta\omega\acute{\eta}$, and knowledge for those of the $\nu\sigma\hat{\upsilon}\varsigma$.

Proclus draws a comprehensive schema of the cosmic reality: first cause, series of participated qualities, autonomy of the three degrees of being, and dependence of their effects delineate the classic world view of those philosophers that Eckhart's generation called simply "the Platonists." Proclus's *Stoicheiosis* is a systematic cosmology. Even in Plotinus, though more spiritual and more complex than Proclus, the starting point and philosophic scaffolding is a cosmology. This aspect

recedes in Meister Eckhart. He converts the three rays of the subsistent
One into a theory of the inner man drawn towards union. He tries to
think of the identity of being between man and God without an intermediary hierarchy. It is true that step "a" of his explanation reads like
a synopsis of the doctrine of the hypostases: the νοῦς, intellect, is
based on the ὄν of the spiritual soul, that is the mind. But even this
synopsis of the world strata is not quite in agreement with that tradition; at the very least, the exposition of the relation between the soul's
being and its life is confused.[18] In any case, the point of the argument
consists in something quite different from this triad.

The point of the argument must be seen in the dialectic between
operation and rest. The faculties of the mind, superior or inferior, operate, but in its being the mind does not operate. The "species," sensible
representations that function as the intermediaries between man and
the world, are formed in the faculties directed towards the outside, and
by these faculties man belongs to the world. The faculties turned inside,
of reflexive nature, render the mind intelligible to itself. Through their
operation man belongs to himself, to his nature. But in the mind's being,
man belongs to God. Here God alone operates: the mind in its ground
does not operate. "Being," "image of God," "ground" (grunt), "abyss"
(abegrunt, ungrunt), or "essence of the mind": all these words designate
the same region of man, eternally at rest, where the mind is closer to
God than to the faculties, closer to God than to itself or to the world.
"The intimacy or the proximity of God and the mind truly entails no
distinction."[19] This, then, is the explanation of the second point ("b").
The mind's being and the intellect, its higher faculty, are opposed like
two universes.[20] The dichotomy between being and acting prepares the
overcoming of the noetics of the gemüete: since "the spark of the intellectual power," or the "higher part of the spirit," is still man's own activity,
what pertains to the mind and is "of" the mind is either the correlate
of the world or the place where the self possesses the self, but not the
locus of deification "in" the mind. Eckhart turns towards the mind's
restful being to identify God's presence in man.[21] The opposition between the active region in man that unites him to what is worldly and
the passive region that unites him to the divine is of Augustinian origin.
Eckhart readily quotes in this matter Augustine's phrase, according to
which God is more intimate to the mind than the mind is to itself.[22]

The mind's being and its operating faculties, empirical and intuitive,
can thus be read as the marks in us of a threefold appropriation. The

mind's being is the trace in man of his possession by God; the interior knowledge or the spark is the trace of the possession by the self; the exterior knowledge or abstractive reason is the trace of the possession by the world. The qualitative leap occurs between the first element and the other two. However, neither in its ground nor in its faculties is the concept of mind equivocal. The mind alienates itself neither in God nor in the world. It would be a misunderstanding to speak of a nonidentity of the mind subject to such a scission between being and acting. The mind is not double; under neither of these modes is it other than itself. The relationship between the active zone and the passive zone in the mind is a relationship of foundation, as proposition "a" indicates. Hence it is an analogical relationship. "The inner knowledge is of an intellectual kind, and it is *grounded* in the mind's being." The mind's being is "the medium and like the center of all faculties."[23]

Thus the antinomy between the "ground," *grunt*, and the faculties of the mind allows for a discourse on the mind's being, which can be grasped indirectly through the negation of change, activity, motion. Yet in a move thoroughly characteristic of his thinking, Eckhart hurries to negate this immutability in turn. The mind, he says, has no ground, it is *gruntlos*. In its being, the mind is entirely passive. But God engenders the Son in it, and he engenders the mind as this same Son. This double and identical birth is the supreme activity of the mind in its being. We have described it through the example of musical listening: just as a hearer is "all ears" before the melodies and the rhythms that reach his ear and touch his sensibility, so the mind in its being is "all reception" —attentive, active, and passive in the extreme—to the Son of God. Due to this dialectic the mind appears first as the immutable condition of possibility in which the activities of the *gemüete* are rooted and immediately afterwards as "life." The brief passage on the life of the mind, another name for its "being," comes to contradict the univocity of repose. Thesis "c" prepares then directly for thesis "e." The life of the mind is to receive and to inseparably bring forth the Son. The opposition between passivity and activity also appears to be provisional. The thought of birth pushes the two terms to their extremes; it abolishes and superelevates them.

The argument of this entire paragraph is complex, but it can be summarized as follows. It is commanded by the underlying dialectic between "operating" and "not operating." At the outset, the dialectic opposes the intellective faculties to the mind's being. At the end, this relationship is again destroyed, but it is also preserved as it is now transposed to the ground of the mind itself, in which the Son is engendered, identically, by man and God. Such is Eckhart's reinterpretation of the Neoplatonic hypostasis of "life." That this life should be qualified as intelligible is only one more example of the intellectualism of Meister Eckhart in this sermon. Point "d," then, has to be read in conformity with the principles developed on this matter in the preceding paragraph.

It can also be said that at the end of this fourth paragraph the relationship between passivity and activity is reversed. Eckhart had spoken of "certain things in our minds which hide this equality from us and veil this knowledge." Certain things—that is to say, all things insofar as they enter the mind from outside. The relation is reversed in that the Son is begotten in the mind's being, while the faculties turned outward remain silenced. This inversion of terms indicates the ascetic aspect of detachment.

[5, 6] Identity and Analogy of Grace

This may be compared to the body, all the parts of which are united in such a way that the eye belongs also to the foot, and the foot to the eye. If the foot could speak, it would say that the eye, though it is located in the head, is as much its own as if it were located in the foot, and the eye in turn would say the same thing. In the same way I consider that all the grace which is in Mary belongs equally and even more properly to the angel; it is just as much his, although it is in Mary, as if it were in him or in the saints. Indeed, all that is in Mary belongs also to the saint and is even more his own. He relishes the grace that is in Mary more than if it were in him.

The dialectic between the faculties of the mind and its "ground" allows us to dismiss as inappropriate some categories that present themselves spontaneously when we deal with the birth of the Word in the mind: the oppositions between the being of filiation and the mind's being, between passivity and activity, between receiving and producing. This dialectic eliminates from our discourse what the mind's being is not, but it is unable to say what it is. It is unable to think for itself the unity of being with the Son. Still another shift in vocabulary is therefore required, and for a brief passage Meister Eckhart adopts Saint Paul's category of the Body of Christ. After the Aristotelian, Platonic, and

Augustinian elements, this is the last of the ingredients from which he will develop his own understanding of being (paragraphs [7] and [8]).

"When someone steps on another's foot, it is the tongue that says: 'you stepped on me.' "[24] Meister Eckhart explicates this analogy of the members of the human body first as a theologian, then as a philosopher. Each of the different organs in man—eye, foot, tongue—performs a specialized function, but it is the whole body that profits or suffers from their activities. The foot does not advance for itself, but man walks thanks to his feet; the eye does not see for itself, but the entire man sees thanks to his eyes. This parable is ancient. We know that in 494 B.C. the consul Menenius Agrippa used it successfully to reconcile the Roman slaves entrenched on the Aventine Hill with the Senate. Ever since, it has served to justify bondage under corporatisms and established hierarchies. Saint Paul had exploited the Greek fable of "the members and the stomach,"[25] and Eckhart is visibly obligated to him when he illustrates the unity of the "mystical body," that is, according to medieval imagery, the saints and angels grouped around Christ and Mary. In our text the Virgin holds the role of the "prime analogate" of grace.

"The grace which is in Mary belongs equally and even more properly to the angel . . . [as much as] if it were in him or in the saints." Mary possesses the fullness of grace. But this grace best profits all the members of the body of Christ. If it were only in themselves, it would only be this angel's grace or that saint's grace. It would be imperfect. For Eckhart, imperfection always means submission to time and to space. As it participates in the perfect grace, "which is in Mary," the Body of those graced is freed from temporality. This doctrine answers not only the problem of communication of merits and of grace, but above all the problem of escaping from time: participation in Marial grace becomes the condition of victory over time. Or again, if we agree to see in the allusion to Mary a conventional manner of expressing perfection: full participation establishes man beyond time, in the eternal now.

If the mystical body is placed outside of time and thus encompasses physical and spiritual beings alike, the result for Meister Eckhart is that immediately in the present man is united to the Son by the intemporal zone within him. After having attempted to understand this region of identity with the divine as "spark," then as "the mind's being," he now proposes a new name to designate the inner man: incorporation into the Body. This new approach permits a more refined thematization of the analogical unity between the mind and God.

"As the Father has sent me, so I send you"; I send you, I say, into the one
and the same, all and each of you; indeed, all are sent or no one is sent,
into all or into nothing. From this it necessarily follows that you enter into
the labor which was theirs, for it is I who send you and who have already
sent you. Here is why: he who receives his identity from the One will
necessarily be one, totally and in all that affects him.[26]

The text of John that Eckhart comments upon describes the historical
mission of the disciples. After the example of the Father, Jesus sends
them through towns and villages. They inaugurate the Body. In the
interpretation of Eckhart, this narrative of mission comes to designate
the "emissions" of the One. The primordial effect of grace, the first
effect granted by the One, is to gather into unity. "Totally and in all that
affects him": this expression is meant to suggest nothing less than the
identity between the mind's being and the One, God. The theologian
will object that Meister Eckhart overemphasizes primary grace, which
is granted to all creatures by the fact of their *esse,* at the expense of
secondary grace, or properly Christ's grace. The primary grace, which
is due to creation, has the effect of "gratuitously" producing all beings;
it acts not upon the faculties, but in "the substance of the mind."[27] It
is this grace that the man described by Eckhart appropriates perfectly:
it "belongs all the more and more properly to the angel . . . than if it were
in him or in the saints." The content and at the same time the manifestation of this grace is the unity of humankind. All "saints," all men
deified, as such *are* the unique emission of the One. And the emission
of the One deifies in their ground all men: "all are destined (into oneness) or no one is, into all or into nothing." The granting of oneness
affects all beings: from the sending of the disciples through Galilee,
Eckhart glides to the grace of the "pleroma," then to the gift of *esse.* All
men possess in their deified zone the oneness that stems from the One,
just as all angels possess the grace that stems from Mary. Belonging to
one another as members of the same body, the human species, they
constitute the analogical Body of grace. In the weak sense this can be
said of secondary grace, Christian holiness. But in the strong sense,
which alone interests Meister Eckhart, this is said of primary grace:
oneness is then the analogical unity of *esse.*

The parable of the organs of the human body leads, by the detour
through the theory of the mystical Body, to the doctrine of the analogy
of being. In the terms of our sermon, this doctrine has to be enunciated

provisionally as follows: uncreated being belongs more, and more properly, to the mind, although it is in God, than if it were in the mind directly. But does this perfect appropriation of God's being by man destroy all distinction between participating and participated? In our Commentary we shall return to this question when we explicate the analogy of being according to Meister Eckhart.

But this interpretation is still too crude and too physical as it is taken from a sensuous comparison. I will now present to you another meaning, still more transparent and spiritual. I say: In the kingdom of the heavens all is in all, all is one and all is ours. The bliss that Our Lady possesses is all mine—when I am there—and in no way as flowing and emanating from Mary, but dwelling in me as my proper good, not as derived from elsewhere. And thus I say: what someone possesses in the beyond, another possesses equally—not as acquired from him or taken from him, but as dwelling in himself, so that the grace which is in the one is fully also in the other, exactly as one's own grace.

"The bliss that Our Lady possesses is all mine . . . and in no way as flowing and emanating from Mary, but dwelling in me as my proper good, not as derived from elsewhere." Eckhart emphasizes again what we have called the perfect appropriation of a participated quality. This theory is in flagrant contradiction to the old doctrine of participation by deficient similarity; according to the latter, the quality of a first, autonomous being, participated by a second, dependent being comes to it precisely "as flowing and emanating" from its source, that is, derived from elsewhere and from another. If one still wants to speak of analogy and participation in Meister Eckhart, it should be clear that this will have to be in a quite particular way and sense.

Eckhart's doctrine of participation through perfect appropriation is now illustrated by the aid of pneumatology, which will lead at last to the thought of the appropriation of being.

[7, 8] Identity and Analogy of Being

In the same way the spirit is in the Spirit. This is why I say: I cannot be the Son of God unless I possess that same being that belongs to the Son of God. It is the possession of this identical being that likens us to him and makes us see him in his divinity. But what we shall be hereafter is not yet manifested. Therefore I say that in the sense of which I have spoken there will be no similarity and no difference, but rather, without any difference, we shall be the identical being and the identical substance and nature that he is himself. But "this is not yet revealed." It will be manifest only when "we shall see him as he is, God."

"In the same way the spirit is in the Spirit." This sentence is the only allusion to the Pneuma in the sermon. At this point of the development it has a precise meaning. Let us replace it in its context: grace engenders the graced ones who, as such, are identical with the bestower of grace; Wisdom engenders the wise man who, as such, is identical with Wisdom itself; God's unity engenders the mind's unity, and as such, as the Son begotten, the mind is identical with the One. This "as such," *inquantum,* which in Meister Eckhart designates the bond between the engendering and the engendered, is the presence of the Spirit in this type of participation.[28] The reciprocal bond in the perfect appropriation of participated grace is expressed in the reduplication, the sign of immediacy and of formal identity between participating and participated. This third term, *inquantum,* refers to the Spirit. Within the Trinity, the Spirit is the reduplication, the bond of perfect reciprocity and appropriation, between the Father and the Son. Thus, in the example of grace, the graced person receives all his being from primary grace: he is its Son, and the primary grace begets him by its missions. In the relationship between grace and the graced, or wisdom and the wise, three elements will necessarily be found: the never-begotten grace and wisdom (Father), man as graced and wise (Son), and the bond between generator and generated, the formal viewpoint of the generation (Spirit).

Located as it is between the exposition of the graced one's identity with grace (paragraphs [5] and [6]) and the identity of the mind's being and God's being (paragraph [7]), this brief allusion to the Spirit affirms the perfect appropriation of the uncreated principle of reflective conversion, the Spirit, by the created principle of reflective conversion, the spirit. Man's complete return upon himself, *reditio completa,* "is" the Holy Spirit, just as the graced one "is" grace and the wise man "is" Wisdom. In Eckhart's philosophy of the mind predicative reduplication not only fulfills all requirements of the perfect return upon oneself, but it also suggests that identity with God is an activity, reflection.

"Without any difference, we shall be the identical being and the identical substance and nature that he is himself." In the light of our remarks on grace and the Spirit, this affirmation is now less astonishing. It means, indeed, the identity of man's being with God's being, the perfect appropriation of the latter by the former. But it no longer describes identity in terms of knowledge or in terms of participation by deficient similarity and formal limitation. As these two approaches converge, they are also overcome: God unites himself to the mind in its "ground," in its "being" which is eternally at rest, in the region of primary grace and of the Spirit. At the same time, this oneness is not the static coincidence of two Aristotelian substances (an explanation of Eckhart's understanding of "substance" will follow) but an active identification; nor is it univocal, but analogical: the uncreated being which is the Godhead belongs all the more and more properly to the mind than if it were its own. The Godhead is the mind's being. Identity and perfect appropriation do not eliminate the distinction between the humanity of man and the Godhead of God. If Eckhart here speaks in the future, this is a simple concession to the biblical text on which he comments: "Beloved, we are Sons of God and we shall be like him."

Being, substance, nature: these words are deeply ambiguous. They seem to be applied here to Christ, but we also read: this "will be manifest only when we shall see him as he is, God." Do they refer to the Son or to the Godhead? Does perfect appropriation of God's being terminate in one Person of the Trinity, or in the *gotheit*? The question should seize our attention; it is a capital piece which must be added to the folder of disputes about Meister Eckhart's Christianism. If identity terminates purely and simply in the ineffable Godhead, doubts about the genuinely Christian inspiration of Eckhart's thinking are permissible. The text of our sermon leads to two contradictory answers.

The concepts used, clarified by one another, refer indeed to the Godhead. First, a remark about *wesene*, being. We have said that in Meister Eckhart's vocabulary of being this notion is the least determined. Its semantic field is even larger than that of *esse*, since it often means "essence." In order to avoid too systematic and traditional schemes of thought, we have at times translated this word by "essential coming forth." Even when applied to Christ's being, it still designates the Godhead. When Eckhart speaks of Christ, he almost always stresses his divinity at the expense of his humanity. Even in scriptural texts clearly describing the humanity of Jesus, he still finds ways of reading his divine nature. When circumstances force him to speak of his human nature, he is largely satisfied with traditional formulations borrowed from some "master." What "comes forth" essentially in Christ is the divine being, the Godhead. It is true, though, that this indication is insufficient if it remains isolated; for classical theology, the divine Persons do not have a being of their own, their being is that of God's essence. "Substance" and "nature" direct us more clearly to the Godhead.

Substance is "that which possesses itself totally in all of itself," says Eckhart; it is "an excellent purity," "neither combined nor mixed with anything," "both because it is related only to itself and not to another, and because it realizes being out of itself and by itself."[29] Such language, particularly the parallelism with *esse*, remains firmly within Aristotelian tradition: "substance" and *wesene* are translations of two aspects of οὐσία, that is, a substance is autonomous, and it possesses being by priority.

Is the Godhead to be thought of as a substance? Not insofar as "substance" designates a category, answers Meister Eckhart. Yet Eckhart also designates God as the "pure and simple substance."[30] Such language does not mean that God falls under the genus of substances, but that he is "something higher, and consequently purer."[31] This supereminence of the divine substance is explained by the absence of relation. If the categorial determination of οὐσία is twice relational— with regard to accidents and with regard to other substances—*Deus substantia* excludes relations as such, even trinitary relation.[32] It is this absence of relation, this exaltation of the *Deus substantia* over the *Deus pater*, which clearly refers to the Godhead.

God as Trinity and as Creator is the term of relations. But as self-sufficient "substance," he is literally detached; without any exteriority or otherness he gathers all things within himself, and he is free from relations to analogized terms. Deprived of proportion and link, he is pure simplicity, desert, *gotheit*. This absorption of all categories in the substance of the Godhead is reminiscent of Maimonides.[33]

Finally, the word "nature," too, is a name for the Godhead. This is even the concept by which the Godhead is defined. We already know the expressions "God must," "whether he wills it or not," "his nature forces him," "God's nature is to give"—these idiomatic expressions of Eckhart point beyond trinitary or creational relationships. Being, substance, nature point beyond God to the impenetrable silence of the Godhead. "We shall be the identical being and the identical substance and the nature that he himself is": Meister Eckhart speaks of the union of the mind's ground with God's ground, a doctrine already familiar to us from the sermons "Jesus Entered" and "Woman, the Hour Is Coming." But in contrast to these previous texts, is not this entire sermon, "See What Love," devoted to man's oneness with the Son, rather than to the Godhead? If Eckhart slides easily from "the Son's being" to "God's nature," is it not because "the identical being," *daz selbe wesene,* designates at one time the union with the unspeakable ground of God, where he is neither Father, nor Son, nor Spirit, and at another time the union with the Son? "The identical being of the Son of God" clearly indicates the perfection of sonship: I have to be Son, the Father must beget me as his Son. But then, how are we to reconcile the identification with the Son, as Son, and the identification with the divine ground? Are not the two theses irreconcilable, since one refers to a theistic, trinitary, christological thought, while the other intends to overcome theism by showing the way of return to the abyss of the Godhead? One leads to Jesus of Nazareth, and his mystery of divine sonship, the other leads into the desert, to the great death of God, of man, of the world. "Being identical with the Godhead" and "being identical with the Son" are two contradictory expressions which we shall have to hold together. We shall have to see if they reflect a pure and simple equivocation of the word "being."

This apparent equivocation points to the very heart of Eckhart's thought. His doctrine of being seems to lead to an aporia: either it is expressed by the call to "break through beyond everything that has a name" (but then being cannot be represented as the union of the mind's being and the Son's being), or it is expressed in the call to "let the Son of God be born in you" (but then being can hardly be the unrepresentable One beyond God). Perhaps we must indeed conclude that two heterogeneous forms of thought, eclectically joined together, coexist in Eckhart's preaching,[34] for we do not see how a henological concept of being—"the very being of the Godhead"—can be reconciled with a Paulinian concept of being—"the very being of the Son." Identity in the first case means total loss, forgetfulness: I am neither God nor creature, but I beget God and the creatures. In the second case, it means, on the contrary, the supreme gain with which man can be endowed: I am the Son of God, I am begotten as the second Person of the Trinity. Is this aporia really impossible to overcome? We shall certainly never be able to solve it by examining exclusively the role played by God: there is no common genus that would encompass the Son and the Godhead. We must then look at it from the side of man. "We shall be the identical being and identical substance and nature that he is himself": to whom precisely does the "we" refer? Does it mean man as a fully constituted being, or only the spiritual part of man? If we can answer, we shall not yet have settled the debate, but we shall have localized the dilemma. The way will then be open to a more detailed presentation of Eckhart's doctrine of the being of God (paragraph [8]).

The question of double identification with God led to harsh confrontations at the trials of Cologne and Avignon. Eckhart's written answer to the objections, his Defense, although it rounds off for the occasion some of the rough edges and angular formulations, is uncompromising as to the aporia mentioned above: Eckhart maintains at the same time the identity by the birth of the Son—"God begets me as his Son (Christ), without any distinction"—and the identity by breaking through everything conceivable—"the mind is one with God." On the other hand, he declares: "To say that deified man is nothing other than God is false and an error."

The consequence is this: when Eckhart says "I am the very Son of God" or "we shall be the identical being . . . ," the "I" and the "we" should be understood as referring to the ground of the mind and not to the mind in its totality or to man in his totality. It is possible to maintain that the mind's being is identical with the being of the Son and that it is identical with the Godhead; this does not allow us, however, to maintain that the mind is the Son or that the mind is the Godhead or that man is the Son or that man is the Godhead. The mind's being is distinct from man just as the Godhead is distinct from God. Concerning the entire human being, body and soul, Eckhart uses a more cautious language, saying that man is "conformed to God," "in some way deified." Yet, between those texts in which "I" and "we" suggest the mind's being and those in which Eckhart speaks clearly of the fully constituted human, the limit is less than clear and stable. One encounters such contradictory statements as: "My essential being is above God" and "It is false to say that I am of divine nature." To understand them, the reader should probably conjecture that, in the first case, Eckhart is thinking of the mind's being and, in the second, of man's being.

The distinction between the mind's being and man's being is less astonishing than it may seem. In traditional Aristotelian doctrine, "the form gives being," *forma dat esse*, and the spiritual soul, Eckhart's *"sêle,"* is the form of the body. Medieval Aristotelians, for whom the immortality of the soul causes no doubt, distinguish this form, mind or spiritual soul, from the "hylemorphic" being, that is, from man in his body. The soul is a form which has being by itself, *forma habens esse per se*; it can therefore subsist independent of the human composite. This distinction, however, never leads the Scholastics either to interiorize the being of God to the point of making it identical with the being of the soul or to spiritualize the soul to the extent of absorbing it in the mind. Eckhart cannot call on their authority when he neglects the soul's bodily function of animation and when, by means of such an intellectualism, he identifies its being with God's being, which is also intellectual. It is not the separate *esse* of the soul that is questionable to a Scholastic (although Aquinas would say that the soul is potentially separate from the body and its animation), but the identity between the soul's participated *esse* and God as *Ipsum esse*.

The distinction between the mind's—or the spiritual soul's—being and man's being does not solve the ambiguity of the union, but it localizes it. The ambiguity of the being of union, in Eckhart, can be stated in two theses: "The mind's being is identical with the divine being, the Godhead," and "the mind's being is identical with the being of the Son." This ambiguity, not yet removed, will allow for a better understanding of the explanations and implications of the paragraph that follows.

> God makes us know himself, and he makes us know himself by his act of knowing, and his being is his knowledge. For him to make me know and for me to know are one and the same thing. Hence his knowledge is mine, quite as it is one and the same in the master who teaches and in the disciple who is taught. Since his knowledge is mine, and since his substance is his knowledge, his nature, and his being, it follows that his being, his substance, and his nature are mine. Thus since his substance, his being, and his nature are mine, I am the Son of God. "See, brothers, what love God has given us: We are called the Son of God and we are."

In an impressive foreshortening this paragraph delivers three keys to the sermon: first, "God makes us know himself, and his being is his knowledge"; second, "since his knowledge is mine, and since his substance is his knowledge, his nature, and his being, it follows that his being, his substance, and his nature are mine"; third, "thus as his substance, his being, and his nature are mine, I am the Son of God."

The first of these propositions, correctly understood, explains all the rest. It repeats, besides, the beginning of the sermon, in part: "It should be understood that to know God and to be known by God, to see God and to be seen by God, are one according to the reality of things. In knowing and seeing God, we know and see that he makes us see and know" (paragraph [1]). Later in the sermon the theory of energetic unity that these lines circumscribe is rejected because it is too directly tied to a relational and abstractive theory of knowledge. However, transformed into a theory of being, it now seems acceptable: "his being is his knowledge." When transposed to the level of a doctrine of being, the vocabulary of the Aristotelian analysis of knowledge promises a rich harvest of affirmations of identity.

The teacher and the pupil are one in the act of learning. The master teaches and the disciple is taught; one speaks, the other listens; one possesses knowledge and the other acquires it. The student is on the way to appropriating knowledge. The teacher begets the science in him, and while one is active and the other "pathetic," the son, wisdom, is born. What is it that properly occurs in such a teaching conceived not only as midwifery, but as begetting? What "is there" properly speaking? Is there a professor on one side, a student on the other? Certainly, but with this not everything is said. To explain that there are two beings, two substances, and that between them words come and go, is still to say absolutely nothing of the teaching itself as an event. To experience this, there is no other way than to sit down on a school bench. But then, in the diligence and the zeal of learning, the face-to-face encounter between teacher and student is abolished. Properly speaking, only the coming forth, the hatching of knowledge "is"; in other words, a process is, rather than a duality of substances. An event gathers together the teacher and the pupil which abolishes the one's superiority and the other's inferiority. To the question "What is there properly?" one will therefore no longer answer with relational determinations, that is, the substantial distinction and the predicamental reciprocity. There is only the event; otherness is no longer. The word is; in all truth the partners in dialogue are no longer. The word initiates the energetic identity of being.

The difficulty in reading Eckhart consists in thinking of this kind of identity in *fluxu et fieri* as an analogical identity of being. We are at the junction of the two paths that Eckhart has followed to reach this point of the sermon, namely Aristotelian identity of the knower and the known and Platonic participation of an inferior in a superior quality. In the event of learning the pupil is "identical" with the teacher and he "participates" by perfect appropriation in the quality of knowing. Eckhart actually betrays both philosophical currents as he joins them on the level of an experience of union expressed in a doctrine of being. The middle term that allows for this philosophical accomplishment is the traditional axiom, "God's being is his knowledge."[35]

This axiom is dear to Eckhart, as it removes the last trace of creation from the relation between man and God. "Being itself" cannot be the highest, or purest, name of God because it still implies the existence of beings that are not by themselves. God is his own, he is totally transparent to himself, only when we speak of him as intellect. God's self-knowledge is his self-possession. But, Eckhart argues, man possesses himself, too, in his intellectual act of return upon himself (the "reduplication" of paragraph [7]). In such an act alone is man properly himself. In Eckhart's version the axiom "God's being is his knowledge" implies a movement away from an ontology in which *esse* means existence to an ontology in which *esse* means primarily essence: God is essentially possessing himself, not creating, and man is essentially appropriating himself, not appropriating things. The mind's being, *wesene*, is thus identical with God's being; essentially both do the same thing, possess themselves through an intellectual act. And as this act of total return cannot be a finite singular act, if it is to be total, but infinite and universal, "it follows that his being, his substance, and his nature are mine." What exactly is the significance of such an argument?

It is fully comprehended only when it is seen in parallel with the third and final proposition: "Thus since his substance, his being, and his nature are mine, I am the Son of God." We see again the very striking juxtaposition of the two formulas of identity: the one apophatic—the mind's being is God's being or the Godhead; the other cataphatic—"I am the Son of God."

We have spoken of detachment. It appeared to us as a path with a goal as unconceivable as the origin of dehiscence. Of the two formulas of identity, only one concludes the reasoning: the apophatic formula. Even more, it not only concludes the preacher's argument, but also brings the itinerary of the detached man to its end; that is, it leads this itinerary to perfection and thereby abolishes it. Union with the Son is subordinated to union with the Godhead. The first union is the preparation and the motivation for the second. The Christian vocabulary and apprenticeship appear as a training, as an *exercitatio animi*, towards the breakthrough. In Augustinian terms: faith seeks, intelligence finds. The subordination also affects the meaning of the word "being." Of the two ontologies that seem to be implied, one is subservient to the other. "I am the Godhead," but the Godhead is nothingness. "I am the Son," but being the Son is a process, just as the begetting of knowledge in the pupil is a process. Eckhart's understanding of being seems to vacillate between being as nothingness and being as a process. It is, however, the latter that naturally leads to the former: in the breakthrough the process of being accomplishes itself as nothingness.

As long as Eckhart's reader attempts to grasp his thought in relations among entities, isolating different philosophical currents like musical motifs, the simple source from which everything springs remains hidden. Eckhart's thinking is such that probably any list of "theses" drawn from his works will provoke objections and rejection for diverse reasons. But why this effort, in Eckhart, to overcome all representational categories, particularly those of relation and gradual participation in being? From the time of the judges of the Inquisition[36] up to some well-known philosophers of today,[37] there has been misunderstanding on this subject. An analysis proceeding from the premises of ousiology will thetically place the entity "Godhead" above the entity "God," or the entity "mind's being" within the entity "soul"; or it will explain that the entity "Son" is born from the entity "ground," that the mind is deified and enters to the core of the Trinity; or finally that the mind's being, encumbered by "images," frees itself and reaches the Godhead. None of these formulations is utterly false, but they bypass the essential matter, that is, the type of identity in question. "One sole identical being": Eckhart, no more than any other speculative mystic, thinks of God and the mind as united by some kind of fusion of entities into a common substance; rather, *Got entwird*: in the disappearance of the God-Person and of the man-person, in detachment and the great forgetfulness of self, being accomplishes itself. Only this process "is." Breakthrough on the one hand, birth on the other, are reconciled in the itinerancy of the detached man. But the reverse formula, man on the one hand, God on the other, is ultimately not tenable. For an opposition of this kind there is no possible resolution.

I possess the being of the Son that constitutes him Son; I possess the being of sonship, the being that is the formation of sonship. When I am reborn Son of God, the mind is one with the Son. This begetting abolishes itself as it fulfills itself in the breakthrough, so that the mind is now nothingness. In either schema the understanding of being is the same. Being enacts itself as an event—only the modes, and therefore the names, of this event are different. What had appeared as an ambiguity in the doctrine of being is resolved into a general and all-encompassing concept of being as self-enacting or self-appropriation. By the formation of the Son the mind returns upon itself, and by the breakthrough it returns into the Godhead. The two steps are but one return, one event, one single appropriation. The birth of the Son and the breakthrough beyond God are neither opposed nor added one upon the other. But "breakthrough" says more than "birth," as it carries the understanding of being as a process to the destruction of all conceivable contents.

Man is disconsolate in his dispersion among images. The mind then returns to its ground. It "tastes" the Son and soon desires his entire nature. It penetrates into the indivisible being of the Godhead, then the *nuda essentia animae* joins the *nuda essentia dei*. God and the mind recognize each other in their perfect nakedness. The core of Eckhart's teaching and the key to his understanding of being lie in the deprivation and divestment that produce the energy for such self-realization. In the sonship, which still allows a part of *eigenschaft*, man is denuded only imperfectly: he remains attached to a Person of the Trinity. Only in the breakthrough is his nakedness perfect.

The temptation is great to confuse the overcoming of Sonship with the overcoming of Christianity altogether. Hegelians,[38] Marxists,[39] Buddhists[40] have taken this step. When it is measured by the criterion of the history of salvation, the thought of Eckhart will appear indeed as hardly Christian.[41] But it may well be that the logic of detachment somehow reflects the logic of the way of the cross. You will follow Jesus on the way of total abandonment; you will renounce yourself and you will renounce God; you will renounce the historical deeds by which God in the course of human action has modelled himself a countenance; and only then will you truly follow Jesus Christ even to the cross. It may well be that the God who vanishes as a motivation for existence also dies as a subject of science. The destruction of systematic knowledge of the highest being would then be the rigorous consequence of detachment; in other words, philosophy would definitely be deprived of its "onto-theological" foundation.

The dynamics of *abegescheidenheit*, which is the point of departure as well as the internal logic of Eckhart's understanding of being, will not fit exactly in the framework of a theory of analogy. In our Commentary on this sermon we shall have to articulate Eckhart's ontology in itself as it results from the indications that have been pointed out.

[9] New Birth and Voluntary Annihilation

Notice by what we are the Son of God: by having that same being that the Son has. How then are we the Son of God, or how does one know that one is the Son of God, since God resembles no one? For this is assuredly true. Indeed, Isaiah says: "To what have you compared him, or what image do you give him?" Since, then, it is of the nature of God not to be like anyone, we are compelled to conclude that we are nothing, so that we may be transported into the identical being that he is himself. When this is achieved, when I cease projecting myself into any image, when no image is represented any longer in me, and when I cast out of myself and eject whatever is in me, then I am ready to be transported into the naked being of God, the pure being of the Spirit. All likeness has to be expelled from it. Then I am translated into God, and I become one with him—one sole substance, one being, and one nature: the Son of God. And after this has been accomplished, nothing is hidden anymore in God which has not become manifest or mine. Then I become wise and powerful. I become all things, as he is, and I am one and the same being with him. Then Zion becomes truly a seer, a "true Israel," that is, "a God-seeing man." Indeed, nothing is hidden from him in the Godhead. Thus man is led into God. But in order that nothing remain hidden from me in God, that all be revealed to me, no likeness nor any image may endure. Indeed, no image will disclose the Godhead or God's being to us. If some image or similitude remained in you, you would never become one with God. Therefore in order for you to be one with God, no image must be represented in you, and you must not represent yourself in any. This means that nothing should stay concealed in you that does not become unconcealed and ejected. Pay attention now to where our inadequacy comes from. It comes from nothingness. Consequently, what pertains to nothingness in man must be eradicated, for as long as there is such inadequacy about you, you are not the Son of God. What man complains about and suffers comes always from his inadequacy. Therefore, in order that man become the Son of God, all this has to be exterminated and expelled. Complaints and sufferings will then be no more. Man is neither stone nor wood, for all this is inadequate and nothing. We shall never be like him so long as this nothingness is not expelled. Only then may we be all in all, as God is all in all.

The explanation of the identity of being that Eckhart extracted from John's text, "we are called Sons of God, and we *are*," ends here. The rest of the sermon is devoted to the moral implications of this theory, that is, the task of becoming nothing (paragraph [9]), and its corollary, suffering no longer (paragraph [10]). Voluntary annihilation and equanimity belong together as the condition and the consequence of detachment.

Meister Eckhart explains his threefold acceptation of "nothingness" as follows:

a) "Since . . . it is of the nature of God not to be like anyone, we are compelled to conclude that we are nothing." This is a fine definition of what we call Dissimilarity. God is unlike anyone: he alone is being; we are nothing: a creature's being resides in God. What is created, insofar as it is created, is nothing. We recognize here the theory of the "creature's nothingness."

b) "When I cease projecting myself into any image, when no image is represented any longer in me, and when I cast out of myself whatever is in me, then I am ready to be transported into the naked being of God." This second acceptation of "nothingness" is no longer an observation about reality, but an exhortation to activity, that is, to actively become the nothing that we are. Since everything created is nothing, Eckhart insists that we rid ourselves of such nothingness. "All that pertains to nothingness in man must be exterminated." Throw out, exclude, expel, exterminate are verbs that sufficiently indicate the violence in Eckhart's teaching. The sermon "Jesus Entered" contained similar recommendations.[42] "You are nothing": that is, insofar as we are created; "become nothing": that is, by voluntary annihilation through detachment. From a formal or structural point of view, the step from the statement of observation to the statement of exhortation is the same as the one above from "being" to "becoming." "You are of divine being," namely in the ground of the mind, is a statement of observation; whereas "Become the Son of God," namely by new birth, is a statement of exhortation. This step from a descriptive to an hortative discourse will have consequences for Eckhart's ontology. What we are, void and divine in our innermost being, we have yet to become. In detachment, what is given becomes ordered; identity by nature becomes the process of identification; nothingness becomes annihilation.

c) "Then I am ready to be transported (or translated: über gesetzt) into the naked being of God." In the nakedness of God, in the Godhead, man and the world return to their nothingness. But in this nothingness they recognize their origin, the unfathomable profusion of embryonic forms. In the nakedness of God, or the Godhead, all things are reinstated in their primitive fullness. There they "are" what they were before being created—they are what they were when they were not yet (sermon, "Jesus Entered"). In the nothingness of origin, I am what I was when I was not yet. I am "all in all, as God is all in all." The third acceptation of "nothing" is the nothingness that the Godhead is, or the nothingness of indistinct fullness from which flow, by Dehiscence, all oppositions and relations. The eyes that want to see this nothingness must be blind.[43]

No less than the concepts of being or detachment, the concept of nothingness can serve as a guiding thread for the exploration of the Eckhartian universe. At each of the four stages of his itinerary, a detached man recognizes himself to be nothing, though in different ways: a creature's nothingness in Dissimilarity; the nothingness of desolation in Similarity and Identity ("all likeness has to be expelled; then I am translated into God, and I become one with him"); the nothingness of the Godhead, or of the indistinct but life-giving fullness beyond God in Dehiscence.[44]

[10] New Birth and Equanimity

There are two births of man: one is into the world, and the other out of the world, that is, spiritually into God. Do you want to know if your child is born and if it is denuded, that is, if you have become the Son of God? As long as you have sorrow in your heart, for whatever reason, be it for sin, your child is not yet born. Does your heart ache? You are not yet mother. You are still on the way to give birth, you are near birth. Do not fall prey to doubt while you are afflicted for yourself or for your friend: if the child is not yet born, it is nonetheless close to being born. It is born perfectly when man no longer feels any torment in his heart. Then he has the being and the nature and the substance and the wisdom and the joy and all that God has. Then the very being of God's Son becomes ours, it comes into us, and we attain the identical being of God. Christ says: "He who wants to follow me, let him deny himself and take up his cross and come after me." This means: throw all anxiety out of your heart, so that in your heart there be nothing but constant joy. Then the child is born. When the child is so born in me, even if I had to see with my own eyes my father and all my friends killed, my heart would not be moved by it. If however my heart were moved by it, the child would not yet be born in me, but it would perhaps be close to birth. I say: God and the angels have so great a joy by every single action of a good man that no other joy could resemble it. This is why I say: When it happens that the child is born in you, you have so great a joy by all good deeds done in this world that your joy reaches to the greatest evenness; it never alters. Therefore he says: "No one can take your joy away from you." And when I am correctly translated into the divine being, God becomes mine as well as everything he has. This is why he says: "I am God, your Lord." I have rightful joy only when neither sufferings nor torments can ravish it from me. Then I am translated into the divine being where no suffering has a place. We see indeed that in God there is neither wrath nor grief, but only love and joy. Even if sometimes he seems to be wrathful against the sinner, this is not wrath but love, for it proceeds from a great divine love. Those whom he loves he punishes, for he is love itself, which is the Holy Spirit. Thus the wrath of God comes from love, for he is wrathful without bitterness. If you reach a state where you feel neither suffering nor vexation from whatever may happen, so that suffering is not suffering for you and that all things are sheer joy for you, then the child is truly born.

Meister Eckhart has explained his understanding of being, followed by that of nothingness. Both have the same structure: Eckhart's thought leaves the realm of representation of substances or fixed entities and enters the realm of process. Being and nothingness can only be understood as a transition, or as birth: we are identical with God, but still on the way to union; we are nothing, but still on the way to annihilation. After this fundamental shift from a representational ontology to an ontology of process has been laid out, not much remains to be said for Eckhart, except for the practical consequences that are always dear to him. He has to present the signal or indicator by which this double actualization and this unique event manifest themselves. As in the sermon "Woman, the Hour Is Coming," the indicator of detachment is equanimity.

"Do you want to know if your child is born and if it is denuded, that is, if you have become the Son of God? As long as you have sorrow in your heart . . . your child is not born." Equanimity is concomitant with the birth to identity. The negative and manifestative face of detachment is concomitant with its positive and germinal face. The event can be missed, or again it can be adumbrated; then the identification is "near" fulfillment: "Does you heart ache? You are not yet mother. You are still on the way to give birth, you are near birth."

When the child is entirely born, you will be entirely mother. You will possess the being of God; with God you will possess all things; and you will so thoroughly be transformed into joy that suffering no longer has a place in you. Eckhart's concept of equanimity has been explained earlier, and its difference from Stoic apathy has been shown.[45] When the child is born, your joy is such that no one will be able to deprive you of it; in a certain sense *gelîcheit,* equanimity or impassibility, turns into its contrary, supreme passibility. Man's sensibility is sharpened to the point of recognizing God in all things.

Here again Eckhart speaks as the syncretist who mixes philosophical theories with biblical promises. On the one hand, the detached man is called impassible because he is "translated into the divine being, where no suffering has a place"; on the other hand, because "God has so great a joy by every single action of a good man that no other joy could resemble it." The first motive for impassibility or equanimity is henological: in the Godhead the perfection of being erases all limitations, all "inadequacies." The second motive evokes the Pauline "pleroma" or the Johannine heavenly Jerusalem: in the communion of saints, there is no suffering because each one lives the divine life itself. "You have so great a joy by all good deeds done in this world that your joy reaches the greatest evenness...." This recalls the theology of the mystical Body as the sole subject of grace.

[11] Being the Son and Becoming the Son

Exert yourself so that the child be not only in the process of being born, but that it be already born, just as in God the Son is always born and in the process of being born. May God help us that this be our destiny. Amen.

The last sentence of the sermon quite admirably summarizes the doctrine of being, the different facets of which Eckhart has presented. "Exert yourself so that the child be not only in the process of being born, but that it be already born...." Being is understood not only as actuality, but as activity. The process that Eckhart speaks of is not accidental, it is not an action added upon man's being. Rather it is man's being itself. In the being of his mind man remains always familiar with his origin; but this being is his only when he commits himself to a becoming. Being and becoming are no longer opposed: the true being is becoming. The true being of science is to be imparted to the student; the true being of language is the process of conversation. Likewise the Son is born from all eternity in God, but his true being is to assimilate the mind to His being. And here is the last parallel: from all eternity there is "something" within man that establishes him in the bosom of the Godhead, but he will truly be what he is only when in perfect releasement he breaks through beyond God. This path of releasement is the condition that makes the union possible. Eckhart's ontology of identity with God is one of wandering, of peregrine identity.

COMMENTARY

THE UNDERSTANDING OF BEING IN MEISTER ECKHART

Identity and Analogy

Man's destiny, in Eckhart's teaching, is to possess "the identical being and the identical substance and nature" which God is himself. But how is this to be understood? Does Eckhart affirm a univocal consubstantiality between man and God,[46] or does this identity leave room for an analogical understanding of being?

Justice, in the just ones, does not encompass them as a univocal genus; it is not abstracted from the sum of subjects. Nor is justice an equivocal concept, designating a purely individual quality which would be different in each being and identical only nominally. As Meister Eckhart understands it, justice is not even a quality that can be abstracted from the irreducible multiplicity of subjects; nor can it be seen as left to their discretion in mere equivocity; rather, it precedes them. Justice does not perfect subjects, but it annihilates the notion of subjects subsisting in and by themselves.

> If the just were many by virtue of an always different justice, the just ones would be just equivocally; or again justice could be related to the just ones in a univocal way. Its relation to them is, however, analogical, exemplary, and a priori.[47]

This relation is said to be "analogical" because just subjects do not possess justice by themselves; it is said to be "exemplary" because justice produces a conformity of the just with the sole and single justice; and it is said to be "a priori" because justice remains identical in God and in the just. In the same way, according to Eckhart, that air becomes luminous when light illumines it, although light is not retained by the air as its own, so justice is never implanted in the just ones but remains entirely in God. Justice is appropriated *in fluxu et fieri*.

We find in Eckhart texts that apply this schema to all the traditional analogical perfections: light, justice, goodness, truth, unity, being. But

172

we also know that he goes further in the affirmation of identity than do the holders of classical analogy. We shall summarize in four theses the teachings of Aristotle on this matter as well as the enlargement that it undergoes in Aquinas. Then we shall confront the results with what we know of Meister Eckhart's thinking.

Analogy according to Aristotle

Aristotle explains the guiding principle of his theory of analogy in the beginning of the *Physics,* where he refutes the Eleatic doctrine of the unicity of being: "being is spoken of in several ways."[48] As a matter of observation, man speaks of being, ὄν, on multiple occasions. What can also be observed are the manifold instances to which the word applies. Aristotle examines human speech and points out the identity of the copula "is" throughout is multiple meanings. In the treatise *Categories* he submits a list of the ten main ways of using the term "being."[49] The first step thus consists in establishing the multiple ways of speaking about being.

The second step is also based on observation: the many ways to speak of being are not irreducible to one another. The ten acceptations of the word "being" are enumerated according to an order: the first among them, being as οὐσία, substance, remains the reference in relation to which the nine others are defined. This "denominative" reference to a primordial acceptation is stated in the *Metaphysics*: "Being is spoken of in several ways, but always with reference to a single term, a single nature, and not homonymously."[50] Aristotle did not give a name to this unity of order by reference to a first, but it is circumscribed by a para-phrase: πολλαχῶς λέγεται, ἀλλὰ πρὸς ἕν: "in several ways, but in reference to one." Logically then, each time the word ὄν is used, a relationship is established between being as substance and the nine other meanings of the copula.[51] This is Aristotle's second observation. In these texts, the term ἀναλογία is never mentioned with regard to the doctrine of being. Later, the Arabic Aristotelians translate the rela-tion to a first, πρός, by the word "attribute"; and two centuries after Meister Eckhart, Cajetan speaks of an analogy of attribution in order to designate the unity between the secondary and primary acceptations of the word "being," that is, the unity between accidents and substance. Aristotle has hardly explained either the conditions of πρός or those of the ground and foundation which the substance provides for disposi-tions, actions, and movements that affect it.

It would be a mistake to confuse the "first" with some real universal entity. For Aristotle οὐσία designates the individual substance, the subject of all determinations. Beyond this substance as subject there is no avenue for seeking a single cosmic foundation. Being as οὐσία is not numerically one. The notion of being is one and universal only insofar as it refers to an intelligible. "The universal is either nothing or it follows from existing singulars."[52] The question of the unicity of a primordial substance (such as the "sphere" in Parmenides), to which the word ὄν would be applied by priority, remains in suspension. The multiplicity of substances appears impossible to overcome; only their predicates are thought of in an analogous relationship. This is the third phase.

The fourth and last step was taken more than a thousand years after Aristotle. It consists in applying the predicamental analogy to the relationship between the created and the uncreated. To Aristotle, such a broadening of his doctrine would have been properly incomprehensible. In medieval Aristotelianism, beings are seen in a relation to God that closely resembles some aspects of the relation between substance and accidents. On the one hand, if creation entailed a complete break between the creator and the creature, the demands of philosophy as well as those of faith would be contradicted. Truth can be communicated from God to man only on the basis of a communication of being. If, on the other hand, God dissolved into the cosmos to form one single substance with it, the very principle of creation would dissolve at the same time.

In his Commentary on the *Sentences*[53] Thomas distinguishes between three types of analogy: the first is according to concept, but not according to being (*secundum intentionem tantum*). The case of "health" traditionally illustrates this first acceptation: health is in the organism, but it has no common being with urine or food, although these too can be called "healthy." The second kind of analogy is according to being, but not according to concept (*secundum esse et non secundum intentionem*). Thomas cites as an example the "body" whose concept is univocally applied to celestial, imperishable bodies and to animal bodies, which are perishable. In these cases "body" designates realities whose being does not fall under a same genus. Thirdly, an analogy can be both according to concept and to being (*secundum intentionem et secundum esse*). This latter type brings together under one name a determination of being that is present to all entities derived from the first, but which the inferior participants realize by mode of a diminished perfection. The concept possesses its full significance only in the first member of the analogy, that which all other members participate but which itself participates nothing. In this way, truth and goodness are found both in God and in the created; they are attributed analogically to what is fully true and good as well as to what is only partly true and good.

In his treatise *On Truth*[54] Thomas calls this kind of agreement between the two terms a "proportion." *Proportio* was the word by which Boethius had translated ἀναλογία. A proportion is a determined relationship between two concrete terms. It concerns primarily substance and accident. The difficulty with Boethius's expression stems from the incomparable, literally disproportionate, greatness of God, when compared to things created: there is no common "proportion" between the finite and the infinite. Thomas prefers, therefore, a scheme of analogy that unites not two, but four members. The relation is established between two different proportionate attributions of the same term—"between two related proportions," says the text. The physical eye "sees," but intelligence, too, "sees." Yet the vision that is proportionate to the physical eye is quite different from the vision that is proportionate to the intellect. Some names taken from the domain of the created can be attributed to God according to the same procedure. Formally, such an analogy of proportionality states that A is to B as C is to D.

Neither the solution of the Commentary on the *Sentences* nor that of *On Truth* seems, however, to allow for real continuity between the two terms of analogy. In his *Summa Theologiae* Thomas proposes a third way of approaching the problem.[55] Here the analogy is drawn between two or more secondary terms and a first one which precedes and includes them *(duorum respectu tertii)*. An ape's intelligence and a human's intelligence can be compared only under the heading of a third term, Intelligence itself. Since neither the ape nor man realizes intelligence perfectly, Thomas finally proposes an analogy in which one of the two terms is strictly first *(unius ad alterum)*. Only in such a type of analogy is there a real communication between the uncreated and the created, as the created is referred directly to its cause. It is this kind of analogy that introduces Aristotelianism into theodicy. Indeed, it applies to the relations between substance and accident, but also to those between God and the world. God infinitely and in fullness possesses the attributes which the creature appropriates in a finite mode through participation.

This rationality of creation goes back in a straight line to Aristotle's predicamental analogy. It allows us to trace the perfections observed in things back into the very being of God. The perfections are the same in the created as in the Creator; they differ only by their mode of realization.

Analogy according to Meister Eckhart

A mind of Thomistic formation, which considers the equilibrium between the identity of perfections and the diversity of appropriations an admirable and insuperable intellectual synthesis, will easily be tempted to see in Meister Eckhart's solution to the problem of universals something akin to Spinoza's opposition to dualism, if not "an anthropological monism both idealistic and Nazi" [sic].[56] But, in Eckhart, God and the world are in no way confused into some single and indistinct fabric. Access to Eckhart's theory of analogy is gained through his elaborations on the type of agreement that prevails between justice and the just. Since "justice is God," this kind of agreement (neither by abstraction nor simply by participation through formal limitation) will make a certain communion of being between man and God understandable. However, from this study it will also become apparent that the theory of analogy is ultimately insufficient to give an account of Meister Eckhart's understanding of being.

Eckhart explicates his theory of analogy in his commentary on the biblical verse, "Those who eat me will hunger still." The creature feeds on God as on its being, he says, and it always has hunger for him since its being never becomes its own, but comes to it from another.[57]

Any analogical perfection, not only justice but also being, will naturally be prior to all that is created. The being of things created springs from the first cause without any mediation. This cause alone is: *Esse est Deus,* being is God.[58] Even when limited in a particular being, these perfections remain general perfections; that is, they remain God. Beings exist by virtue of that being which is God; beings are just, good, true, by virtue of justice, goodness, truth, all of which are God. Thus, the concrete, individualized transcendental always expresses the abstract, universal transcendental. Not only is each transcendental, convertible with every other, God, but it is God himself even in the finite mode in which a particular being realizes it, in "this and that." The structure of the act of being of beings is not measured by, but identified with the one being that is God. Thomas was careful to maintain a more radical difference between God and things: he taught that they are alike and unlike God as being is communicated to them by decreasing intensity and increasing limitation. Eckhart destroys the concept of an analogy by deficient similarity and limitation: if being is God, then beings are what they are entirely in God and by God; outside of God they are nothingness. Much more, insofar as they are, they are God. Insofar as man is just, he is justice.

The construction of a proportionality inspired by the predicamental analogy between the substance and its accidents is thus rejected by Eckhart. Under this particular point of view his metaphysics is neither Aristotelian nor Thomist, but Neoplatonic. He considers things not "from below," starting with the sensible world, but "from above," starting with God. On the other hand, his destruction of all intermediaries between God and the world, the elimination of justice, goodness, truth, etc., as ideas or prototypes subsisting by themselves, estranges him also from Neoplatonic systems. Plotinus, Proclus, Dionysius, and Erigena have in common at least a certain realism of universals. To Eckhart, there is no intermediary that can resist the effectiveness of releasement. Gilson has gone so far as to call the perfections, in Eckhart's thinking, simply "imputed" to the created.[59] Eckhart himself speaks rather of "borrowing." Being and all perfections are allotted to the created things *ze borge,* on loan.[60]

"The identical being and the identical substance and nature" that God is himself: what else is there that we could be, since all being is God? The act that makes each thing exist is God's; outside of God no perfection subsists. For Aristotle, the accident is still a certain ὄν, an additional entity; for Thomas, too, the created is a being in its own right; *esse* designates first of all the finite sensible substance—so much so that the finite being enjoys a definite autonomy with regard to the divine *ipsum esse.* Both philosophers understand being as appropriated according to different degrees of perfection. This is not so for Eckhart. The radicalism of releasement allows for nothing but perfect appropriation: God appropriates man to Himself, perfectly, by imputing to him the being that He is himself. Man points to God in the same way as a crown of vine leaves at the entrance of a tavern points to the wine:[61] without participation and by an extrinsic relationship. Being, that is, God, is "in the mind," not "of the mind." The gap between the mind's being and the rest of man reduces our ontological autonomy (not our freedom of choice) to nothingness.

Everything created should be loved for the sake of God, not for its own sake. To love things for themselves is indeed to love nothingness and to become nothingness. The analogy between God and man appears "intentional" *(secundum intentionem tantum)*, as a signalization. Things created receive their being, which is God, *in fluxu et fieri,* [62] just as, according to Eckhart, the air receives the sunlight "in passing, passively, and in a process." [63] In one of the German sermons Eckhart says:

> God has indeed infused sufficiency and pleasure into creatures, but the root of all sufficiency and the essence of all pleasure God has kept within himself. . . . The sun, although it illumines the air and penetrates it by its light, does not take root there. Thus the brightness of the air ceases when the sun disappears. That is how God communicates himself to his creatures. [64]

As the light is preserved in the air by the unceasing influx of sun rays, so the being of beings is always an actual continuation of God's creative deed, which confers being upon them.

Together with Aristotle and Thomas, Eckhart affirms that the first term of the analogy possesses being by priority, *per prius,* the second *per posterius.* Eckhart follows his predecessors insofar as this difference of modes opens the realm to which analogy is applied. But "mode" *(modus* or *wise)* does not mean the same thing in Eckhart and in his predecessors. Aristotle and Thomas think of a secondary mode of being, that is, one of diminished intensity, whereas Eckhart has in mind subsequent attributions of the sole being which is God. [65] In his view attribution no longer falls within the realistic context of an analogy by proportionality. Attribution does not refer to a mode of being, but to a mode of presence of that single being which is God. The mind's being is really "the identical being and the identical substance and nature" that God is himself. Or again, the goodness of the good man is really goodness itself, which is God. [66] Eckhart practices a realism that is neither the Aristotelian and Thomist realism of the sublunar and the created nor the Platonic realism of subsisting universals, but the mystical realism of the uncreated and uncreatable. Still more, God is not chiefly considered by him in Christian terms, as the Creator, but as the infinite dimension that offers itself to man. According to the analogy of proportionality as well as according to all Platonic schemes of participation, a good man's goodness would have to be different from the divine goodness. Only the analogy of attribution allows us to think the identity of what is participated with what participates; it is the identity of a transcendental quality in itself and as it is imputed "on loan" to a finite creature.

Compared with the Aristotelian tradition, Eckhart's ontology is thus characterized by the fleetingness of borrowed being—evanescent like a ray of the sun in the air—as opposed to the permanence, the duration, and the autonomy of analogical beings according to Thomas. In such a vision of precarious being, the concept of transcendental analogy loses its meaning. One sole and same determination is found at all levels of the analogy: the perfection of the first.[67] Being is formally and numerically one. To be "this or that" adds nothing to being; the individuation of the just man adds nothing to justice.[68]

Does such a theocentrism—some say: such a monism of being—abolish all analogical relations between being, which is God, and created beings? Is there still place for analogy when the created order loses all autonomy, or is all this not rather a matter of "genial deception"?[69] The theory that negates any finite realization of the transcendental perfections implies an analogy of a dynamic dependence where the uncreated possesses everything and the created nothing, apart from its insatiable hunger for God.[70] Three elements, however, still make this an authentic doctrine of analogy: being *qua* being, as well as all transcendental perfections as such, are encountered formally only in one of the terms considered, and created beings receive being itself, God; beyond these perfections things created possess nothing, they are nothing in themselves, and they exist only by the "eating" of uncreated *esse*; finally, such a radical dependence is comprehensible only in the context of a continual "ebullition" of perfections out of their source. This last point gives, of course, arguments to those who see Meister Eckhart as a Neoplatonic thinker; but they would then have to explain how he can completely dispense with a formal hierarchy of essences, without which any Neoplatonic world view loses its most characteristic feature and its principle of cohesion. The analogy of attribution does not allow us to speak of such a hierarchy. Rather, analogical causality here entails an exterior and contradictory relation: exterior because being does not really take root in the created, contradictory because being can belong only to one of the terms. This point can be schematically illustrated by Erigena's classification of four realms of being. To the question "What is being?" a Neoplatonist would reply: "The nature that is not created, but which creates," as well as "The natures that are created and create," that is, the ideas or prototypes; an Aristotelian would reply (although not in this language): "The nature that is created, but does not create," that is, finite things. But Eckhart would say: "The nature that neither is created nor creates"—God's being, the Godhead, into which releasement returns.

The Scholastic theory of analogy is derived from Aristotelian ousiology and Neoplatonic cosmology; but Eckhart's understanding of being can be reduced to neither of these, and actually transcends both. The vocabulary of analogy is therefore in itself and necessarily incapable of making us grasp his ontology at its core. This radical insufficiency is what we must now devote our attention to. But beforehand Eckhart himself should again be allowed to speak. The sermon "Proclaim the Word" outlines the theory of analogy which we have just explained and indicates at the same time the ways to overcome it. Unfortunately the text, as it is transmitted, is defective; the notes taken by the audience simply enumerate the subdivisions outlined by the preacher. All that remains of the sermon is therefore its skeleton. Its argument is nevertheless clear: being is not mine; "if I take it from another, it is not mine; rather it has to belong to him from whom I take it."

SERMON,
"PROCLAIM THE WORD"

(PRAEDICA VERBUM, 2 Tim. 4:2)

Today and tomorrow a text is read which concerns my master Saint Dominic. It is taken from a letter of Saint Paul's. Here is what it says in our language: "Proclaim the word, pronounce it, produce it, and beget the word."

That there be things which flow out from a being and at the same time remain within it may sound surprising. Words are like that, amazing: they are uttered and yet they remain within us. Also, that all creatures flow outside their origin, and yet remain within it, is quite amazing. What God has given and what God has promised to give is indeed amazing, incomprehensible, and unbelievable. This is indeed as it should be, for if these things were comprehensible and believable something would be wrong. God is in all things. The more he is in things, the more he is outside of them; the more he is within, the more he is outside. I have already said many times that God creates this entire world fully and totally in this present now. All that God created six thousand years ago and more, when he made the world, he creates right now and all together. God is in all things. But insofar as God is divine and insofar as he is intelligible, he is nowhere more appropriately than in the mind, and also, if you wish, in the angels. He is in the innermost and the most sublime part of the mind. And when I say the innermost, I mean the most sublime; and when I say the most sublime, I mean the innermost part of the mind. I mean the innermost and the most sublime part of the mind together and as one. Here, in the innermost and the most sublime part of the mind, into which time has never penetrated and into which no image has ever cast its reflection, God creates

181

the entire universe. All that God created six thousand years ago, and all that God will create six thousand years from now, if the world exists that long, he creates in the innermost and the most sublime part of the mind. All that is past and all that is present, as well as all that is to come, God creates in the innermost part of the mind. Whatever God operates through all his saints, he operates in the innermost part of the mind. The Father begets his Son in the innermost part of the mind, and he begets you together with his only Son, and in no way as inferior. If I am to become the Son, I must become it in the very same being which is the Son's and in no other. I am a man, and I could not be one in an animal's being. It is the being proper to man that makes me be a man. And to be this particular man, I have to be this man in this particular being. Indeed, Saint John says, "You are children of God" (1 John 4:4).

"Proclaim the word, pronounce it, produce it, beget the word!" Pronounce it: an utterance that enters the mind from outside is always coarse; but that word is spoken within the mind. "Pronounce it": that is, become aware of what is in you. The prophet says: "God says one [word], but I understood two" (Ps. 62:12). That is true; God always pronounces one sole and single [word]. His speech is one. In this unique utterance he pronounces his Son and at the same time the Holy Spirit and all creatures; and yet there is only one sole speech in God. The prophet, however, says: "I heard two," that is, I understood God and the created. At its origin, where God pronounces the created, this speech is God himself; here below, however, it appears as things created. People fancy that God became man only formerly. That is not so. Indeed, God becomes man right here and now exactly as before. The reason why he has become man is that he may beget you as his first-born Son, and nothing less.

Yesterday I was sitting at some place, and I said this little phrase from the Our Father: "Your will be done!" But it would be better to say: "May the will be yours." That my will be his will, that I be he—this is what the Our Father means. This phrase has a twofold meaning. First: "In all things, sleep!" That is, know nothing of time, creatures, images. The masters say that if a man remained sound asleep for a hundred years, he would be ignorant of every creature, and he would be ignorant of time and images; only then could you begin to see what God effects in you. This is why the soul says in the Book of Love: "I sleep, and my heart is awake" (Cant. 5:2). Hence, if all creatures sleep in you, you can begin to perceive what God effects in you.

The phrase also means: "Apply yourself in all things!" This again has three meanings. It wants to say as much as: "Realize your advantage in all things!" Its first sense is: grasp God in all things, for God is in all things. Saint Augustine says: God has created all things; not that he has brought them into being and then gone his own way, but he has remained in them. If people own things and God, too, then they imagine that they possess more than if they possessed God without things. But that is not correct. To add the sum total of all things to God will not make more than God alone. And if someone, possessing the Son and at the same time the Father, imagined having more than if he had only the Son without having also the Father, that would not be correct. Indeed, the Father taken together with the Son is not more than the Son by himself, and so the Son together with the Father is not more than the Father by himself. Therefore grasp God in all things, and that will be the sign for your new birth, by which you will have been begotten his first-born Son, and not less.

The second sense of "Realize your advantage in all things" is this: "Love God over and above all things and your neighbor as yourself" (Matt. 22:37–39). This is one of God's commandments. But I say that this is not merely a commandment. Rather God has given it to you, and he has promised to give it. If you prefer to keep a hundred marks for yourself rather than let someone else have it, that is not correct. If you love one human being more than another, that is not correct. And if you love your father, your mother, and yourself more than another human being, that is not correct. If you love your own happiness more than another's, that is not correct. "God forbid! What are you saying there? I must not love my own happiness more than another's?" There are many learned people who do not understand this, and it seems far beyond their comprehension. But it is not difficult. On the contrary, it is very easy. I wish to show you that it is not difficult. Look, a member of the human body naturally fulfills a double purpose. The first purpose it fulfills is to serve the body's functioning as a whole. Only secondarily is it to serve each member individually as itself, and no less than itself; and in its operations it pays no more attention to itself than to some other member. How much more should that be so in the domain of grace! God should be a rule and a foundation for your love. The first intention of your love should be purely for God and only then for your neighbor as for yourself, and no less than for yourself. But if you love your own happiness more than another's, you love yourself, and wherever you love yourself God ceases to be your pure love, and that is not correct. So, if you love Saint Peter's and Saint Paul's happiness as much as your own, you possess the same happiness as they do. If you love the angel's happiness as much as your own, and if you love Our Lady's happiness equally as your own, then you enjoy the same happiness quite properly as she does; it is your own as it is her own. Therefore it is said in the book of Wisdom: "He has made him equal to his saints" (Ecclus. 45:2).

In its third sense the phrase "Realize your advantage in all things" means: love God in all things equally, that is, love God as willingly in poverty as in riches, and cherish him as much in sickness as in health, hold him as dear in temptation as without temptation, in suffering as much as without suffering. Even more: the greater the suffering is, the smaller the suffering is—like two buckets: the heavier one is, the lighter the other will be. The more man abandons, the easier it will be for him to give things up. A man who loves God would renounce this entire earth as easily as an egg. The more he gives, the easier it will be for him to give, as with the apostles: the heavier their suffering was, the more easily they bore it.

"Apply yourself in all things" means finally that you have to start working on yourself whenever you find you are grounded in things manifold rather than in the pure One. It means: apply yourself in all things in order to fulfill your service. It also means: raise your head! That again has a twofold meaning. The first is: rid yourself of all that is yours and give yourself over to God, then God belongs to you as he belongs to himself, and he is God for you as he is God for himself, and not less. What is mine, I owe to no one. But if I take it from another, it is not mine; rather it belongs then to him from whom I take it. The second meaning of "raise your head" is: direct all your works towards God.

There are many people who do not understand this. That is not surprising to me. Indeed, whoever wants to understand this has to be very detached and raised above all things. May God help us that we may attain this perfection. Amen.[71]

The limits of the analogical understanding of being

a.) Throughout our interpretation of Eckhart we have adopted a single hermeneutical criterion in order to discover his authentic thought beneath the currents of doctrines which intersect in his teaching. This single criterion is the imperative, incitive call to perfect detachment, that is, to releasement. "Rid yourself of all that is yours and give yourself over to God, then God belongs to you as he belongs to himself": the sermon "Proclaim the Word" deliberately opposes, once again, the indicative doctrine of a Scholasticism already turned into Inquisition. Does the analogy of attribution verify this crucial role of releasement?

Yes and no. To understand being as incessantly bestowed upon beings without ever taking root in them certainly reflects an ancient and beautiful vision of things: being is granted in a process, in a continuous outpouring from the Source, and any existence is possible only in the lifegiving stream of this procession. This is how the Neoplatonists viewed the cosmos, and assuredly Eckhart is of their lineage. Furthermore, just as Plotinus and his followers taught, so Eckhart seems to preach an interior asceticism in order to reascend the sequence of emanations and draw life from where it originates. Thus understood, analogy of attribution undeniably resembles the call to active releasement. Nevertheless, we have seen that ἐπιστροφή and *gelâzenheit* or *abegescheidenheit* do not say the same thing.[72] Fully understood, releasement both precedes and consumes the understanding of being; it realizes it entirely. Only full releasement allows for a correct grasp of the single and simple intent behind all of Eckhart's sermons. In particular, release-ment alone unifies the two doctrines of the birth of the Son in the mind and the breakthrough beyond God. In order to preserve the primacy of releasement in the theory of being it is not enough then to cite the Neoplatonic *exitus* and *redditus*. What Meister Eckhart understands by "being" will remain unintelligible as long as the meaning of being is not experienced and verified in the course of releasement. Our first reserve, then, with regard to the analogical system, concerns the insufficient place that it assigns to *gelâzenheit,* releasement.

b.) The analogy of attribution is unsuited to manifest the under-standing of being in Meister Eckhart for still another reason. Through-out the three sermons analyzed, we have detected not only evidence of Platonic doctrines but also some important Aristotelian vestiges: "His knowledge is mine, exactly the same, one sole and identical knowledge: in the master as he teaches and in the disciple as he is taught." Being had appeared to us as an energetic identity, *einheit im gewürke.* "Acting and becoming are one. God and I are one in operation: he acts and I become."[73] This identity, not of a substantial "suppositum" but of event, is the place from which the question of being must be raised. Ἐνέργεια is the other side of releasement: no longer peregrination, but union; no longer voluntary detachment, but fulfillment beyond all hu-man faculties. Something like an identity by process is traditionally thinkable only in two cases: with regard to knowledge or with regard to the act of being through which a being that does not exist by itself participates a being that exists by itself. But being, in Meister Eckhart, precisely excludes distinctions such as those between the knowing sub-ject and the object known, and between first act and second act. Being as *einheit im gewürke* requires an intelligibility other than what the systems derived from Plato and Aristotle can offer. It is our under-standing that ultimately Eckhart's ontology is irreducible to these two currents in philosophy. Our second objection, then, is that analogy of attribution does not honor the eminent place that the sermon "See What Love" reserves for being as ἐνέργεια, taken in the precise sense of birth and breakthrough.

The complexity of Eckhart's vocabulary of being has been shown above.[74] It now has to be shown how it yields a residual factor for which the theory of analogy cannot account. *Iht,* we said, designates the being of finite beings, the perfection of being that makes a created thing exist. We have translated *iht* by "something" and *ihtes iht* by "this individual being." The analogy of attribution teaches us that *iht* is *niht*, nothing in itself, and that *ihtes iht* is *nihtes niht*, nothingness. This has already been explained.

c.) The infinitive of the verb *wesene*, sometimes used as a noun, reflects the *ens commune* of the Scholastics. Its exact meaning fluctuates; at times it designates existence, at times essence. In the history of the German language, Meister Eckhart adopts this word at the moment of transition, when it no longer translates *esse* in all its doctrinal rigor but is not yet the modern *Wesen*, which is often a synonym for "human being."[75] In Middle High German dictionaries the first equivalent of *wesene* is *bleiben*, to remain, to maintain, to live; that of the present participle *wesende* is *anwesend*, present.[76] To render the nuance of process, we have translated it at times by phrases such as "essential presencing" and "essential coming forth." When being is called *wesene*, this always suggests an event or a process by which a thing reaches its full essence. The word thus means both coming forth and fulfillment. It is true that the analogy of attribution excludes neither of these two aspects: uncreated and uncreatable being is incessantly granted from elsewhere, and it fixes the created in its fulfillment or dwellings. But to speak of analogy is to represent relations between at least two proportionate terms. Eckhart wants to do away with any such definable proportion as he thinks of one sole and unique breaking forth of whatever is: *wesene*, coming, dwelling. It is understandable that in this line of thought *wesene* swallows up *iht*:

As long as there is any *iht* within the *wesene* of a thing, this thing is not recreated.[77]

It is also understandable that *wesene* should be the proper name of God:

"I am": here [the text] speaks of *wesene*. The masters say: all creatures can very well say "I"; this is a universal word. But the word *sum*, "am," is different: no one can pronounce it properly except God alone.[78]

d.) The third group of words, *istic* and *isticheit* or *istikeit*, all derived from the verb *sîn*, applies still more exclusively to God.[79] One may be tempted to translate *weselîche isticheit* by: the being "whose essence is

existence"; but this would be a mistake, as *isticheit* terminates the movement of releasement and designates therefore the pure and formless
being of the Godhead, the ὑπέρ-ὄν of Pseudo-Dionysius.

> You have to completely founder in your "yourness" *(in diner dinesheit)* and
> to dissolve into his "hisness" *(in sine sinesheit)*. Your proper self has to
> become so totally one Self with his proper self that you understand
> eternally his being *(istikeit)* without any becoming, and his nothingness
> without any name.[80]

The adjective *istic* is more difficult to circumscribe. One thinks of
Augustine's phrase that "God is more intimate to me than I am to
myself." Eckhart seems to borrow even the grammatical structure of this
phrase as he, too, uses the comparative:

> If God's nature is my nature, then the divine being is my being. Thus God
> is more intimately present *(istiger)* to all creatures than the creature is to
> itself.[81]

The intimate presence of God is expressed by a derivative of the verb
to be. *Istic* should therefore be understood as indicating the "intensity
of being." God's being within me is more intense than my own being.
This intensity is so strong that God himself and myself become unified
in one identical Self, called *wesene*.[82] God is supremely *istic*, present to
himself, and a perfectly released mind is introduced into this *isticheit* or
divine presence. Saint Paul, says Eckhart,

> abandoned God for the sake of God; then God became his such as he is
> present *(istic)* to himself, neither given nor received, but in the presence
> *(isticheit)* that God is in himself.[83]

In these texts, Eckhart thinks of being as presence: not as the received
or given presence of one particular being to another,[84] but as the very
content of releasement. To let God be, to break through and beyond
him, is a process in which the dialectic of immanence and transcendence
actually vanishes together with the hierarchy of analogically deciphera-
ble degrees. If releasement and presence are to be the most acceptable
titles for being, then being can no longer be represented as the universal
foundation or the inherent reason of all things. A perfectly released man
literally represents nothing. Being as presence and as nothingness arises

on the path which Eckhart describes as that of solitude, of the desert, and of forgetfulness. Both the philosopher of analogical identity and the thinker of peregrine identity articulate some kind of presence. But while, according to the former, beings represent being which makes them be, the latter has experienced the breakthrough and its nothingness. For him, presence means the simple showing of things; the quest for causes is forgotten. Releasement knows that things are there for nothing. Hence nothingness is as valid a title, in Eckhart's ontology, as being.

Being as coming forth and as a process *(wesene)*, as a presence that is nothingness *(isticheit)* directs us away from theories of analogy. And there are still more reasons to look for a new direction in analyzing Eckhart's concept of being.

e.) Another departure from analogy is due to Eckhart's intellectualism. He says that the intellect breaks through beyond God into his ground and that the highest name that he can give to God is "intelligence." What exactly is at stake in such an identification between God's act of being and his act of knowing? Under the title "God Is Intelligence" Eckhart writes:

> Some say that being, life, and intelligence can be viewed in two ways: firstly in themselves, in which case being is first, life second, and intelligence third; secondly in relation to that which participates them, and then intelligence is first, life second, and being third. But I believe the exact opposite to be true. "In the beginning was the Word" (St. John), which belongs entirely to intelligence. Consequently, among perfections in themselves intelligence comes first, and then determinate or indeterminate being. . . . On the basis of this I show that in God there is no being, determinate or indeterminate. Indeed, if a cause is a true cause, nothing is formally both in the cause and in its effect. Now, since God is the cause of all being, it follows that being is not formally in God. Of course if you wish to call intelligence "being," that is agreeable to me. Nevertheless I say that if there is anything in God that you want to call being, it belongs to him through his intelligence.[85]

If in God you wish to call intelligence "being," that is agreeable to me! What is at stake is self-possession. In knowing himself, God possesses himself totally. If being, as a synonym for intelligence, is "agreeable," then the emphasis in Eckhart's ontology has to lie on the movement of self-appropriation. As pure intelligence, God is entirely transparent to himself. Everything else is either appropriated by him (things created in general) or appropriates him (man in particular). The Christian doctrine of the uncreated Logos (Word), in this reinterpretation according to the dynamics of releasement, becomes a doctrine of being as a process. The utterance of a word, Eckhart says, is a matter of the intellect. God pronounces his Word from all eternity; and man does what God does: "Announce the Word, pronounce it, produce it, bring forth the Word!"[86] Thus man enters the being of God, that is, God's self-possession by his intelligence and by the utterance of his ineffable Word. When man becomes an "adverb" *(biwort)* to the "Verb" *(wort)*, he takes possession of God through what is the proper activity of an intellect, namely to pronounce a word. We actually know that in Eckhart God's utterance and mine are identical: "If I were not, God would not be either: that God is God, of this I am a cause. If I were not, God would not be God."[87]

Such a verification of Eckhart's intellectualism by means of releasement shows clearly why Aristotelian analogy has to step aside when it comes to defining Eckhart's understanding of being: the theory of analogy provides no conceptual tool for articulating self-appropriation as the common "ground" of God and man. "Among perfections in themselves intelligence comes first, and then determinate or indeterminate being," because intelligence is by its very nature a movement. An ontology based on intelligence will never become a static ontology. If intelligence is the most appropriate name for being because self-appropriation as a movement is essential both to man and to God, then being cannot be represented any longer according to Aristotelian schemes of analogical attribution. Hegel seems to have sensed this transformation of ontology in Meister Eckhart quite clearly.[88]

f.) If a new approach to the question of being is to be attempted in Meister Eckhart, it will have to take into account a first conclusion: the failure of God represented as the cause and reason of beings. The word that creates is "announced," "pronounced," "produced," "brought forth," but it is neither founded upon the uncreated ground nor does it found the created. In the silence of the original word, in the nothingness of its being, God, man, the world, are uprooted. The Three let each other be. Releasement has nothing to count or to base itself upon. When the origin is thought of as the word, or as intelligence, all metaphysical buttresses become provisional. The word speaks, but it does not pose anything. It does not pose itself under beings as their foundation: it supports nothing; and further it does not precede beings as their cause;

it presupposes nothing. The origin neither poses, nor supposes, nor presupposes anything. But it bespeaks all that there is. Its saying arises "without a why."[89]

Analogy requires a First as its support. It institutes God as the supreme support of totality, the foundation both of being and of knowing. The Roman Pantocrator holds in his hand the globe of the universe: in the hand of God all things are, and are explicable. Supreme science is the science "by the causes." Being, as the cause of beings, procures their necessary and sufficient condition of possibility.

Under the "without a why" of releasement this foundation gives way. The ground of things is then abyss, nothingness. The analogy of attribution speaks of nothingness as nothingness of essence: the creature is nothing in itself. We shall have to see how nothingness must be thought of if the origin is event, word, self-appropriation.

The polemic that turns the Eckhartian "without a why" against the theory of the analogy of attribution certainly does not pretend that Meister Eckhart speaks neither of foundation nor of cause. But the former, the *grunt*, is thought of as the locus of the birth of the inner Word and of the great death of God, man, and the world; and the latter, the cause understood as *causa sui*, is an epithet not of God, but of man in the Godhead.[90] Thus it is the very vocabulary of analogy in Eckhart which indicates the new orientation of research.

We have expressed six reservations against those commentators who wish to explain Eckhart's understanding of being exclusively by recourse to the theory of analogy: releasement *(gelâzenheit, abegescheidenheit)*, energetic identity *(einheit im gewürke)*, being as process and as appropriation *(wesene)*, presence under the mode of nothingness *(isticheit)*, word *(in principio erat Verbum)*, without a why *(sunder warumbe)*. These are reasons enough to attempt a comparison between Meister Eckhart and Heidegger on these points.[91]

Confronted with a particular experience of thought, certain philosophical categories can suddenly appear inadequate. This does not mean that they are "false." But we can ask ourselves if they reflect the authentic core of an author's thought, or if in using such categories the author does not simply fulfill a "program" of teaching. The authentic core of Meister Eckhart's thinking is releasement. In the history of ideas, each epoch has its own language, and perhaps releasement precedes its own epoch. Our experience is that it reveals the framework of established metaphysics as too narrow, for releasement is as inexhaustible as being itself. In the course of our reflections we have already had to abandon antinomies such as subject–object, action–passion, I–you: they proved unable to lend a satisfactory vocabulary to releasement. These six reservations point to an interval in the itinerary of Eckhart into which the theory of analogy cannot reach. Its failure is not surprising if we remember that the original task of this theory was to establish the ontological primacy of the sensible substance.

Wandering Identity (Meister Eckhart and Heidegger)

Die Gelassenheit zu den Dingen und die Offenheit für das Geheimnis gehören zusammen.
Die Gelassenheit zu den Dingen und die Offenheit für das Geheimnis geben uns den Ausblick auf eine neue Bodenständigkeit.
Die Gelassenheit zu den Dingen und die Offenheit für das Geheimnis fallen uns niemals von selber zu. Sie sind nichts Zu-fälliges. Beide gedeihen nur aus einem unablässigen herzhaften Denken.
Wenn die Gelassenheit zu den Dingen und die Offenheit für das Geheimnis in uns erwachen, dann dürften wir auf einen Weg gelangen, der zu einem neuen Grund und Boden führt.[92]

Whoever wishes to obtain decisive answers from an ancient author most pose decisive questions. Lacking a vigorous foregoing surmise, the interpretation of an author can never be successful. Here is the surmise that will now guide us: in our six-point program of contestation, something has left its trace; something which, through Eckhart, eminently concerns the actual situation of man and thought, at least if the latter is at all to be characterized by the recollection into being. The following remarks on Heidegger's, as compared to Meister Eckhart's, understanding of releasement are made neither in order to prove Eckhart's influence on Heidegger,[93] nor in an attempt to turn Eckhart into a modern philosopher. But it appears clear that releasement unveils being. In our effort to extract from Eckhart's sermons the truth of being as it was granted to him, we have come to surmise that the essence of being is itself releasement. It is this paradox of releasement as the condition for thinking and as the essence of being that will be better suited than the theory of analogy to reveal the truth of Eckhart's experience of thought. Perhaps the reader of today, to whom the sense of mystery seems contradictory with the demands of reason, will gather from this paradox a sign for his own way of thought.

As has been our procedure with Eckhart, we shall comment on the passage quoted under the heading above. These sentences were spoken by Heidegger, as is well known, in his natal village on the occasion of the 175th anniversary of the German composer Conradin Kreutzer. The meditation on these lines will cast a new light on the six questions raised earlier.

There are innumerable ways to enter a philosopher's thought. For our purpose access through the trial of translation will be most appropriate. Indeed, the translator has to be perfectly released himself if he is to collect the truth from a text. A translation entails more than an effort at literary precision: to translate is to yield one's thought to the demand of truth that originates with the text. In such a trial the text becomes summons, apostrophe. Literally, to translate means the same thing as to transfer, that is, to carry across. A translation fords our thinking from one bank of language to the other. It is legislative for thought; here, thought cannot escape the law of *Gelassenheit.* The most appropriate equivalent for *Gelassenheit* has appeared to be "letting-be"; as the translation *lets* truth come forth in the text, it experiences this truth already as letting-be. The act of translation is the paradigm (which does not mean the epitome) of mysticism: one must let truth be in order to understand truth as letting-be. As Eckhart said: "He who wants to understand my teaching of releasement has to be himself perfectly released." In this crossing over, the truth of being addresses our thought and claims it as it is by itself: "naked," "detached," without property *(eigenschaft).* Truth translates us before its own legislative instances. Not that it imposes some eternal laws which translation would have to abide by—rather, the translation enacts its own law. But within the limits of a philosophy of language, translation fulfills the paradox of releasement: it is thoroughly receptive and passive and thoroughly legislative and active; in other words, it is "virgin" and "wife" at the same time.

Translation thus introduces us to an original experience with language. You do not come out of a dialogue unaffected; nor do you come out of a translation unaffected. Both are modes of the single way in which being grants its truth. We shall expose ourselves first to the trial of Heidegger's words, then, in a brief return to Meister Eckhart, we shall measure the two courses against each other.

Die Gelassenheit zu den Dingen und die Offenheit für das Geheimnis gehören zusammen.

The first of Heidegger's sentences seems easy to render in English: "Letting-be before things and openness to the mystery belong together."

Two words, however, stop us: *zu* and *für*. Are we to assume an attitude "before things," as someone might be said to keep his composure "before"—that is, when faced with—a scene of violence? *Zu* does not exactly indicate an opposition, a face-to-face encounter. And what is the meaning of "to" in the phrase "openness to the mystery"? One who is hungry is "ready to" take in proteins, fats, and starches. And one who moves from the countryside to the city becomes "open to" the prevailing crazes of the day. Is Heidegger speaking of some predisposition in man which seeks to be filled or overwhelmed by mystery? The text would then advocate a disposition for mystery in the sense of a space or a readiness for some kind of secret knowledge; in other words, it would recommend that we cease to be moved by things as they appear and turn towards their hidden connections, inaccessible to reason. The "openness to" would then refer to an ultimate end of man that appears when emotions "before" things are controlled or transformed.

Frequently Heidegger builds his verbs with the prefix *zu*: *zueignen*, to appropriate, *zugehören*, to belong to or to adhere, *zugehen*, to accede.... Both *zu* and *ad* designate a transitive: a complement is expected in which a movement terminates. The book title *Unterwegs zur Sprache* [On the way to language] suggests a similar movement: the way "translates" us towards language. *Zu* denotes an inclination for a term—in the sentence quoted, for things. *Zu*, then, does not mean "before," "faced with," "in opposition to," but rather the contrary, namely an approach or a destination. The sentence now reads: "Letting ourselves be destined towards things and the openness for the mystery belong together."

Heidegger invites us to hold such an attitude in the midst of a technical world in which anything but releasement prevails. We can say yes to the utilization of technical objects, he writes, and yet remain free. We can leave objects and their manipulation to themselves as something that does not concern us intimately. To refuse to let them take us under their exclusive domination is to say yes and no at the same time to their universe. He who lets them be inaugurates a simple and peaceable relationship to things; he lets them enter into his daily world and nevertheless leaves them outside.[94] If the term of this "destination" is clear —the multiple products of technology—its origin is not. Our translation, "letting ourselves be destined towards things," does not mention man as the subject of releasement.

Openness to the mystery has to be understood out of the same yes and no. The technical universe is not the only way in which a world arises from things. Other epochs, other languages knew other worlds. The technical universe is that particular rising of a world which today predominates. But the spontaneous equation between the world and its technical yards is not evident. It covers a forgetfulness. The world is not reducible to the sum of known and unknown objects at our disposal, nor to the setting of representation in which they are enclosed. The triumph of technology has covered up forms of the world which we no longer inhabit or which have become less actual. Man settles in an always particular opening of beings which is granted to him; in that sense he has his world. When beings manifest themselves to him under the traits of technology, the world opens itself in such a way that it closes and precludes other possibilities of settlement. It grants and re-fuses itself at the same time. The contemporary universe such as we know it is one of the historical possibilities in which the world manifests and conceals itself in beings. The technological universe shows and hides the world.

As "openness," in our text, refers to a way of existing within technol-ogy, it indicates a way in which the world discloses itself. Destiny and openness appear less and less as human attitudes or dispositions. It is not so much man who says yes and no to the technical universe; rather, in this universe, the world as possibility grants and denies itself. The advent of the world is essentially ambivalent, essentially mysterious— like the sayings of "the lord whose Oracle is at Delphi," and of whom Heraclitus is reported to have said that he "neither speaks nor conceals, but gives a sign."[95] This, properly, is the mystery: something that veils itself while unveiling itself. "The meaning pervading technology hides itself."[96] Indeed, domination, production, and organization mask the primitive openness. But that which dissimulates it also shows its traces: in domination, production, and organization the world discloses itself as openness. What the openness is in itself remains hidden; but it comes forth under the mode of this retention.

"Openness to the mystery" is no longer an appropriate translation if technology is understood as one possibility for the world to unfold. No space, no readiness for the mystery is meant, but the openness in which technology becomes possible is itself mysterious as it happens in the mode of concealment-unconcealment. The openness of which Heideg-ger speaks can only secondarily be man's. Heidegger does not exalt the inner dispositions of an *honnête homme* who is open to the mystery as he may be open to the suffering of others or to music. If openness does, however, imply a human attitude, this will be a response. Such a man responds and corresponds to the favor of that which grants itself to him all the while refusing itself. The openness is in favor of the mystery. To underline that the openness as an attitude of man's is only a response to a more primitive favor, we translate: "Opening ourselves to the favors of the mystery."

"To let ourselves be destined towards things and to open ourselves to the favors of the mystery belong together." It should be understood that the importance of the exercise lies in the way that this translation has come to be. In such an exercise it remains true, of course, that a German sentence has been carried over into English. But the aspect I am more interested in is that thinking has been carried over into the matter that the text speaks of: releasement as a theme in a text has changed into releasement as a necessary attitude. And not only that. Not only have we been translated into the truth of the text, rather than the text from one tongue into another, but this truth itself has appeared in its concreteness. Who, or what, destines letting-be to things? And who grants the openness in the mode of the mystery? On the way on which we have been "set over" (translated) to the truth of the text, an event has occurred; in Eckhart's vocabulary, a birth has taken place. At the outset, man as the subject of releasement was the unquestioned evidence: in front of things he practices letting-be, and in front of the mystery, openness. But now an ignorance is born. The words "destiny" and "favor," which we have introduced, confuse this relationship. The grammatical subject of letting-be and of openness is suddenly unknown.

The exercise of translation turns out to be a schooling of thought. We sought to render the *zu* of letting-be and the *für* of the openness, and we ourselves have been submitted to both. *The translation has abandoned man as the subject* of such or such a disposition; it has led the thinking under the favor of the mystery. Translation, according to the ancient definition of the symbol, realizes what it signifies. It has led us to the very heart of the question that we pose to Meister Eckhart and to Heidegger. The one preaches, the other gives a memorial address. Superficially the words they use resemble each other; with a little levity, one might exchange this or that term, for example, *gelâzenheit* with *Gelassenheit*. But a comparison of themes and terms stays outside of what the matter is in Eckhart and Heidegger. The historian of ideas misses the violence that releasement imposes on the mind and the will; his attitude of investigation would destroy everything. A sermon and an address, on the other hand, issue a call: Leave there whatever there is. . . . The sermon and the address manifest the *same*. In the course of the translation, the selfsame has taken us into its school.

"Not the like, but the *same*." The call of the selfsame shows a way which has to become ours. The study of Meister Eckhart and of Heidegger remains in vain if it does not lead to the appropriation of this path. "Whoever wants to understand this has to be very detached."[97] What counts is not the understanding of a doctrine which then is lived up to as honestly as possible. The teaching of releasement is not moral. Rather, the experience of the selfsame is what counts. The selfsame counts on us, claims our effort. To undergo the trial of hearing is to find ourselves directly exposed to letting-be. The ignorance concerning the subject is now the shadow that adumbrates the favor of the mystery. In a world dominated by sciences and technology, by the transformation of things into commodities, releasement discloses an alternative way of thinking where we are the recipient rather than the actor of a transitive movement towards beings.

To speak of the selfsame that claims our thinking (and therefore our living) in Meister Eckhart and in Heidegger is not to draw subtle lines of comparison between one element or the other in their doctrines. The thought of the selfsame locates our effort in a realm that is at the same time earthier and loftier than such parallels. It locates us in the place that has been ours at all times, where we are summoned to let be whatever is and thus to respond and to correspond to the mystery of releasement that lets historical worlds be what they are.

> Die Gelassenheit zu den Dingen und die Offenheit für das Geheimnis geben uns den Ausblick auf eine neue Bodenständigkeit (To let ourselves be destined towards things and to open ourselves to the favors of the mystery gives us the perspective of a new ground-hold).

To be *bodenständig*, to find oneself firmly standing on the ground, is to be at home; the dictionary meaning is "native." The ground where a man is native is his fatherland. Letting-be and openness prepare a fatherland. What kind of "ground" is this? The "ground" as fatherland can hardly be Leibniz's principle that "nothing is without foundation" *(nihil est sine ratione),* or Eckhart's *grunt der sêle,* ground of the mind.

We need not be content with Heidegger's rural idyll, in which man's ground is his fields, and his native land the familiar countryside in which he feels at home. As the country-born has "his" plot, so the city-born has "his" neighborhood. From this we understand what it means to have a horizon. The scientist has "his" domain in reality: it is life if he is a biologist, language if he is a linguist, society if he is a sociologist. . . . Each thinker has "his" horizon of thought. The philosophical horizon of Aristotle is the sensible substance, which grounds the accidents that alone appear. The horizon of Kant is the transcendental capacity of reason and the noumenon, which ground intuition and the phenomenon. The horizon of western metaphysics altogether, as Heidegger thinks it, would then be transcendence in general, as the reason and foundation of all that there is.

Man's ground is his horizon. But is today's world not characterized by a global reach? Is it correct, then, to represent man at home on this or that particular soil, under such or such a horizon only? Does rootedness require as its complement the segmentation of the earth? It is difficult to be a citizen of the universe; the fatherland is always "this or that," this country or culture and not another. At the same time we have become uprooted. The segment of the globe which is ours has become permeable. Contemporary residences are hardly a stable ground. We know what happens in countries never visited, but we no longer know very well where we are at home. Would not our fatherland, our ground and horizon, soon be the entire cosmos?

Heidegger invites us to think of the ground otherwise. A horizon is what encircles our visual field. The visual is the familiar. The non-visual is elsewhere and strange, it is the beyond, the invisible. But what is it that gives the horizon its disjunctive quality? What is it that separates the invisible from the visible? Who has traced the line of partition? The question is that of the essence of the horizon. No representation can resolve it, as the horizon itself is never perceived. It is conceived and represented out of the perceptible. Its line is the limit of representation and is itself based on representation. "In this way what *lets* the horizon *be* what it is has not yet been experienced at all" (emphasis added).[98]

Is the essence of the horizon to be construed out of representation? Objects perceived would then by their presence trace a circle around the mind. The limit of perception would trace man's rootedness and ground. But if the horizon is determined by the appearance of things as objects of perception, then the perceived constitutes the horizon. Our territory ends where we can see no further. Thus we seem to speak of the horizon, but in fact we only represent the subjectivity among sense-objects: to perception and representation the horizon appears as the background to a foreground which is ready to hand or present at hand. To properly think its essence, a new attitude is required. "That which *lets* the horizon *be* what it is": things appear no longer under the exclusive mode of disposability to the senses, but under that of letting be, and the horizon will show forth in its truth. It will eventually show forth as the truth itself, that is, as the openness or the region in which beings grant themselves to thought. Only a thinking that lets the horizon be (that dissociates it from perception) can think of the horizon as "let" (*gelassen*) and as letting-be.

If the openness is thought of as the possibility that lets the horizon be, then we have actually stepped back behind the horizon. Our study of it has *turned away* from the beings that are present, and it has *turned towards* that which lets them be present. The horizon appears as an event: as letting-be present, as releasement. This decisive turn, once again, is towards an alternative attitude of thinking. Here things are not represented as sense-objects, but they are released to be. The elucidation of the groundhold, or the native land, in Heidegger's text has led us to reflect on the horizon. This reflection has suddenly brought us back to releasement; it now gives another meaning to the word "mystery." Letting-be and mystery have changed their constellation. Things no longer appear only as sense-objects; a more primitive openness lets them be. The openness, the condition of their appearance and the essence of the horizon, shows itself. Its showing is "mysterious," that is, it comes forth while withdrawing into the objects. Insofar as the openness that lets things be discloses and conceals itself in them, it is our oldest and our newest fatherland. In Eckhart the precise meaning of *heimelich* is "familiar," " benevolent."[99] Mystery is our fatherland: the *Geheimnis* is the *Heimat*.

"Mystery is our fatherland": such a phrase has meaning only in the active—or existential, if that is the word—process of releasement. The phrase yields no philosophical thesis. It says that as long as man holds things in his obstinate disposition, as long as his thinking remains calculative, he errs in the quest for a presence that would be everlasting, fulfilling, grounding—a presence understood as durable *(beständiges Anwesen)*, as a noun, and not presencing understood as an event

($\pi\alpha\rho o\upsilon\sigma\acute{\iota}\alpha$), as a verb. Detachment from techniques of disposition is the condition for mystery to manifest itself as well as for man to return to himself. The "translation" or the turning is accomplished when the openness in which beings appear is freed from the dominance of representation and possession. Meister Eckhart would say: the breakthrough is accomplished when the Godhead in which beings appear is freed from the dominance of attachment and possession.

Letting-be and openness to the favors of mystery have first appeared to us as belonging to one another. Now we have taken this one step further: letting-be is the condition for mystery to manifest itself. The step further is a step backwards, namely from the horizon into the essence of the horizon. The step backwards leads into the open, where thinking becomes meditative. At this point, releasement designates identically man's thinking and being's openness. In releasement so understood all things are gathered together, they enter into relationship with each other, and they dwell in their proper locus. Thus they are left to their being. To think of being as the openness itself—"clearing" as it is understood in Heidegger's later writings—is to reach a new ground-hold. The "ground" is no more the foundation on which man can count, but rather the absence of all counting and calculating; it is the homeland that is both absent and present. Its "epochs," its impartations and retentions, are the favors, or the historical ways of being, which being bestows upon man. In this identical releasement things are no longer determined by perception and representation, but by their coming into the open and their historical dwelling in it. Thus releasement is the truth of things. But as releasement remains a process, truth is always ahead of us; the "new" groundhold, says the text, appears only as a "perspective."

Two other texts by Heidegger help us to better understand this openness as the condition of the manifestation of the mystery and as that which "lets" things be as they are. We have noted that the German verb *wesen*, to be, indicates a process (*"er west"* is archaic for "he roams about," but the sense is still there in expressions like *"sein Wesen treiben,"* to go about, *"viel Wesens machen,"* to make much ado). In a lecture of 1953 Heidegger recalls that this verb is of the same origin as *wahren*, to stay or to dwell.[100] As being unfolds, it makes beings dwell in the open. The difference between being and beings is one of letting-be. Releasement is thus both what being does and what thinking, or man, does. In that sense, being and thinking are the same. "With no difference, we are the same being *(daz selbe wesene)*, the same substance and nature," Eckhart said of the Godhead.

In Eckhart, beings receive their dwelling or their stay as they are released from the Godhead. It is this identity of being and thinking in releasement, insofar as it assigns to all things their place and stay, which I see as the underlying structure in both Eckhart's and Heidegger's ways of understanding being.

If being is understood out of beings, it is nothing. Being is no thing; it can never be encountered among beings. Releasement opens the perspective of that way of philosophizing and of living in which the new groundhold is recognized in its mysterious structure: as absent and present, as nothingness and being.

The second text speaks of the difference between being and beings.[101] If it is not enough to think being out of beings, if a step backwards is necessary, this step leads thinking towards what is properly its lot: the difference as such. Being comes to presence as the passage or transition towards beings. Not that beings are originally separated from being and must be reached by it. But being is not itself, and beings are not themselves, except in this transition. Being takes shelter in this coming into day; it makes itself present by granting beings their dwelling.

Thought, too, is itself only in this transition in which being comes to beings and settles them within the difference. Here thinking is at home. The new groundhold presaged by the thought of the difference is being itself as coming into the open and as dwelling. The essence of being is nothing other than this difference; but it will only be our "homeland" when we begin to think it for its own sake—when we begin to be perfectly released ourselves. We can conclude: letting-be as the present–absent rootedness of thought is the condition as well as the essence of the manifestation of being itself.

This brings us remarkably close to Meister Eckhart. In the course of the reflection, two more points of our initial surmise have found an answer: the significance of the words *wesene*, "to be" as coming into the open and as dwelling, and *isticheit*, "to be" as presence under the mode of nothingness.[102] With regard to the first of these two words, Heidegger himself suggests the relation to Eckhart;[103] the content of the second, however, changes drastically from one author to the other. It suffices to recall that it is *eigenschaft*—selfhood, attachment, property—that Meister Eckhart principally denounces as nothingness because it darkens peregrine joy by making being into that particular being, man into that individual, and God into that divine person.[104] The kinship between the two thinkers bears on the way being grants itself: under the condition (for man) and according to the mode (in itself) of letting-be.

> Die Gelassenheit zu den Dingen und die Offenheit für das Geheimnis fallen uns niemals von selber zu. Sie sind nichts Zu-fälliges. Beide gedeihen nur aus einem unablässig herzhaften Denken (To let ourselves be destined towards things and to open ourselves to the favors of the mystery never happen of themselves. They do not befall us accidentally. Both flourish only through persistent, hearty thinking).

Heidegger had characterized *Gelassenheit* first by its reciprocity with the openness to the favors of the mystery. Then he has shown it as preparatory for a new rootedness, the one that being, as present–absent in beings, offers to thought. Now the relation between releasement and thought is articulated more explicitly: letting-be and the openness to the favors of the mystery flourish only through persistent, hearty thinking.

This manner of speaking does not mean that intelligence must enrich itself by some affective complement. The "heart" does not refer here to the seat of the sentiments. "The widest orbit of beings becomes present in the heart's inner space," says Heidegger in memory of Rilke.[105] The heart is the place where the totality of beings renders itself essentially present: it is the center or the core of thinking. This "heart of thought," then, maintains a nonfortuitous relation with letting-be and the openness to the favors of the mystery.

It is essential to thought to let beings be. Since Aristotle, man in his most genuine capacity has been defined by this openness to all that there is. And it should be clear, in passing, that Heidegger's late expression "thought" or "thinking" stands for his earlier title *Dasein*, that is, for what is most essential in man—just as the "ground of the mind," in Eckhart, stands for what is most essential in man. It will have to be shown how far the agreement between the two views reaches before they part company. But this much is clear: releasement is the very essence of thought. Originally, thinking does not take hold of things. Rather, it gathers them together into its brightness and renders them to themselves, that is, to the mystery of the difference. According to Heidegger, this attitude of gathering is so much at the "heart" of thinking that *Denken* appears originally as *Gedanc.* This latter word does not mean *Gedanke,* a thought, but rather "to thinking pertains thanking,"[106] gathering and gratitude. Being gives itself to thinking. Its gift requires gathering and gratitude.

If, in itself and essentially, thinking lets beings be, why should a persistent and hearty effort be asked of it? There seems to lie an ambiguity in thought. Naturally it says "beings are," and thus lets them be; but it also must correspond to its nature by a free and incessantly renewed persistence. Lacking such an agreement, "there might go hand in hand with the greatest ingenuity in calculative planning and inventing indifference toward meditative thinking, total thoughtlessness."[107] The new thinking, which prepares the new rootedness, requires a complete reversal of habits. This reversal is the very apprenticeship of thinking: only meditative thinking deserves to be called thought. Calculative thinking ignores the attitude of releasement.

A very similar ambiguity characterizes the mind as Eckhart sees it. In the essence of your mind, he says, you are already *gelâzen*; but the destiny of the ground of the mind is to become its nature, to return to itself, and to learn *gelâzenheit.*

We can take this a step further. Both thought and being let beings be: their essence, releasement, is the same. *Gelassenheit* shows what thought and being are all about: they are naturally the same. We must now examine the Parmenidean implications that seem to accompany this identity.

From the side of thought first: thought is no longer seen as a faculty of man, it is no longer one being among others that confronts the others by voluntary "adequation" or conformity. Thought can no longer be represented as that being which faces objects. It owes them nothing; rather, it owes itself to being. In a parallel fashion, letting-be ceases once and for all to figure among the attitudes of man. That which lets beings be exposes them to thought in one and the same process.

From the side of being, then: like thought, being can no longer be represented as one being among others, even if it is understood as the greatest. A supreme being, such as speculative thinking represents it, stands behind beings as their foundation. On such a founding principle man can always count. He can even consecrate a place in the city and devote a cult to it. He can also proclaim the supreme being the purpose for which the city works and to which it is devoted, its highest reason for living. Being thus enters into the horizon of man. But when being appears to, and as, releasement, it neither founds nor explains nor justifies anything. It grants beings, without a why, *ohne Warum*. [108] From this angle, the overcoming of being as supreme foundation answers our last reservation concerning analogy, namely Eckhart's *sunder warumbe*. "Why are you living? I do not know, but I am happy to live."[109]

From releasement's point of view, thought and being are the same. This understanding of identity now marks the limits of a rapprochement between Meister Eckhart and Heidegger. To be sure, thought does what being does: it lets beings be. Their nature, *Gelassenheit*, is the same. Yet, however broadly in extension and comprehension Heidegger may want his title "thinking" to be understood, tending to subsume even man's actions under it, he still uses "thinking" as a translation of νόειν, and in that sense noetically. The new groundhold is *Seinsdenken*, the thought of being, and it may be reached only "through persistent, hearty thinking." For Meister Eckhart *gelâzenheit* as an attitude of man refers to thought only secondarily. Primarily it is a matter of a way of life—a life without representation of ends and purposes.

The point of departure, in Heidegger, is the question of being. The openness in which beings appear manifests itself as mystery when and insofar as beings are "left" to what they are. Then the difference properly grants itself to thought. Or inversely: when thought returns to what is properly its own—the difference between beings and their openness —then beings are left to what they are, and being manifests itself as present and absent, as the mystery. The truth of being and the truth of thought are the only and same releasement.

In Meister Eckhart the point of departure is different. The one theme throughout his preaching is man's proper relation to God. Releasement "forces" God towards me: "Rid yourself of all that is your own, then God will properly be your own as he is his own."[110] A reader trained by this master in living and in thinking recognizes without hesitation the authentic path of releasement in the three steps of Heidegger's text that we have followed: first "letting ourselves be destined towards things" and "opening ourselves to the favors of the mystery," as well as the reciprocal belonging of letting-be and openness; then the perspective of a new groundhold where releasement becomes the condition for the concealing–unconcealing nature of being to manifest itself; finally the nonaccidental character of both. But an ambiguity prevails through all this. Meister Eckhart speaks of God close to man; Heidegger speaks of being close to thought. If Eckhart submits the traditional representation of God to the same treatment by which Heidegger destroys the metaphysical representation of being, he does so only for the sake of a more divine discourse on God, that is, the abolition of all discourse on God. Much more importantly, Eckhart and Heidegger understand releasement quite differently. When he is driven by the Inquisition to justify the philosophical implications of his doctrine, Eckhart declares: "this is something moral." This trait of releasement, thought of in the schemes of a philosophy of the will, is precisely what Heidegger points to as the element to be overcome.[111] Heidegger's "releasement" signifies the favors that grant being to thought; Eckhart's "releasement" refers to a persistence which is not only that of thought, but that of man's general commerce with things and people in daily life. This new life can be learned; then the Godhead is the being in which man encounters beings.

In Heidegger, on the other hand, releasement has a decidedly secular meaning. Not that Heidegger takes the counterposition to any religious concern, but his thinking locates itself underneath the various contents vehicled by our civilization. It remains neutral with regard to the great causes that motivate and mobilize human endeavors, and thus it is in contradiction neither with the most abject political regimes nor with the most authentic experience of God. The step backwards from cultural contents to the "clearing" that makes them possible pertains to Heidegger's philosophical project itself. The understanding of the translation may illustrate this secularization of releasement. When Eckhart says *übersetzen,* he has in mind a very precise trajectory, the mind's transition into God.[112] Heidegger, too, speaks of *übersetzen,* but here the passage simply leads thinking to its "food," which is the manifestation of being in time—or (later in his career) the manifestation of language in historic utterances.[113] In Eckhart, translation leads the ground of the mind back into the ground of God; in Heidegger, it simply reunites man to being (or to language) as to his "homeland," in which forms of life, ever renewed, are possible.

In other words, in Meister Eckhart releasement for the most part has the meaning of detachment; that is, it most often refers to an attitude of man. Only an interpretation that explicitly pursues Eckhart's understanding of being reveals that voluntary detachment, when perfect, leads into releasement as revelatory of being's way to be. In Heidegger, on the contrary, releasement primarily has the sense of letting-be as it designates identically the essence of being and the essence of man.[114] It refers to a life-attitude only in a derivative way.

Wenn die Gelassenheit zu den Dingen und die Offenheit für das Geheimnis in uns erwachen, dann dürften wir auf einen Weg gelangen, der zu einem neuen Grund und Boden führt (When we awake to letting ourselves be destined towards things and to opening ourselves to the favors of the mystery, then we may become engaged on a path that leads to a new ground and soil).

The new soil, as we have seen, is that of our oldest rootedness: the openness that lets be whatever is. Heidegger speaks of a path. With the exploration of this path we conclude our research on releasement in Meister Eckhart and Heidegger.

When Heidegger writes a preface for one of his books, it almost always contains an allusion to his own path of thinking. What initiated this path was the question of being. This question was first raised out of human existence, then out of the Greek concept of truth in relation to the beginnings of western civilization, and later in relation to the essence of language. From the time of the early thinkers, being is the preferred theme of philosophy. But at the same time the contemporary need for foundations suggests that since Plato this question has clouded itself with complex preoccupations whose modern version may be described as a quest for security, certainty, and salvation. The inner logic of this question may thus appear historically as one of occultation and exinanition. Hence the surmise that western thought has not reached its ground, that it still has to attain its groundhold. Only poets may at times have hinted at this ground that resists representation. The path they point out, at first sight, leads backwards, near the unthought origin of metaphysics. The path that was Heidegger's is one of verification. The presuppositions of the transmitted philosophy are to show themselves in their truth. The "path" that Heidegger speaks of is thus first of all his own.

But the isolated itinerary of a present-day thinker is decisive for his entire period: if western thought during more than two thousand years has been what it was, that is not an accident; and if today the whole of this tradition offers itself to pervasive verification, that is not an accident either. A thread has been traced throughout western thinking in general: the self-revelation of the essence of metaphysics. This is the second acceptance of the "path" in Heidegger. "At each phase of metaphysics is unveiled an end of the road which the destination of being has blazed on beingness, in unexpected periods of truth."[115] To many contemporaries Heidegger's own path of meditation has been revelatory of the road that philosophy as a whole had to follow since its birth in Greece. In this sense, the path is the "method" of philosophy, that is, the tracing of a truth which is perilous (*gefahrvoll*) because its experience (*Erfahrung*) is peregrination (*Fahren*) itself.

The third acceptance of the "path" results from the two that precede. Here the question is again one of history and its occultation. Being "sends" itself unto man, but the modes according to which beings are present conceal the sending. This occultation and this presencing are thought of as one single event. They say what metaphysics neither does nor can think of: how the openness that lets beings be, how the epochal favors that being bestows upon thought yield their own oblivion. The forgetfulness of being is not due to some human failure. Rather, in philosophy, being itself withdraws into hiding. The truth of being as nonconcealment remains itself concealed. But this historic concealment that is imparted to us is being itself: the peregrine identity, or the "method" (from ὁδός, the path) of the advent of being.

These three meanings of the "path" in Heidegger can be seen in their unity only when they are clearly separated from representations of subjects (human or divine) and relations between subjects (e.g., the mind's itinerary to God). This anonymity of peregrination is developed mainly in Heidegger's courses on Nietzsche.[116] In the text that serves as a guide for our reflection, he speaks of the history of "that-which-regions," or of the "expanse."[117] This history (*Geschichte*) and this destiny (*Geschick*) temporalize the event (*Geschehen*) of releasement.

According to the epochs of the history of its truth, being lets, or grants, beings to thought. For each epoch, being emerges differently. Only a meditation which returns upstream, i.e., which follows backwards this path of emergence, leads to the origin. The condition of viability of such a path is that the origin be represented neither as a point of departure nor as a term, but as present–absent to the road itself. In the law of the present–absent, or of identity and peregrination, thinking recognizes the normal status of its proceeding. Thought and being are the same in the commitment to the sendings of truth in history. Identity is intermittent, a process, anonymous—peregrine identity. Intermittence (momentary detachment), process (birth and the breakthrough), and anonymity (Godhead beyond God) again bring us close to Meister Eckhart.

In and as history, being emerges under the mode of a calling. The discovery of releasement's temporality, that is, of the epochs of truth, renders an address. Truth is not the correctness of a proposition, but the given constellation of things and thoughts among which we live. To such a constellation we are urged to respond and correspond. Thinking is thus originally listening, as the process of being is originally a calling. Earlier, releasement appeared as the identical essence of both being and thought; so listening and calling must now be seen as one and the same event, as peregrine identity. The way being commits itself, sends itself over to us, is releasement. So is man's response. "It is manifest that man's nature is released to the expanse, because this nature belongs so essentially to it that without man the expanse cannot achieve its essence, as it does."[118] If I were not, Eckhart says, God would not be God.

When the hearer becomes a thinker, that is, when being is questioned for its own sake, then man becomes what he is naturally. Authentic thinking fulfills man's nature as well as being's nature. Both are determined exclusively and identically as letting-be present. Releasement, Eckhart says, is the identical discovery of the ground of the mind and the ground of God.

When thought is so allied to releasement it is serene; then man's word brings forth beings in their very being. A released man, Eckhart says, becomes "adverb to the Verb," and in the eternal sheerness of the Godhead he begets Him of whom he is begotten.

When his word lets all things be and brings them forth, man experiences himself as spoken rather than speaking. The silence of the vast expanse speaks him, it gathers together all that there is. In the desert of the Godhead, Eckhart says, a released man is and possesses all things.[119]

When the silent word gathers originally all things into their being, then being becomes an event, and the space of history opens itself to man. I beget the Word in God, Meister Eckhart says, and in the event of this birth, God and I are *ein einic ein,* one unique unity.

With this original word and the event, the two last reservations that we formulated in opposition to the theory of analogy are now confirmed.[120] But another opposition is also confirmed, this one between Eckhart and Heidegger, which sweeps away all similarities: Heidegger's thinking is historical through and through; Meister Eckhart's is not; the path on which he experiences peregrine identity is that of existence, not that of history. From this point of view, "event" does not mean the same thing in both. When Heidegger says "event," he speaks of something historic, namely the epochs in which being grants and refuses itself to thought under diverse figures. This giving and denying opens the difference which being itself is. The ever-changing modes of gift and denial are our history. Epochal appropriations trace out the way in which being lets or grants itself to the difference. As in Eckhart, appropriation and releasement coincide, but both are historic.

When Meister Eckhart says "event," he speaks of God. Again an amphibology of being declares itself, namely between the nothingness of the created and the *wesene* as original and undetermined being. In the created, being becomes *iht,* beingness. Thus Eckhart, too, experiences a difference. But this duplicity of being is the consequence of attachment. It is to be overcome. One could even paraphrase Eckhart by saying that the core of his demand is an existential resolution of the ontological difference into identity. To say that being is an event (*gewürke*) does not exclude a monism of being. It is this monism that leads Eckhart to view the difference as something to be overcome, as an opacity rather than grace. The abolition of the difference would mean that *iht,* the beingness of beings, shows itself for what it is, *niht,* nothingness. Identity would then be experienced in the very course of this abolition. The breakthrough is that appropriating event in which all otherness is annihilated. A contemporary reader may situate this understanding of the difference within a historical perspective; he may see that Eckhart's "energetic" monism has its own epoch. But to the medieval that Eckhart is, such a perspective remains alien. The history of being itself forbids Eckhart to think about the temporality of releasement.

It remains true, though, that the understanding of being as a "path," in Meister Eckhart, daringly forestalls its epoch. Like Heidegger, Eckhart thinks the identity of being as wandering ("peregrine"), not in order to better know beings, nor to better understand man, but in the service of something more original which within this thinking gives and refuses itself to thought. And as Heidegger turns against the Idealism which precedes him and which he strives to complete and overcome, Meister Eckhart turns against Scholasticism. His preaching is seditious: it rises up against the project of a culture which reduces the Indeterminate to the disposition of man, which makes it serviceable to spiritual comfort, collective security, academic erudition, and institutions. Both Eckhart and Heidegger have experienced how in their time the unique mystery, which manifests itself only in the interval between forgetfulness and presence, is fragmented into the mystery of man, the mystery of God, the mystery of the world. To this dislocation they oppose releasement. Thus the one's preaching and the other's thinking apostrophize us across the drift of the identical. Their word shows the advent of the *same* in all the scattered ways. The riverbed becomes its source and also its estuary. A man who has thus experienced the *same* no longer has a place to establish himself. He has settled on the road, and for those who have learned how to listen, his existence becomes a call. This errant one dwells in joy. Through his wanderings the origin beckons.

Conclusion: Releasement and the "There Is"

We may summarize the different aspects of releasement in Eckhart and Heidegger as follows:[121]

1) In Meister Eckhart, releasement is primarily a voluntary emptiness of man's preoccupation with things and images, in order to do God's will. In Heidegger, it is the condition for a thing's truth to happen.

2) In Meister Eckhart, releasement discloses the creature's nothingness; it urges death to individuality and birth to beingness in general. In Heidegger, it is the condition for all things' truth, openness, or unconcealedness.

3) To Meister Eckhart, perfect releasement puts an end to the difference between created beingness and uncreated, trans-divine, being. In Heidegger, being is understood as the historical issue of the difference that is released into its epochal horizons but never to be overcome.

4) In both Meister Eckhart and Heidegger, releasement becomes the name of being's way of being. Process and nothingness are its two faces. But is not this ultimate accord entirely due to an equivocation of "being"? We must examine what Heidegger means when he says that being, as nothingness and as accomplishment or process, lets beings be.

During a seminar held in Le Thor, France, in 1969, Heidegger distinguished between three acceptations of "letting-be." To let be, *lassen,* he said, may be understood in relation either to a being, or to its presence, *Anwesen,* or to its coming-to-presence as such, *Anwesen lassen.* The first of these meanings points towards a singular being and results from the attitude which "lets something be." Phrases like "there are peasant shoes," "there are corn and wine," and "there is a jug" show the familiarity of our language with this form of releasement. In the second sense, attention is drawn to that which makes things present, to their presence in general, to their beingness. To "let all things be" is to experience their presence for its own sake; Meister Ekhart said: it is to experience the *iht* that is God in creatures. Heidegger writes one word, *Anwesenlassen,* and emphasizes the *Anwesen.* These two meanings signify the ontological difference between beings and their beingness as occidental philosophy is accustomed to think it.

In the third acceptation of "letting-be," Heidegger hyphenates the word *Anwesen-lassen* in order to emphasize the *Lassen.* This is releasement in its nonmetaphysical sense. The difference that is now thought of is between being and beingness (*wesene* as accomplishment and *iht* in Meister Eckhart, and *Sein* and *Seiendheit* in Heidegger). Being is understood as letting beingness be. This letting-be is already hidden in the *Wesen* of *Anwesen;* it is, Heidegger said in Le Thor, the "excess of presence."

In the lecture "Time and Being" (1962), Heidegger asked what is thought of when we say "there is Being." The German language does not say "there is," but rather "it gives," *es gibt Sein.* This idiomatic turn of speech reveals to Heidegger being's way of being. What is experienced when one says *es gibt Sein*? What is given? Being is given. But what is it that gives? "We try to bring the 'It' and its giving into view and capitalize the 'It.'"[122]

"There is being." Traditionally, philosophy considers being as the presence of beings (beingness). But what makes the presence come to presence? Our task consists of thinking that which gives presence. "It" allows for presence, grants presence. It lets presence open up beings. It brings beings into unconcealedness, into being. To "give" and to "let" mean the same phenomenon: "It" gives, "It" lets.

As long as being is represented as the ground and foundation of beings, to speak about the "It" that gives remains as mythological as an unmoved mover behind everything that comes to presence. The theologian will hasten along to detect an anonymous faith. This is not our intention in comparing Meister Eckhart and Heidegger. It is rather to follow their common enterprise of "destruction."[123] For both, neither beings nor beingness can answer what being is. The equations "being is beings" and "being is beingness" are dismantled. Thus releasement shows its original way to be: "It" lets beings be present, and "It" lets beingness be their presence. Such letting-be is being. Releasement brings being into its own.

What is it that gives being? The verbs to let and to give say nothing about "It." However, we remember an early answer: *Geschick,* destiny or mittance. The history of being sends us epochs as possible modes of existence. What is "It" that gives, now? Destiny refers to being and its history; thus the "It" that gives being appears to be being. Release-ment's way to be would now be: being gives being. But this does not say anything more than "being is," and we remember rather that being "is not." "It" and being seem to remain hidden within releasement as destiny and being.

When the difference between beingness (presence) and being (the being-given of the presence) is thought of, "It" comes into sight as that which tolerates no name. However, "It" brings being into its essential difference, into its proper way of being. "Proper," the German *eigen*, suggests a belonging or appropriation, *Ereignis*. Unconcealedness is being's proper way to be. But unconcealedness has appeared as what "It" lets be. Being comes into its own as "It" appropriates being. Thus we have seen releasement turn into its contrary: appropriation. This turning, however, does not result from man's taking possession of any-thing; it is only the return into being's original way to be. Releasement and appropriation, now, are names for one and the same event. But these names no longer refer to any attitude of man or to anything human. They interpret the phrases "It gives being" and "there is being." Only secondarily do they imply a claim made upon man's thought. This claim is what earlier quotations from the lecture "The Turning" and the course "What Is Called Thinking?" indicated.[124]

The event—releasement and appropriation—is as different from be-ing as an *a priori* is from an *a posteriori*.[125] A third understanding of the difference now appears: that between the event and being. Each of the three modes of the difference mentioned must be thought of as modes of releasement and appropriation: beingness lets beings be present, be-ing lets beingness be their presence, "It" lets being be. Beings, being-ness, and being come into their proper way of being. However, this process of dismantling is not a regression of hierarchical degrees. The inquiry proceeds towards a *neutrale tantum*,[126] not towards a more and more original ground. Heidegger traces these steps backwards from beings to the event that gives being, as follows:

Being by which all beings as such are marked, being means presencing. Thought with regard to what presences, presencing shows itself as let-ting-presence. But now we must try to think this letting-presencing ex-plicitly insofar as presencing is admitted. Letting shows its character in bringing into unconcealment. To let presence means: to unconceal, to bring to openness. In unconcealing prevails a giving, the giving that gives presencing, that is, Being, in letting-presence.[127]

Commenting on this difficult text, Heidegger excludes the possibility of a gradation, in the sense of an ever greater originality, from presence, though letting-be-present, unveiling and giving, to appropriation.[128]

"It" is not, but "It" gives being; "It" accomplishes being properly. Nothingness and accomplishment were the two facets of releasement in Meister Eckhart, not-being and event are the two facets of the "It" that gives being in Heidegger. Beyond all the incongruities that oppose medieval to contemporary experience, is it not the urgency of a new existence and thought, releasement, that brings Meister Eckhart and Heidegger close to each other? Heidegger is indebted to the mystical tradition when he thinks being, not as reason or foundation, but in terms of an event, *Wesen* and *Anwesen*. Meister Eckhart attempts to think the vanishing of all reasons. A mode of thinking flares up in his German sermons that does not only question man in order to know being, but questions being itself as a happening. In the silent desert of the Godhead, where no God and no man are there to confront each other, only the breakthrough "is." Eckhart came too early to succeed in his daring design. He is not a modern philosopher. But his understanding of being as releasement prepares the way for modern philosophy. The religious authorities of his age, although they could not follow his teachings, sensed a destructive power in his words. Today, this destruction has already taken place: the metaphysical God is proclaimed to be dead. Releasement can now be thought of otherwise than within the realm of man's experience. Perhaps it is only now that the time has come for Meister Eckhart's thought.

The following sermon probably contains the boldest formulations of the "breakthrough" by which man "lets" God be. To the old metaphysical question, "What is being?" this sermon answers: it is neither things, nor the mind, nor God, but the act of passing beyond beings, as well as beyond knowing, willing, and having. Eckhart's point is that such an act is neither human nor divine: "there is," properly speaking, only the transition beyond everything representable, only the "impulse" (a reinterpretation of the Neoplatonic *reditus*), only "the strictest poverty" in which God and man join. Eckhart's understanding of being (*wesen*) as an event has its counterpart in the destruction of the representable God. In order to think being as the nameless event of identity, "I pray God to rid me of God."[129]

SERMON,
"BLESSED ARE THE POOR"

(BEATI PAUPERES SPIRITU, QUONIAM IPSORUM EST REGNUM CAELORUM, Matt. 5:3)

Blessedness opened its mouth of wisdom and spoke: "Blessed are the poor in spirit, for theirs is the kingdom of heaven."

All angels and all saints and all that were ever born must be silent when the wisdom of the Father speaks, for all the wisdom of the angels and of all creatures is pure foolishness before the groundless wisdom of God. And this wisdom has said that the poor are blessed.

Now there are two kinds of poverty: an external poverty, which is good and is to be much praised in a man who willingly accomplishes it through the love of our Lord, Jesus Christ, because he was himself poor on earth. Of this poverty I do not want to speak any further. Yet, there is still another kind of poverty, an inner poverty by which our Lord's word is to be understood when he says: "Blessed are the poor in spirit."

Now I beseech you to be just so poor, so as to understand this speech. For I say to you by the eternal truth: So long as you do not equal this truth of which we now want to speak, you cannot understand me.

Various people have asked me what poverty is in itself and what a poor man is. That is what we want to answer.

Bishop Albrecht says that a poor man is he who finds no satisfaction in any of the things that God ever created—and that is well said. But we say it better still and take poverty in a yet higher understanding: A poor man is he who wills nothing, knows nothing, and has nothing. Of these three points we are going to speak, and I beseech you for the love of God that you understand this truth if you can. But should you not understand it, do not worry yourselves because of it, for the truth I want to speak of is of such a kind that only a few good people will understand it.

First we say that he is a poor man who wills nothing. What this means many people do not correctly understand. It is those people who in penitential exercise and external practice, of which they make a great deal, hold fast to their selfish I. The Lord have pity upon such people who know so little of the divine truth. Such people are called holy on account of their external appearance; but internally they are asses, for they do not grasp the actual meaning of divine truth. Indeed, these individuals, too, say that he is a poor man who wills nothing. However, they fancy this to mean that one should never fulfill one's own will in any way, but rather strive to fulfill the ever beloved will of God. These people are right in their way, for they mean well and for that let us commend them. May God in his mercy grant them entry into heaven. But in all divine truth I say that these people are not poor people nor do they resemble poor people. They are highly considered only in the eyes of those who know no better. I, however, say that they are asses, understanding nothing of divine truth. Because of their good intention may they receive the kingdom of heaven. But of that poverty of which we now want to speak, they know nothing.

If someone asks me now what a poor man is who wills nothing, I answer and say: So long as a man has this particular wish to fulfill the ever beloved will of God—if that is still a matter of his will, then this man does not yet possess the poverty of which we want to speak. Indeed, this man then still has a will with which he wants to satisfy God's will, and that is not the right poverty. For a human being to possess true poverty he must be bereft of his created will as he was when he was not yet. Thus I say to you in the name of divine truth: as long as you have the will to fulfill God's will, and as long as you have the desire for eternity and God, you are not poor; for he alone is a poor man who wills nothing and desires nothing.

When I still stood in my first cause, I had no God, I was cause of myself. There I willed nothing and desired nothing, for I was a pure being and a knower of myself in full enjoyment of the truth. There I willed myself and willed nothing else. What I willed, I was, and what I was, that I willed. There I stood, clear of God and of all things. But when by free will I went out and received my created being, then I had a God. Indeed, before there were creatures, God was not yet God, but he was what he was. But when creatures came to be and received their created being, then God was no longer God in himself, rather he was God in the creatures.

Now we say that God, so far as he is God, is not a perfect goal for creatures. Indeed, even the lowliest creature possesses that high a rank within God. And were it that a fly possessed reason and could intelligently seek the eternal abyss of divine being out of which it has come, then we would say that God, with all he is as God, would still be incapable of fulfilling and satisfying this fly. Therefore we beg God to rid us of God so that we may grasp and eternally enjoy the truth where the highest angel and the fly and the mind are equal. There I stood and willed what I was, and was what I willed. So then we say: If man is to be poor in will, he must will and desire as little as he willed and desired when he was not yet. And in this way a man is poor who wills nothing.

Furthermore, a poor man is one who knows nothing. We have said on occasion that man's life should be such that he lives neither for himself, nor for the truth, nor for God. This time, however, we say it differently. We want to go further and say: whoever is to be so poor [as I am describing it] must live so that he not even know himself to live, neither for himself, nor for truth, nor for God. He must be bereft of all knowledge to the point of neither knowing nor recognizing nor perceiving that God lives in him; even more: he should be devoid of all knowledge that lives in him. For, when man still stood in God's eternal being, nothing else lived in him [than that being]. All that was alive, there, was he [that man] himself. Hence we say that man should be so devoid of his own knowledge as he was when he was not yet. He should let God accomplish whatever God wills, and man should stand void.

All that ever came out of God is set to unmixed activity. The activity proper to man, now, is to love and to know. It is a point of controversy, though, in which of these happiness consists primarily. Some masters have said that it lies in knowing, some say it lies in loving, still others say that it lies in knowing and in loving; these are closer to the mark. We say, however, that it lies neither in knowing nor in loving. Rather, there is a oneness in the mind whence flow knowing and loving. It itself does not know and love, as do the forces of the mind. Whoever comes to know this [oneness] knows what happiness consists in. This [oneness] has neither before nor after, and it is in want of nothing additional, for it can neither gain nor lose. That is also why it is deprived of understanding that God is acting within it. Even more: it is itself that identical self which is its own fruition, quite as God. Thus we say that man shall keep himself rid and void so that he neither understand nor know that God works in him. Only so can man possess poverty. The masters say that God is a being, an intelligent being, and that he knows all things. We say, however: God is neither being nor intelligent nor does he know this or that. Thus God is free of all things, and therefore he is all things. Whoever is to be poor in spirit, then, must be poor of all his own understanding so that he understand nothing either of God or of creatures or of himself. That is why it is necessary for man to desire that he become unable to understand or know anything at all of the works of God. That is the way to be poor of one's own understanding.

Thirdly, he is a poor man who has nothing. Many people have said that this is perfection that man possess none of the material things of the earth. And indeed, that is certainly true in one sense: when one holds to it with resolve. But this is not the sense that I mean.

I have said before that he is a poor man who does not even will to fulfill God's will, that is, who lives in such a way that he is devoid both of his own will and of God's will, quite as he was when he was not yet. Of this poverty we say that it is the highest poverty. Secondly, we have said he is a poor man who himself understands nothing of God's activity in him. Whoever stands as devoid of understanding and knowing as God stands void of all things, then that is the purest poverty. Thirdly, the poverty of which we are now going to speak is the strictest: that man have nothing.

Now pay close and serious attention. I have often said, and great masters say so too: Man must be so clear of all things and all works, be they inward or outward, that he can become a proper abode for God, wherein God may operate. But this time we say it differently. If man comes to actually keep himself free of all creatures, of God and of himself, but if it is still the case that God can find in him a site for acting, then we say: So long as that is so, that man is not poor in the strictest poverty. For in his doings God does not strive for a site that man leave him to work in. Rather, only that is poverty of spirit when one keeps oneself so clear of God and of all one's works that if God wants to act in the mind, he [God] is himself the place wherein he wants to act—and this he likes to do. For if God finds man so poor, God operates his own work and man suffers God in him, and God is himself the site of his operation, since God is an agent who acts within himself. Henceforth, in this poverty, man recovers the eternal being that he was, now is, and will eternally remain.

There is a saying of Saint Paul which reads: "But by the grace of God I am what I am" (I Cor. 15:10). My own saying, on the contrary, seems to hold itself above grace and above being and above knowing and above willing and above desiring—how then can Saint Paul's word be true? To this one must answer that Saint Paul's words are true. God's grace was necessarily in him: for the grace of God effected in him the completion of accidental into essential being. When grace finished and had completed its work, Paul remained what he was [that is, what he had been from eternity].

Thus we say that man must be so poor that he is not and has no place wherein God could act. Where man still preserves some place in himself, he preserves distinction. This is why I pray God to rid me of God, for my essential being is above God insofar as we comprehend God as the principle of creatures. Indeed, in God's own being, where God is raised above all being and all distinctions, I was myself, I willed myself, and I knew myself to create this man [that I am]. Therefore I am cause of myself according to my being which is eternal, but not according to my becoming which is temporal. Therefore also I am unborn, and according to my unborn being I can never die. According to my unborn being I have always been, I am now, and shall eternally remain. What I am by my [temporal] birth is to die and be annihilated, for it is mortal; therefore with time it must pass away. In my [eternal] birth all things were born, and I was cause of myself as well as of all things. If I had willed it, neither I nor any things would be. And if I myself were not, God would not be either: That God is God, of this I am a cause. If I were not, God would not be God. There is, however, no need to understand this.

A great master says that his breakthrough is nobler than his emanation, and this is true. When I emanated from God, all things spoke: God is; but this cannot make me happy, for it makes me understand that I am a creature. In the breakthrough, on the other hand, where I stand devoid of my own will and of the will of God and of all his works and of God himself, there I am above all created kind and am neither God nor creature. Rather, I am what I was and what I shall remain now and forever. Then I receive an impulse which shall bring me above all the angels. In this impulse I receive wealth so vast that God cannot be enough for me in all that makes him God, and with all his divine works. For in this breakthrough it is bestowed upon me that I and God are one. There I am what I was, and I neither diminish nor grow, for there I am an immovable cause that moves all things. Now God no longer finds a place in man, for man gains with this poverty what he has been eternally and evermore will remain. Now God is one with the spirit, and that is the strictest poverty one can find.

Those who cannot understand this speech should not trouble

their hearts about it. For, as long as man does not equal this truth, he will not understand this speech. For this is an unhidden truth that has come immediately from the heart of God.

That we may so live as to experience it eternally, so help us God. Amen.[130]

APPENDIX

MEISTER ECKHART AND ZEN BUDDHISM

Daisetz T. Suzuki has drawn some parallels between Zen Buddhism and Meister Eckhart's teaching which, in my opinion, require a few clarifications. The ideas expounded in Eckhart's sermons, he says, closely approach Buddhist thought, "so closely indeed, that one could stamp them almost definitely as coming out of Buddhist speculations." I can judge only what Suzuki says of Eckhart. The following remarks refer to specific statements in his book *Mysticism: Christian and Buddhist.* [1]

1. *Time.* The first parallel, according to Suzuki, lies in a certain understanding of time to which both Eckhart and Zen Buddhism testify. The historicity of the facts related in the Bible, creation and redemption, do not count for Eckhart. The birth of the Word in the ground of the mind must accomplish itself in an instant, in "the eternal now." [2] The same holds true in Zen, Suzuki says. Awakening reduces duration to instantaneity. Suzuki concludes from these facts that Eckhart's "God is not at all like the God conceived by most Christians." One would have to reply to Suzuki that the doctrine of the atemporal birth of the Word in the ground of the mind, in Eckhart, is rooted directly in the catechesis of the Fathers of the Church. [3]

2. *Is-ness.* Suzuki translates Eckhart's *isticheit* quite correctly as "is-ness": "Eckhart's experiences are deeply, basically, abundantly rooted in God as Being which is at once being and not-being: he sees in the 'meanest' thing among God's creatures all the glories of his is-ness (*isticheit*). The Buddhist enlightenment is nothing more than this experience of is-ness or suchness (*tathatā*), which in itself has all the possible values (*guna*) we humans can conceive." [4] It has been shown above that *isticheit*, the intermediary between *iht* and *wesene*, properly designates the non-being of the Godhead. [5] One may doubt here the resemblance suggested by Suzuki. The Buddhist "is-ness" seems to refer to a thing's fact of being; if enlightenment discovers that is-ness is in truth nothingness, then what is negated is properly the common fact of being of things. Rinzai Buddhism, as Suzuki explains throughout his writings,

attempts indeed to think pure nothingness. But this is not so in Eckhart who, in this case, uses the language of the Neoplatonists, particularly of Pseudo-Dionysius: God's nothingness is his "super-being," ὑπέρ-όν. As Eckhart's vocabulary and thinking remain thoroughly theocentric, there seems to be a pure equivocity of nothingness as between Suzuki and Eckhart. The Godhead's *isticheit* is a negation of all quiddities; it says that God, rather than non-being, is at the heart of all things. The question is exactly what Suzuki calls "all sorts of mythological paraphernalia" in the Christian tradition. If Eckhart's theocentrism[6] is to fall into this class, if it is one "unnecessary historical appendix" among many others,[7] then we disagree. The *isticheit* of the Godhead and the is-ness of a thing then refer to two opposite experiences in Meister Eckhart and Suzuki: in the former, to God, and in the latter, to "our ordinary state of the mind." On this point at least I have difficulty following Suzuki's statement: "The Christian experiences are not after all different from those of the Buddhist. Terminology is all that divides us."[8]

3. *Pantheism.* Both Meister Eckhart and Mahayana Buddhism, Suzuki writes, have been unjustly accused of pantheism. We have explained that Eckhart's statements of identity between man and God must be read as referring to a process, "birth" or "breakthrough," rather than to a unicity of substance. From this point of view, it would be more appropriate to speak of panentheism. As to the Zen experience, we are told that it culminates in the overcoming of all dualisms by the inner man, quite as in Eckhart: "The difference between God and Godhead is that between heaven and earth and yet Godhead cannot be himself without going out of himself, that is, he is he because he is not he. This 'contradiction' is comprehended only by the inner man, and not by the outer man."[9] This is an appropriate description of the dialectical method followed by Meister Eckhart. The kinship between Eastern and Western mysticism would thus appear in a definite form of thought. It is striking indeed that other medieval mystics, such as Scotus Erigena and Nicholas of Cusa (to say nothing of Hegel), quite naturally argue in sharp dialectical oppositions. If the vitality of Zen consists in the overcoming of such antitheses as transcendence and immanence, theism and atheism, etc., and if the "ignorant misinterpreters" mentioned by Suzuki have recourse to these false oppositions to denounce Zen Buddhism as a form of pantheism, then at least Meister Eckhart's (as well as many others') type of thinking was "singularly Mahayanistic."[10] I agree with Suzuki

that the entire debate about pantheism is actually one about forms of thought.[11] Suzuki's point would thus be that a pantheistic and a dialectical form of thought are mutually exclusive. This point seems well taken.

4. *Releasement and Emptiness.* Only a perfectly released person, Eckhart says, comprehends, "seizes," God. The most apparent determination of releasement is negative: one has to be devoid of all *eigenschaft*, of one's own and of one's belongings, in order to be God's own. Only a human being that is "void," *ledig,* of individuality can be full of God. Does this concept resemble the Zen concept of emptiness? Suzuki writes: "While Buddhist emphasis is on the emptiness of all 'composite things' (*skandha*) and is therefore metaphysical, Eckhart here insists on the psychological significance of 'pure nothingness' so that God can take hold of the soul without any resistance on the part of the individual."[12] What is at stake, if my reading is correct, is something quite similar to what was mentioned with regard to the notion of "is-ness," namely Eckhart's theocentrism. The Buddhist "emptiness" seems to concern man's relation to things; in Soto Zen, riddance of representations is in fact the explicit purpose of the seated meditation. This is assuredly one side of releasement, its voluntary or ascetic side, which we have called detachment. But at the end of the road opened by detachment the mind espouses the very movement of divine "dehiscence." It does what the Godhead does: it lets all things be. Not only must God also abandon all of his own—names and attributes—if he is to reach into the ground of the mind (this is already a step beyond the recognition of the emptiness of all composite things), but God's essential being, releasement, becomes the being of a released man. The disturbing power of Eckhart's theory of releasement consists precisely in the transformation of a psychological or moral concept into an ontological one. Man's way of being turns into God's way of being. The mind can achieve total vacuity of attachment only because God follows the mind on this road and leads it back into the divine "desert." The double annihilation of human and divine properties constitutes one and the same conquest of releasement, as being's essential way to be. Whether or not such a widening of the meaning of releasement is most appropriately labeled as metaphysical, to interpret releasement merely as a human attitude would be a pure and simple misinterpretation of both the letter and the spirit of Eckhart's sermons. The attitude of releasement is the condition for the understanding of being as releasement.

5. *Tao and Godhead.* Literally *Tao* means "way" or "road" or "passage." The Taoists use it in the sense of "truth," "ultimate reality," "logos." Suzuki comments on a pasage from *The Way and Its Power* in which Lao-tzu describes his *Tao Te Ching* as follows: "The Way is like an empty vessel. . . . It looks as if it were prior to God. . . . No name is to be given. It returns to nothingness. It is called formless form, shapeless shape. . . ." Suzuki then cites several phrases from Eckhart which all refer to the Godhead beyond God.[13] But if Chinese Taoism and medieval speculative mysticism speak of the same distinction between God and the emptiness that is prior to him, then Zen Buddhism appears as still more radical in its negations than either of these religious doctrines. According to Suzuki's presentation of it, Japanese Zen refuses categorically to speak of God. If that is so, then what is said of Lao-tzu cannot be said of Zen, namely that "Lao-tzu is expressing in his classical Chinese way what the medieval Dominican preacher would talk about in his German vernacular." Elsewhere Suzuki quite rightly distinguishes Zen Buddhism from all religions: "As I conceive it, Zen is the ultimate fact of all philosophy and religion. . . . What makes all these religions and philosophies vital and inspiring is due to the presence in them of what I may designate as the Zen element."[14] This Zen element, in itself neither religious nor philosophical, would thus be found not in the content (Godhead, Tao) which either Eckhart or Lao-tzu teach, but in the very fact of their teaching and preaching. The sermons would have an effect similar to the strokes given with the master's staff, or to the koans. Such a way of reading Eckhart makes any effort of conceptual clarification, and indeed philosophy, superfluous. Needless to say, in this perspective the intimate link that Eckhart sees between existence and reason ("speculative mysticism") is broken.

6. *Learned Ignorance.* Zen masters, Suzuki says, are all unknowing knowers or knowing unknowers. The resemblance to Western medieval mysticism on this point is beyond dispute. The "learned ignorance," an expression of Nicholas of Cusa which has its roots in Eckhart, is the mode of knowledge that belongs to whoever has unlearned to objectify God in extrinsic relations. As suggested above, the dialectic that pushes both knowledge and ignorance to their extremes probably constitutes one of the unquestionable similarities between Eckhart and Zen. It should be understood, though, that this similarity is purely formal. *Docta ignorantia* is far from always meaning the same thing even among the Western authors who use this, or a comparable, expression. The

refusal to find a name for the divine which can only be approached by simultaneous negations and affirmations does indeed constitute a "family" among spiritual authors. But if different authors refuse to give a name to the divine, that does not mean that they think the ineffable in the same way. This is so even among Western authors: the ineffable in Eckhart is not the same as in Plotinus, which again differs from that in Augustine, which in turn must be distinguished from that in Cusanus. . . . We are certainly not to suppose that because all Zen masters are unknowing knowers and knowing unknowers the ineffable which they approach dialectically is also the ineffable Meister Eckhart speaks of in his sermons.

7. *Birth and Nirvana.* The reciprocity between God and man has been called a reciprocity of birth: God begets me as his only Son, and I in turn beget the only Son in Him. Likewise, Suzuki says, a Japanese painter "becomes the plant itself" that he paints. "This identification enables the painter to feel the pulsation of one and the same life animating both him and the object." The way this identification between the artist and his object is stated here is indeed strikingly similar to many of Eckhart's formulations of identity. "How does the painter get into the spirit of the plant?" Suzuki asks. "How can a human being turn himself into a plant? Inasmuch as he aspires to paint a plant or an animal, there must be in him something which corresponds to it in one way or another. If so, he ought to be able to become the object he desires to paint."[15]

Is this to say that the painter is "born" again as the plant the way a perfectly released man, according to Meister Eckhart, is born again as the Son of God? Like Meister Eckhart, Suzuki considers that man here "ceases to be the one outside that object" and that he "transforms himself into that object itself." The two terms, subject and object, are abolished by a process of active identification. In other words, the true relation to things, for instance a hibiscus, abolishes relations of exteriority. If it is true that "Oriental art consists in depicting spirit and not form," then the artist catches in the hibiscus "a zero full of infinite possibilities, an emptiness of inexhaustible contents." The true relation to things thus reaches nothingness, nirvana. Some Japanese paintings represent simply a big black circle: the painter's new birth has been a birth into the originary fullness of things which "holds in it infinite rays of light and swallows all the multiplicities there are in this world."[16]

It seems to me that the resemblance between Zen and Eckhart can be defended here on two conditions. The first is that nirvana must be understood not as absence or death, but as a radical affirmation beyond all oppositions. Certain formulations in Suzuki seem to assign to nirvana the role of a transcendental condition of possibility for things to appear: nirvana "is that which makes all things possible." In the *Ten Oxherding Pictures*,[17] the picture that represents nothing corresponds to the seminal fullness in the Godhead. The second condition is that one has to overcome the definition of nirvana as "a psychological state realized through enlightenment."[18] It is totally insufficient to interpret the birth of the Word in us, according to Eckhart, as a psychological state. If these two conditions are met, the parallel is probably viable; it would illustrate what we have called the horizontality of Eckhart's mysticism: that it is thoroughly a matter of releasement before things.

8. *The spark and the satori.* Eckhart's vocabulary concerning the ground of the mind is rich: the little castle in the mind, spark, guardian, light, little point. Suzuki writes: "A 'little point' left by God corresponds to what Zen Buddhists would call *satori*. . . . This 'little point' is full of significance, and I am sure Eckhart had a *satori.*" He defines *satori* as the "opening of a new eye," as "an intuitive looking into the nature of things in contradistinction to the analytical or logical understanding of it."[19] Suzuki understands Eckhart correctly when he interprets the ground or "little point" in the mind as the demarcation between the uncreatable zone in man and everything created. Still, these formulations must not remain confined to their gnoseological context: they indicate less a faculty of knowledge than man's ontological identity. The metaphors of the eye and of looking are thus misleading. In some texts Suzuki does suggest that *satori* consists in "looking into our own nature." This is very convincing, as the spark is not only that which sees in us, but also that which is seen. The following line could have come directly from Eckhart's sermon "Jesus Entered": "Let us once see into our own original nature and we have the truth, even when we are quite illiterate, not knowing a word."[20]

Notes

The following abbreviations are used in the notes:

Bull   Bull *In Agro Dominico* of March 27, 1329, in *Archiv für Literatur-und Kirchengeschichte des Mittelalters,* ed. Heinrich Denifle and Franz Ehrle, vol. II, Berlin, 1886, and in Heinrich Denzinger and Adolf Schönmetzer, *Enchiridion Symbolorum, Definitionum et Declarationum de rebus fidei et morum,* Freiburg, 1963, nos. 950 to 980, pp. 290–295, quoted as Denzinger-Schönmetzer.

DW   Meister Eckhart, *Die deutschen Werke,* ed. for the Deutsche Forschungs-gemeinschaft by Joseph Quint, volumes I, II, III, and V, Stuttgart 1958–1976, vol. IV in progress.

Lexer   Matthias Lexer, *Mittelhochdeutsches Taschenwörterbuch,* Stuttgart, 32nd ed., 1966.

LW   Meister Eckhart, *Die lateinischen Werke,* ed. for the Deutsche For-schungsgemeinschaft by E. Benz, K. Christ, B. Decker, H. Fischer, B. Geyer, J. Koch, E. Seeberg, K. Weiss, A. Zimmermann, volumes I to V, Stuttgart 1938 to 1975, in progress.

Pelster   Franz Pelster, "Ein Gutachten aus dem Eckehart-Prozess in Avi-gnon," in *Aus der Geisteswelt des Mittelalters, Festgabe Martin Grabmann,* Mün-ster, 1935, pp. 1099–1124.

Pf   Franz Pfeiffer, *Deutsche Mystiker des vierzehnten Jahrhunderts,* 2 vol.; vol. 2, *Meister Eckhart, Predigten und Traktate,* Leipzig, 1857, and Aalen, 1962.

PG   J. P. Migne, ed., *Patrologiae cursus completus. Patrologia Graeca,* 161 vol., Paris 1857–1866 (quoted by volume and column).

PL   J. P. Migne, ed., *Patrologiae cursus completus. Patrologia Latina,* 221 vol., Paris 1844–1855 (quoted by volume and column).

Quint   *Meister Eckhart, Deutsche Predigten und Traktate,* ed. and transl. into modern German by Joseph Quint, Munich, 1955.

RS   Rechtfertigungsschrift, Eckhart's 'Defense,' edited by Théry.

Théry   Gabriel Théry, "Editions critique des pièces relatives au procès d'Eckhart contenues dans le manuscrit 33 b de la bibliothèque de Soest," in *Archives d'histoire doctrinale et littéraire du Moyen Age,"* vol. I, 1926–27, pp. 129–272.

INTRODUCTION

1. See the corresponding indications in the bibliography at the end of this book and below, ch. 3, n. 39.

2. There are several translations of Eckhart's German sermons into English. Some of them, unfortunately, present serious handicaps. C. de B. Evans, *Meister*

Eckhart by Franz Pfeiffer, 2 vols., London, 1931, is based on the insufficient
German text edition arranged by Pfeiffer in 1857. A comparison with the critical
edition, begun in Germany in 1936, shows that Pfeiffer's edition is no longer
usable. Evans gives a complete, but archaizing and therefore difficult, translation
of Pfeiffer's text. Raymond B. Blakney, *Meister Eckhart, A Modern Translation*,
New York, 1941, presents a more critical attitude towards Pfeiffer's text. However, Blakney's desire to produce a "modern" translation has all too often
carried him away both from the letter and from the meaning of the text. James
M. Clark, *Meister Eckhart, An Introduction to the Study of His Works with an
Anthology of His Sermons*, Edinburgh, 1957, and James M. Clark and John V.
Skinner, *Meister Eckhart, Selected Treatises and Sermons Translated from Latin and
German with an Introduction and Notes*, London, 1958, are the two most recommendable translations. Clark points out the faulty character of Pfeiffer's text,
and he considers that Blakney's translation does not represent any real advance.
His own version is based on the critical German edition. But these two volumes
give only a relatively small selection from Eckhart's German sermons. DW I, II,
and III together contain 86 sermons, and one more volume is announced.

3. See for instance the text from St. Augustine quoted below, ch. 2, n. 14. See
also Heidegger's remarks on this matter, below, ch. 3, n. 28.

4. E.g., Thomas Aquinas, *Summa Theologiae*, Part I, question 75, art. 2, the
phrase "animam humanam, que dicitur intellectus vel mens," "the human soul
which is called intellect or mind." In his translation of *Master Eckhart, Parisian
Questions and Prologues*, Toronto, 1974, Armand Maurer is therefore correct in
translating *anima*, in this Latin treatise of Eckhart's, as "mind," cf. the text
quoted below, ch. 3, n. 5.

CHAPTER 1

1. The Middle High German text has been published in DW I, pp. 21–45. M.
Pahnke, "Meister Eckhart's Predigt über Lukas 10, 38" in: *Nachrichten der
Akademie der Wissenschaften in Göttingen*, I, #9, Göttingen, 1951, pp. 169–206,
has contested the homogeneity of the text published in DW; he sees in it a
compilation of at least two sermons, a "Binnenpredigt" and a "Rahmenpredigt."

2. Albert the Great, whose courses of theology Eckhart had taken at Cologne,
gives for the same passage of the Gospel of Luke an equally allegorical interpretation of the name of Martha, although in another sense: "She is called 'Martha'
because 'Martha' means 'provoking' or 'inciting'; her eagerness provokes indeed
many virtues, and by her heroic virtue she incites indeed her eagerness." Translated from *Opera omnia* (ed. Borgnet), vol. 23, p. 76.

3. Prologue of the *Liber parabolarum Genesis* (LW I, p. 447,4–9). Konrad Weiss,
"Meister Eckharts biblische Hermeneutik" in *La Mystique rhénane*, Paris, 1963,
p. 95, sees here a connection with Bede the Venerable: Beda, *In Esdram . . .
allegorica expositio*, PL, vol. 91, col. 308 B. Henri de Lubac, *Exégèse médiévale*, vol.
4, Paris, 1964, p. 164, calls the domain of exegesis in which people so proceed
"threshing floors of symbolism." Also p. 489: "It can be estimated that it entered

into the mission of Eckhart to recall to Christian consciences some great inexhaustible texts about God, about His uncreated Word. . . . It cannot be asked of each generation, nor *a fortiori* of each individual, to put in highlights at the same time all the aspects of a complex and fertile tradition."

4. Saint Augustine, *Holy Virginity* (John McQuade, transl. in: "The Fathers of the Church," vol. 27, New York, 1955, pp. 143–212, PL, vol. 40, col. 397–428), has doubtless served as a source for this spiritual comprehension of virginity.

5. *Meno* 81b, transl. B. Jowett, New York, 1949, p. 37.

6. *Republic* 517c.

7. Thomas Aquinas, *Commentary on Aristotle's De Anima*, ch. III, lecture 7, transl. K. Foster et al., New Haven, 1951, pp. 402–410. Cf. Bernhard Welte, "Meister Eckhart als Aristoteliker," in: *Auf der Spur des Ewigen*, Freiburg, 1965, pp. 197–210. To this article we owe the parallel with Aristotle. Welte writes: "[in this doctrine of the receptive intellect] we see the Aristotelian model for the Eckhartian exhortation and doctrine of detachment, of the void, of the emptiness of the spirit" (p. 201).

8. 1 Cor. 13:1.

9. Plotinus, *The Enneads* IV, 8,1; transl. Stephen McKenna, 4th ed., rev. B. S. Page, New York, 1969, p. 357.

10. Epictetus, *Enchiridion* #16. In: *The Work of Epictetus,* transl. E. Carter and T. W. Higginson, Boston, 1865, p. 381.

11. Aristotle, *De Anima*, book I, ch. 2; 404 b 17; transl. R. D. Hicks, Amsterdam, 1965, p. 15. According to a quotation in Proclus, *In Timaeum,* ch. II, p. 298,8–10, this axiom would go back at least to Empedocles (Diehls, 31 B 109); cf. also Proclus, *Théologie Platonicienne,* ed. Saffrey-Westerink, Paris, 1968, p. 15, note 3. This axiom is at the origin of Eckhart's identification between God's being and his knowledge. C. F. Kelley, *Meister Eckhart on Divine Knowledge,* New Haven, forthcoming, correctly presents this identification as one of the central purposes in Eckhart's teaching. From this axiom Kelley derives the notion of principial knowledge, which he defines as "the consideration of all things and all manifestation from *within* the Godhead." Unfortunately Kelley's book suffers not only from loose translations and apologetic speculations but also from some ignorance of the tradition in which Eckhart stands: on the identification of *esse* and *intelligere* in God, Eckhart literally repeats traditional Scholastic doctrine; cf. below, ch. 3, n. 35.

12. Thomas Aquinas, *Commentary on Aristotle's De Anima*, book I, ch. 2, lecture 4, n. 43; op. cit., p. 71.

13. Aristotle, *On the Heavens,* 310 b 2; transl. W. K. C. Guthrie, Cambridge, Mass., and London, 1960, p. 345: "like moves the like."

14. Plotinus, *The Enneads* VI, 9,11; op. cit., p. 625.

15. Thomas Aquinas, *Summa Theologiae,* Part Ia IIae, questions 1–5, transl. Blackfriars, New York and London, 1969, vol. 16.

16. Aristotle, *De Anima*, book III, ch. 5; 430 a 18; op. cit., p. 135.

17. Thomas Aquinas, *Commentary on Aristotle's De Anima*, book III, ch. 5, lecture 10, n. 739; op. cit., p. 430: "It is an active immaterial force able to

assimilate other things to itself, i.e., to immaterialize them; in this way it makes the potentially intelligible actually so."

18. Saint Augustine, *The Trinity,* book XV, ch. XI, 20; in: *Basic Writings of Saint Augustine,* transl. W. J. Oates, New York, 1948, vol. 2, pp. 847–848. Cf. ch. XIII, 22: "As our knowledge is unlike that knowledge of God, so is our word, also, which is born from our knowledge, unlike the Word of God which is born from the essence of the Father." Ibid., p. 852. Also ch. XVI, 26: "Wherefore, since we have found now in this enigma so great an unlikeness to God and the Word of God, wherein yet there was found before some likeness . . .," ibid., p. 856.

19. When Eckhart had to defend himself about his theory of the simultaneous production of the Word, he invoked a passage from book XV of Saint Augustine's *The Trinity*: "The just man is also called the begetter of the eternal Word; Augustine says so, because between the knower and the known a word is produced, as well as between the lover and the beloved," translated from Pelster, p. 1120. The quotation is very vague; Pelster gives a reference (*The Trinity,* book XV, ch. XI, 20), but no text is found there which literally corresponds to it. The objectors make the following remark: "His reference to Augustine is not appropriate, because although a word is produced from the knower and the known, it is still heretical to say that a creature be the begetter of the divine Word," Pelster, p. 1121.

20. John 15:1–8.

21. Richard of Saint Victor writes in *Of the Four Degrees of Violence in Love*: "Man's spirit is ravished in the abyss of the divine light so that the human mind forgets all things in this ecstasis (*status exterior*), hardly knows itself any more and goes entirely over into its God," translated from PL, vol. 196, col. 1220 D. Or again, in the *Mystical Annotations on the Psalms*: "The mind of the contemplator, which rises above itself, becomes totally settled among heavenly things; it hardly knows itself and forgets whatever is beneath it; . . . it looks at nothing except heaven," translated from psalm 28, PL, vol. 196, col. 308 D. Meister Eckhart does not teach such a mysticism of contemplation.

22. Aristotle, *De Anima,* book III, ch. 4; 430 a 3; op. cit., p. 135. Cf. this text in Aristotle's *Metaphysics,* book XII, ch. 9; 1075 a 3–5: "Wherever things are immaterial the mind and its object are not different, so that they are the same; and knowing is one with what is known." Transl. R. Hope, New York, 1952, p. 266.

23. Thomas Aquinas, *Commentary on Aristotle's De Anima,* book III, ch. 4, lecture 9, n. 724; op. cit., p. 423.

24. Thomas Aquinas stresses, indeed, that this actual unity is verified in the entire field of knowledge: "This saying of the Philosopher is universally true in every kind of intellect." *Summa Theologiae,* Part I, question 87, art. 1, ad 3; op. cit., 1922, vol. IV, p. 219. The *verbum Philosophi* being precisely this: "That what knows and what is known are identical." However, Thomas Aquinas does not even consider drawing from this law, universal though it may be called, the ultimate consequences with regard to the knowledge of God. For that, time was ripe only with Meister Eckhart.

25. *Letter to Diognetes,* XI, 3–5; Sources chrétiennes, vol. 33, Paris, 1962, p. 80.

26. *The Pedagogue,* III, 1; PG, vol. 8, col. 556 C.

27. *Homily on Jeremiah,* 9,4; PG 13, col. 357.

28. *Symposion* VIII, 9 GCS, p. 91,11,14–21.

29. *Commentary on the Song of Songs* I, GCS VIII, p. 91, 1,5: the desire of the soul is "to be united and to associate with the Word of God and to penetrate into the mysteries of his Wisdom and of his Knowledge as in the nuptial chamber of the heavenly Spouse."

30. *Fragment on the First Letter to the Corinthians,* LXXII.

31. *Quaestiones ad Thalassium,* question 22; PG 90, col. 320 B.

32. The expression returns often: ibid., question 56; PG 90, col. 584 C; question 18, col. 306 D.

33. Ibid., question 47, col. 424 C.

34. *Expositio Orationis Dominicae,* PG 90, col. 889 BC.

35. *Ambiguorum Liber,* PG 91, col. 1081 D.

36. This schema has been proposed by Hugo Rahner, "Die Gottesgeburt. Die Lehre der Kirchenväter von der Geburt Christi aus dem Herzen der Kirche und der Gläubigen," in: *Symbole der Kirche,* Salzburg, 1964, pp. 11 to 18; cf. esp. pp. 40f.

37. It is true that, much closer to him, Joachim of Fiore also spoke of the spiritual Son of God who was reborn each day (sanctus spiritus . . . de quo et renascuntur quotidie qui sint filii dei), *Introduction to the Apocalypse,* c. 5.

38. RS, #11, art. 13 (Théry, p. 204).

39. *Apex mentis:* Bonaventure, *The Mind's Intinerary to God,* I. Albert the Great says *pars superior animae* (in 1 Sent., ed. Borgnet XXV, 121). Thomas, *altissimus animae* (*De Veritate,* 10,1).

40. Saint Augustine, *The Trinity,* book XV, ch. VII, 11: "If we think of the soul by itself, the mind is somewhat belonging to the soul, as though its head, or eye, or countenance," in: *Basic Writings of Saint Augustine,* op. cit., vol. 2, p. 839.

41. This manner of characterizing the intellect is ancient; cf., e.g., *Liber de Causis*: Anima . . . est in horizonte aeternitatis inferius et supra tempus; ed. Bardenhewer, Freiburg, 1882, p. 165, 1,8f. In one of his Latin sermons, Eckhart says: "Notice how, according to Augustine, there is something within us, that is to say within the mind, into which nothing bodily or body-like may enter and which is dedicated solely to God." Translated from Latin sermon XLVII, n. 482.

42. RS, #I, 4, art. 5 (Théry, p. 179).

43. "The Father begets his Son in me, and thus I am this selfsame Son and not another," RS, #I, 4, art. 1 A (Théry, p. 176). "The Father begets his Son in the mind in the same way he begets him in eternity, and not otherwise," RS, #II, art. 38 (Théry, p. 241). "The Father begets his Son unceasingly. I say more: He begets me as his Son and as the same Son. Whatever God makes, that is one; therefore he begets me as his very own Son with no difference," RS, #II, art. 39 (Théry, p. 242). "Man must live thus that he be One in the firstborn Son, and that he be that firstborn Son himself. There is no distinction between that

firstborn Son and the mind," RS, #II, art. 59 (Théry, p. 266). These articles have to be compared to the numbers 20 to 22 of the Bull of condemnation; cf. Denzinger-Schönmetzer nos. 970 to 972.

44. M. H. Laurent, "Autour du procès de Maître Eckhart" in *Divus Thomas*, Piacenza, XXXIX (1936), p. 345. The reference *doctores meas collegas* no doubt points to Albert the Great and Thomas Aquinas: for this latter, cf.: *Summa Theologiae*, Part I, question 54, art. 1 and 2; question 79, art. 1.

45. RS, #III, prologue (Théry, p. 186).

46. This is a pantheistic form of thought, a decadent but faithful offshoot of the "indicative" thought or thought of substances. A proposition which would say "the mind = God," by the simple juxtaposition of two substantives, would push to the extreme and thus would manifest the malaise of this type of thought desirous of pronouncing itself about the "real." Pantheism is found at the antipodes of the form of imperative thought, which is wandering, or thought of process; consequently, at the antipodes of the thought of Meister Eckhart. Rather than in the "unique substance" of Spinoza, we find a resurgence of Meister Eckhart in the understanding of being as event, or its "verbal" understanding in Heidegger. For Eckhart's alleged pantheism, cf. below, ch. 2, n. 96, and ch. 3, "Identity and Analogy."

47. "Vel certa malitia, vel crassa ignorantia," RS, #III, art. 3 (Théry, p. 196); "ruditas et brevitas intellectus illorum," RS, #IV (Théry, p. 205); "brevitas et imbecillitas intellectus eorum," RS, art. 43 D (Théry, p. 248).

48. Beginning of the Bull, Denifle, p. 636.

49. Denifle, p. 639; Denzinger-Schönmetzer no. 977.

50. The minutes of the trial note: "He rejects this article because, as he says, it is stupid (*stultum*) to hold that the mind is patched up (*peciata*) with created and uncreated elements." This, however, does not convince the Curia: "What he negates is nevertheless found in many quotations, and it is proved that he has said what this article contains. Therefore we declare this article to be heretical according to its letter (*ut sonat*) because it would entail that the mind be God with some part of itself, since there is nothing uncreated but God." Pelster, p. 1111 s. The paraphrase "ut sonat, hereticum reputamus," is repeated in the Bull, which condemns twenty-eight propositions, declaring eleven of them rash, that is, only "suspect of heresy," not directly heretical. Of these articles that receive the benefit of mitigating circumstances, the pope writes that one can yield a catholic sense from them on the condition that one holds them "with correct explanations and complements." But the article on the divine nature of the intellect does not fall under this category; it is declared incompatible with Christian truth. Cf. Denifle, p. 639. The Bull, given at Avignon in 1329, after the death of Meister Eckhart, mentions also at the end a retraction by him with regard to all that in his oral or written teaching could appear erroneous: "The same Eckhart has at the end of his life confessed the catholic faith, and he has retracted the twenty-six articles stated above—which however he has acknowledged to have taught—as well as many others contained, insofar as they yield such a meaning (i.e., heretical). He has submitted himself as well as all his writings and sayings to our and the Apostolic See's authority." Denifle, p. 640.

51. Bernhard Welte, "La métaphysique de saint Thomas d'Aquin et la pensée de l'histoire de l'être chez Heidegger," in *Revue des sciences philosophiques et théologiques*, 50 (1966), p. 164. Joachim Kopper, *Die Metaphysik Meister Eckharts*, Saarbrücken, 1955, has seen, too, that around Meister Eckhart two forms of thought are given up to combat; his thesis, however, inspired by Kant, according to which Eckhart would prefigure transcendental criticism (cf. esp. pp. 26–28), has not convinced us. C. F. Kelley, op. cit., who reads Eckhart quite correctly in the light of the intellect's relation to God, does not draw, however, the decisive consequence from his discovery: the incompatibility between a metaphysics of substance and Eckhart's understanding of being as 'birth,' 'operation,' 'becoming,' as 'intelligence' in a process. Kelley's intention, on the contrary, is "pure metaphysics" "from the standpoint of unrestricted knowledge."

52. Aristotle, *Physics*, book IV, quoted by Thomas Aquinas, *Quaestiones Quodlibetales*, II, 3, 5.

53. "It is apparent that, since time possesses no continuity except from movement, such a time (namely that of a spritual being) is devoid of continuity, and that it is different from the time of physical things." Indeed, "discontinuous and continuous beings cannot be submitted to the same measure," ibid., the Response.

54. *Commentary on the Gospel of Saint John*, #192, LW III, p. 161.

55. Aristotle, *De Anima*, book III, ch. 4; 429 a 27; op. cit., p. 131.

56. When Plato treats of "ideas" in an epistemological context, he defines them as the immutable or exemplary reasons, connatural to the human spirit and source of all knowledge of the movable. They are the archetypes latent in the spirit, whose revival makes known the truth of things. This "connaturality" is developed for example in the famous allegory of the Cave: *Republic*, VII, 514 a ss; cf. et.: *Timeus* 51, b-e; *Phaedon* 100, c.

57. Thomas Aquinas, *Summa Theologiae*, Part I, question 15, art. 1: "Whether Ideas exist"; op. cit., 1964, vol. 4, p. 63.

58. Article 13 of the Bull condemns as heretical the following proposition: "All that belongs to the divine nature belongs also totally to a just and divine human being; therefore such a man does whatever God does, and together with God he has created heaven and earth. Also he is the begetter of the eternal Word, and God can do nothing without such a man." Denzinger-Schönmetzer n. 963. As such, this formulation is not found anywhere in the works of Meister Eckhart.

59. Proclus, *The Elements of Theology*, ed. E. R. Dodds, Oxford, 1963; the expressions pointed out are found in propositions 113–117, Dodds, pp. 101–113.

60. Ibid., prop. 24; Dodds, p. 29.

61. Cf. this dialogue in Martin Heidegger, *Gelassenheit*, Pfullingen, 1959, p. 36: "Teacher: . . . the nature of releasement is still hidden. Scholar: Especially so because even releasement can still be thought of as within the domain of will, as it is the case with old masters of thought such as Meister Eckhart. Teacher: From whom, all the same, much can be learned." Transl. J. M. Anderson and E. H. Freund, *Discourse on Thinking*, New York, 1966, pp. 61f.

62. The Greek and Latin authors knew several equivalent expressions: in the *Capita centum de perfectione spirituali* of Diadochus of Photice (ed. Des Places,

Sources chrétiennes, vol. 5 bis, Paris, 1955, p. 77), we read expressions like βάθος τῆς ψυχῆς, "abyss of the soul," βάθος τῆς καρδίας, "abyss of the heart," βάθος τοῦ νοῦ, "abyss of the mind." Proclus, *Platonic Theology,* ed. Saffrey-Westerink, Paris, 1968, p. 11, likewise speaks of τὰ τῆς ψυχῆς βάθα and indicates in this regard the Chaldean oracles from which he had drawn this expression; the editors indicate another source: Damascus, *In Phil.,* #180, 4 (Ibid., p. 133, note 4). Pseudo-Dionysius, *The Divine Names,* knew the expression πυθμὴν παντοκρατικός, the "basis" which governs all things (ch. IV, PG 3, col. 700 B), but also βάθος τῆς σοφίας (ibid., col. 872b); transl. C. E. Rolt, New York, 1920, pp. 103, 108. Saint Augustine, finally, often speaks of *abyssus:* "Quid profundius hac abysso?" he asks in reference to the heart of man (*Enarr.* in Ps. 103, sermon II, no. 6, Corp. Christ., PL vol. 40, col. 1494, l. 11).

63. *Summa Theologiae,* Part I, questions 77–83: Thomas here enumerates the "powers of the soul," the intellect, including the memory, understanding, synderesis, conscience, then the appetites, choice, and free will, op. cit., 1970, vol. 11, pp. 119–124.

64. *Dionysiaca. Recueil donnant l'ensemble des traductions latines des ouvrages attribués à Denys de l'Aréopage,* vol. II, Bruges, 1950, p. 1479. The Greek word is σπινθήρ. Richard of Saint Victor comments on the "mystical theology" of Dionysius by establishing a hierarchy in the powers of the soul: the lowest, according to him, is the imagination; then follow the *ratio* and the *intellectus,* and then the *principalis affectio,* "and this is the spark of synderesis which alone can be united with the Holy Spirit," quoted in E. von Ivanka, "Apex mentis," in *Zeitschrift für katholische Theologie,* 1950, p. 169.

65. Seneca, *On Leisure,* ch. V, 5: "Whether this is true, by which it appears most clearly that men are of divine spirit, that a part, or rather sparks of holy fire, have reached the earth and originate in some foreign place?" The expression πῦρ τεχνικόν is found in Diogenes Laertius.

66. From [13] and [15] the most alarming passages were extracted and, translated into Latin, submitted to the commission of the Inquisition, first at Cologne (RS, I, 4, art. 13, Théry, p. 183), then in Avignon (RS, II, art. 51, Théry, p. 253).

67. Proclus, "De Providentia et Fato," transl. G. de Moerbecke, ed. Cousin. *Opera inedita,* Paris, 1864, col. 146–195; *unum animae* (col. 171,33), *super intelligens* (col. 172,2), *flos intellectus* (col. 172,15). The Greek terms corresponding to these expressions are in the Commentary of Proclus on Plato's "Alcibiades," ἐν τῆς ψυχῆς, ὑπὲρ νοῦν, ἄνθος τοῦ νοῦ; H. Ebeling, *Meister Eckharts Mystik,* Freiburg, 1960, pp. 270–276.

68. *Cognitio super intellectum,* Cousin, op. cit., col. 171,31.

69. Νοῦς, ἐπιστήμη, ἐν ψυχῆς; Moerbecke translates *scientia, intellectus, uniale,* Cousin, op. cit., col. 170,36.

70. Proclus, *Platonic Theology,* I, 3; ed. Saffrey, Paris, 1968, p. 15.

71. RS, #II, art. 51, Solution; Théry, p. 28. The sentence of Paul, "By the grace of God I am what I am" is taken from 1 Cor. 15:10.

72. "Der alte Lebe- und Lesemeister Eckehardt," Martin Heidegger, *Der Feldweg,* Frankfurt, 1962, p. 4. This aphorism is found in a proverb attributed to

Meister Eckhart himself, Pf. 599,19. In his dissertation for habilitation Heidegger had already stated that medieval mysticism reveals the living basis of the speculative problems in Scholasticism: "In the medieval world-view, scholasticism and mysticism belong essentially together. The two pairs of 'opposites,' rationalism—irrationalism and scholasticism—mysticism, do not coincide. And where their equivalence is sought it rests on an extreme rationalization of philosophy. Philosophy as a rationalist creation, detached from life, is powerless; mysticism as an irrationalist experience is purposeless," Martin Heidegger, *Frühe Schriften*, Frankfurt, 1972, p. 352.

73. The Middle High German text of this sermon has been published in DW I, pp. 281–293.

CHAPTER 2

1. The Middle High German text of this sermon has been published in DW II, pp. 18–36.

2. *Commentary on the Book of Wisdom*, #34, LW II, pp. 354f.; this text is not isolated; for parallels see ibid., #7.

3. "Creavit enim ut essent omnia," Ecclus. 1:14.

4. Sermon "Every Good Gift," DW I, pp. 69,1–70,4. The condemned proposition #26 was extracted from this text: "All creatures are mere nothingness; I do not say that they are small or anything at all, but that they are mere nothingness." Denzinger-Schönmetzer #976. The minutes of the trial relate the following dialogue: "[Eckhart] affirms the article above in many instances, and he declares that it is true that the creatures in themselves and by themselves are nothing, because 'by Him all things are made, and without Him, nothing has been made' (John 1:3). Thus everything would depend on God, so that it would vanish into nothingness if he did not maintain everything at every single moment.—[The Curia:] That still does not exclude error. Although creatures depend indeed on the Creator God, they are nevertheless something in themselves and by themselves; this is due to the activity of the Creator. From their real dependence on God, and as this real dependence is grounded in their real being, it appears clearly that the creatures possess a real being . . .," Pelster, pp. 1112–1113; cf. RS, #2, 4 art. 15 (Théry p. 184). The use of the word "real," which returns unceasingly in this accusation of error, illustrates satisfactorily the opposition between the "imperative" thought of Meister Eckhart and the "indicative" thought of the theologians of the Curia. The thought of nothingness conveys the hearer on a road, that of detachment; the thought of the "real," on the other hand, perceives entities and points them out (cf. above, ch. 1, "The Divine Destiny of the Intellect").

5. Eckhart is not the first who has taught that the creature is nothingness. This doctrine is dear to spiritual authors. It constitutes the philosophical basis of the "contempt of the world," cf. Bonaventure, *Breviloquium*, Part I, ch. II, #3: "Of itself the creature is nothing. What it has, it is indebted for to another. Thus it is that the creature, because of its deficiency, always remains dependent upon

its Principle; and that this Principle, because of its benignity, never ceases to support the creature." Transl. J. De Vinck, New York, 1963, p. 186. Gregory the Great had already said: "All things would fall into nothingness if the hand of the Founder did not hold them back," *Moralia* book XVI, ch. 37, #45; PL, vol. 75, col. 1143. Thomas Aquinas repeats, especially in his moral teaching, this notion; he does not, however, exploit its metaphysical basis. *Summa Theologiae,* Part Ia IIae, question 109, art. 2, second answer: "Every created thing has being only from another, and considered in itself it is nothing," transl. Blackfriars, New York and London, 1972, vol. 30, p. 77. Also: *De Veritate,* question 8, art. 7, second answer (Leonina Edition, Rome, 1970, p. 244, resp. 12): "When one says that every creature, taken in itself, is a shadow or false or nothing, this is not because its essence is dark or false, but because of whatever act of existence, light, or truth it has, it is from another being; consequently, only considered apart from what it has from the Other is it nothing, darkness, and falsity," transl. R. W. Schmidt, *Truth,* vol. I, Chicago, 1952, p. 354. The objection to which this text responds is a false quotation from Origen: "Omnis creatura tenebra est," "all creature is a shadow." The quote seems rather to be taken from John Scotus Erigena.

6. *Summa Theologiae,* Part I, question 6, art. 3.

7. "Bonitas nec est creata nec facta nec genita, sed tantum generans et generat bonum." RS, II, I, art. 1 (Théry, p. 157); Eckhart defends his thesis: "I say that this is absolutely and simply true." RS, III, I, art. 1 (Théry, p. 187). The main texts of this debate have been collected by Quint in the notes that accompany his publication of the *Book of Divine Consolation: "Anmerkugen zu Bgt.,"* DW V, pp. 62–70.

8. Sermon "Justi vivent in aeternum," DW I, p. 103 1s; cf. the numerous parallels, ibid., note 1.

9. Thomas Aquinas, *Summa Theologiae,* Part I, question 5, art. 6, op. cit., vol. 2, 1964, pp. 79f. We have slightly modified the translation. Aquinas only repeats here the distinction between "fine, beneficial, and pleasant" in Aristotle, "Nicomachean Ethics," book II, ch. 3; 1104 b 31, op. cit., p. 955.

10. Ibid., second Reply: "Those things are properly called delightful which are desirable solely because they give delight and can at times be harmful and unworthy. And those things are said to be useful which are desirable not in themselves but solely as means to other things—for example, the drinking of bitter medicine. Those things are called worthy which are desirable in themselves." Transl. p. 81.

11. See, above, the analysis of the sermon "Jesus Entered" [10], ch. 1, notes 54–58.

12. Sermon "Jesus Entered" [15], DW I, p. 44,1–2; see this text above, ch. 1.

13. J. Quint, *Die Überlieferung der deutschen Predigten Meister Eckharts,* Bonn, 1932, p. 166. In the place "suochest du got alleine," this Ms. has "Sô du den vater suochest, daz ist got alleine." This variant has been adopted by Quint, DW II, p. 29,1–2.

14. Saint Augustine, *The Trinity,* book XII, ch. VII, transl. W. J. Oates, *Basic Writings of Saint Augustine,* New York, 1948, vol. 2, pp. 814f. Thomas Aquinas

makes reference to this text, from which he draws his distinction between *ratio superior* and *ratio inferior,* cf. *Summa Theologiae,* Part I, question 79, art. 9.

15. Cf. the sermon "Jesus Entered" [8], DW I, pp. 32–35; see this text above, ch. 1, and the analysis: "The Divine Destiny of the Intellect."

16. For the hesitations, in Meister Eckhart, in the attribution of the primacy either to the intellect or to the will, see our remarks above, ch. 1, "The Divine Destiny of the Will"; as an example, here is a text where Eckhart takes exactly the opposite position of what he affirms in the sermon "Mulier, venit hora": "Knowledge transports God in the mind and leads the mind to God. But it is powerless to lead it to the bosom of God. So, God performs his divine works not in knowledge . . . but the supreme faculty advances, that is, love, and breaks through to the interior of God," sermon "In omnibus requiem quaesivi," Pf. p. 153, 27–32. Why this precedence given to love and the will over knowledge and the intellect? The reasons are the same ones that in our text constrain him to the inverse option, namely, the wording of the biblical text on which he comments. This sermon is entitled: "In omnibus requiem quaesivi," "in all things I have searched for rest" (Ecclus. 24:11). Eckhart asks himself about the faculty capable of leading man to rest, and he gives priority to the will. Rest, in man, is the will overwhelmed by "delight." When he preaches on the verse "Woman, the hour is coming when the true adorers will adore the Father in spirit and truth," the word "truth" is given to him, and he then exalts the intellect.

17. Gilbert de Poitiers had been accused of teaching such a real distinction, in God, between God and Godhead. But his doctrine is limited to a problem of theological grammar; it was condemned by the synod of Reims, in the presence of Pope Eugene III, in 1148. In late antiquity, the question of knowing "if God and the being of God are identical or something different" was raised, for instance, by Marius Victorinus, *Adversus Arium,* I, 33, 4–5; this text is quoted by Hadot, *Porphyre et Victorinus,* Paris, 1968, vol. 1, p. 66.

18. Cf., e.g., *The Divine Names,* IV, 1; PG 3, col. 693b: "The Sovereign Good . . . by the simple fact of being, sends to all beings, and with proportion, the rays of absolute Good. These rays have created, in the intelligible order and the intelligent order, substances, faculties, and their operations. By them they are, by them they have life incessantly and without lessening . . ."; in P. Chevalier, *Dionysiaca. Recueil donnant l'ensemble des traductions latines des ouvrages attribués au Denys de l'Aréopage,* vol. I, Bruges, 1939, pp. 147f.

19. Cf. above, ch. 1, "The Birth of the Son in Detachment."

20. M. Lexer, *Mittelhochdeutsches Taschenwörterbuch,* Stuttgart, 1966, p. 59; Quint, pp. 386f. For gelîcheit as "likeness," see our Commentary, below.

21. This acceptance of the concept is to be distinguished from the impassibility of which the medieval theologians speak: a quality of the glorious body and especially of the risen Christ.

22. Epictetus, *The Manual,* ch. 12, 2; transl. P. E. Matheson, Oxford, 1916, vol. 2, p. 217.

23. Plotinus, *The Enneads* I, 2,3; transl. Stephen MacKenna, New York, 1969, p. 32. In *The Enneads* IV, 3,32, we read: "But the memory of friends, children, wife? Country too, and all that the better sort of man may reasonably remem-

ber? All these, the lower man retains with emotion, the authentic man passively. . . . The good soul is forgetful. It flees multiplicity, for only thus is it free
from entanglement, light-footed, self-conducted," p. 287. This is indeed apathy:
indifference, forgetfulness, a flight from "lower" experiences.

24. See, e.g., Clement of Alexandria, *Stromata* I, ch. 7, 37-38 (Sources chrétiennes vol. 30) Paris, 1951, pp. 73-75. None of the Greek fathers has been so
strongly attached to the ideal of apathy as Clement.

25. Evagrius the Pontian, *Capita practica ad Anatolium,* ch. 64; PG vol. 40, col.
1237 D.

26. Gregory of Nazianzus writes: "I praise the courage and the nobleness of
soul of the Stoics who consider all exterior things incapable of disturbing them
and declare man blessed even if he were burned in the tomb of Phalaris," Letter
XXXII, PG vol. 37, col. 71.

27. Origen, *Homily on Jeremiah,* vol. III, frag. 30, ed. Klostermann, Leipzig,
1901, p. 214.

28. Jerome blames Evagrius for having written "a book *On Apathy,* or as we
may say impassibility or imperturbation, according to which our spirit is to stay
unmoved by any reflection and any affection, which means in brief that it
becomes either a stone or God," "Letter 133 to Ctesiphon," ch. 3; PL vol. 22,
col. 1029. In the same letter Jerome describes apathy further and is still more
severe: "What could be more presumptuous than to claim for oneself, I do not
say similarity with God, but equality, and to embrace with a short catchword
[apathy] the mischiefs of all heretics ever since philosophers followed the Stoic
principles of, above all, Pythagoras and Zeno? Indeed, the Stoics profess that
what the Greeks name *pathé,* and what we may call perturbations—namely
bitterness and joy, hope and fear—can be removed from our minds by meditation and assiduous exercise of the virtues, so that not a single fibre, not a single
root of vices remains in man," ibid., cols. 1025f. This text gives an excellent
description of Stoic apathy. The twofold pretension against which Jerome rebels
—to make of man a stone or God, and to vindicate not only similarity, but
equality with God—has been repeated against Meister Eckhart, at the price of
the simplifications which we have already seen.

29. Augustine's argument is the following: the pathetic faculty is an integral
part of terrestrial life. It would rather be a defect not to feel any such sentiments
as pain and joy. With regard to the Eastern doctrines of apathy he states very
bluntly: "If that *apatheia* is a state in which no emotion of any kind can affect
the mind, surely it is nothing but a state of stupor, and, as such, is worse than
any vice," *The City of God,* XIV, 9,4; transl. G. G. Walsh and G. Monahan in:
"The Fathers of the Church," vol. 14, New York, 1952, pp. 370f.

30. Sermon "Moyses orabat Dominum," DW II, pp. 7,12–8,2.

31. Isa. 53:7.

32. Matt. 27:13–14.

33. Sermon "Quasi stella matutina," DW I, p. 148, 2f.

34. "A man who commits himself to God and carefully pursues His will,
whatever God may give such a man will be the best. It has necessarily to be the
best . . . for God wills it this way and not another. Be it sickness, poverty, hunger

or whatever—all that God allows to occur or to happen to you, or again not to happen, is the best, no matter if that is a feeling of piety or inner joy or whatever you possess or do not possess." RS II, art. 41 (Théry, op. cit. p. 245), quoted DW I, p. 61, n. 1.

35. Thomas Aquinas, *Summa Theologiae*, Part I, question 21, art. 1, ad 3m: "The free is that which is cause of itself"; transl. Blackfriars, *Summa Theologiae*, vol. 5, New York and London, 1967, p. 75 ("a free man is one who belongs to himself") is erroneous. Ibid., question 82, art. 1; op. cit., vol. 11, 1970, p. 217: "The necessary is that which cannot not be."

36. *Summa Theologiae*, Part I, question 19, art. 3 c; transl. T. Gilby, New York, 1964, vol. II, pp. 104f.

37. Angelus Silesius, physician and poet, who died in 1674, was one of those who no doubt have best understood the Eckhartian preaching on detachment. In his *Cherubinic Pilgrim* he adopts even the vocabulary of the Master. He is, so to speak, Meister Eckhart's versifier. *Abgeschiedenheit, Lauterkeit, Eigenschaft, Bildlosigkeit, Jungfrauschaft*—all the Eckhartian terms are known to him:

> Weil Abgeschiedenheit sich niemand macht gemein
> So muss sie ohne Sucht und eine Jungfrau sein.
> Vollkommne Lauterkeit is bild-, form-, liebelos,
> Steht aller Eigenschaft wie Gottes Wesen bloss.

Since detachment makes itself familiar to no one / It has to be without desire and virginal. / Perfect exemption has neither figure, nor form, nor love, / It is devoid of all property, as the being of God (Angelus Silesius, *Der Cherubinische Wandersmann*, ed. J. Schwabe, Basel, 1955,p. 41). There exists an English translation of selections from this work: Frederick Franck (ed.), *The Book of Angelus Silesius*, New York, 1976.

38. Saint Bernard speaks sometimes of "five regions" which the "mystic" must go through; for instance his sermon "On the fivefold commerce and the five regions." These regions are: the region of dissimilarity; the hidden paradise; the region of atonement; the infernal region; paradise beyond heaven; PL vol. 183, col. 661–665. The Spanish mystics speak of spiritual "dwellings." Yet these authors bespeak an itinerary of perfection, while Meister Eckhart considers four steps of intelligibility of how man appears in relation to God. There is no question in him of progressive purification or of initiatory asceticism.

39. "Alle crêatûren sint ein lûter niht." Sermon "Omne datum optimum," DW I, pp. 69, 8–70,1. Cf. also the article 26 of the Bull which literally repeats this sentence; cf. RS II 4, art. 15 (Théry p. 184) and Pelster, p. 1112.

40. "Alle crêatûren hânt kein wesen, wan ihr wesen swebet an der gegenwerticheit gotes: ibid., p. 70,2–4.

41. "...Würket diu sêle in unwesene und volget gote, der in unwesene würket." Sermon "Quasi stella matutina," DW I, p. 151, 11f.

42. "Die Seiendheit des Seienden (wird) als die Anwesenheit für das sicherstellende Vorstellen gedacht, Seiendheit ist jetzt Gegenständlichkeit," *Vorträge*

und Aufsätze, Pfulligen, 1954, pp. 74f; cf. also ibid., p. 240. "The beingness of beings is thought as presence *for* the guarantee of representation. Beingness is now objectivity," in M. Heidegger, *The End of Philosophy,* transl. Joan Stambaugh, New York, 1973, p. 88.

43. In the mystical German poetry of the 13th and 14th centuries, we sometimes meet with a play on the oppositions between *iht* and *niht.* Mechthild of Magdeburg writes:

> Du solt minnen das niht,
> Du solt vliehen das iht . . .

Thou shalt love nothing, / Thou shalt flee everything . . . (quoted by G. Lüers, *Die Sprache der deutschen Mystik des Mittelalters im Werke der Mechthild von Magdeburg,* Munich, 1926, p. 293). Angelus Silesius writes:

> Mensch, sprichst du, dass dich Ichts von Gottes Lieb abhält,
> So brauchst du noch nicht recht, wie sich's gebührt, der Welt.

Man, do you say that something holds you back from the love of God? / You do not yet use the world correctly and as you ought (op. cit., p. 39).

44. Cf. the sermon "Intravit Jesus in templum": "When the mind penetrates into the unmixed light, it falls into its non-being *(nihtes niht),* and it is so far removed in this non-being from its created something *(iht)* that its own powers are incapable of bringing it back into its created something. So God places his uncreated being under the mind's non-being *(nihtes niht)* and maintains the mind with his something *(ihtes iht)."* DW I, p. 14,2–6.

45. Ibid., p. 19,1.

46. Sermon "Justi vivent in aeternum," DW I, p. 106,1–3: "Gotes sîn mîn sîn und gotes isticheit mîn isticheit."

47. "Von der übervart der gotheit," Pf. p. 503,15–17. The authenticity of this text is not certain.

48. Sermon "Unus deus et pater omnium," DW I, p. 358,2. "Uzer gote enist niht dan niht aleine."

49. E.g., *Expositio Libri Sapientiae,* n. 166: "Sin is, in truth, nothingness. The psalm says: 'Salvation is far from the sinners,' and Augustine finds himself far removed from God. What can be farther away than being and nothingness?" LW II, p. 500,9–11.

50. E.g., the sermon "Et ecce, homo erat in Ierusalem," Pf. p. 85,15–17.

51. Saint Augustine, *Confessions,* book VII, ch. X, n. 16: "I found myself to be far off from Thee, in the region of dissimilarity," *Basic Writings of Saint Augustine,* vol. I, p. 101.

52. Ps. 137:4.

53. *Expositio Libri Sapientiae,* n. 294; LW II, p. 652.

54. Sermon "Ave, gratia plena," DW I, p. 376, 7f.

55. "Allez, daz geschaffen oder geschepflich ist, daz ist niht." Sermon "Con-vescens praecepit eis," DW II, p. 88,7–10 and elsewhere.

56. Sermon "Convescens praecepit eis," ibid., p. 89,4–7: "This is why man has to be dead, absolutely dead, to be nothing in himself; he must be alien to all similarity and must resemble no one. Only then does he properly resemble God."

57. "Lâzet niht," sermon "In diebus suis," DW I, p. 170,4.

58. Y.-M. Congar, "Langage des spirituels et langage des théologiens" in *La Mystique rhénane*, Paris, 1963, p. 22.

59. H. Rombach, *Substanz, System, Struktur*, Freiburg, 1965: "Die Funk-tionenontologie tritt an die Stelle der Substanzenontologie," p. 180. J. Koch, "Zur Analogielehre Meister Eckharts," in *Mélanges offerts à Etienne Gilson*, Paris, 1959, p. 346, speaks likewise of the "function" of created beings, understood here as a reference by which the created points beyond itself.

60. Sermon "In hoc apparuit," DW I, p. 80,7–17. Angelus Silesius summarizes this teaching about nothingness when he writes:

> Mensch, so du etwas liebst, so liebst du nichts fürwahr;
> Gott is nicht dies und das, drum lass das Etwas gar.

O man, as long as you love anything, you in truth love nothing. / God is not this or that, therefore abandon all something (op. cit., p. 22).

61. Sermon 'Quasi stella matutina," DW I, p. 156,7–9.

> Die Schöpfung ist ein Buch, wer's weislich lesen kann,
> Dem wird darin gar fein der Schöpfer kundgetan.

Creation is a book: who knows how to read it wisely / Will find the Creator subtly revealed in it (Angelus Silesius, op. cit., p. 63).

62. G. Théry, "Le 'Benedictus Deus' de Maître Eckhart," in: *Mélanges Joseph de Ghellink*, Gembloux, 1951, p. 927.

63. Sermon "Ego elegi vos," DW II, p. 66,2–11.

64. Michel Henry, *The Essence of Manifestation*, transl. G. Etzkorn, The Hague, 1973, p. 319.

65. Cf. above, our Analysis in ch. 2, "Birth of the Son and Equanimity."

66. Sermon "Impletum est tempus Elisabeth," DW I, p. 180,7–13.

67. *Expositio libri Exodi*, n. 117; LW II, p. 112,7–12.

68. "Bilde enmac niht gesîn âne gelîcheit." Sermon "Quasi vas auri solid-um," DW I, p. 265, 4f.

69. Ibid., p. 269,2–7.

70. Ibid., p. 271,1–3.

71. "Lauffet allein zu der ersten lauterkeyt." Sermon "Haec dicit dominus: Honora patrem tuum," DW II, p. 475,3–4.

> Wer Gott will gleiche sein, muss allem ungleich werden,
> Muss ledig seiner selbst, und bloss sein von Beschwerden.

He who wishes to be like God has to become unlike everything, / He has to be void of himself, and delivered from all pains (Angelus Silesius, op. cit., p. 74).

72. Sermon "Quasi stella matutina," DW I, p. 154,1–3.

73. Sermon "Quasi vas auri solidum," DW I, pp. 265,9–269,1.

74. Sermon "Justi vivent in aeternum," DW I, p. 105, 2f.

75. Ibid., DW I, pp. 99ff.

76. Ibid., p. 104,5–7.

77. Sermon "Quasi stella matutina," DW I, pp. 154,7–155,3.

> Ein einzges Wort hilft mir, schreibts Gott mir einmal ein,
> So werd' ich stets ein Lamm mit Gott gezeichnet sein.

One single word can help me, if God one day inscribes it in me, / I shall be for always a lamb marked with the seal of God (Angelus Silesius, op. cit., p. 114. This single word is God's Word).

78. Sermon "Justi vivent in aeternum," DW I, pp. 106,4–107,4.

79. Sermon "Sta in porta," DW I, p. 318,4–8.

80. The Middle High German text of this sermon has been published in DW I, pp. 263–276.

81. Sermon "Vidi supra montem Syon," DW I, pp. 215,10–216,7.

82. Sermon "Et ecce, homo erat in Ierusalem," Pf. p. 86,11.

83. Sermon "Quis puer iste erit?" Pf. p. 196, 40f.

84. Fire "suochet in ime daz eine"; Pf. p. 431,19–34. Angelus Silesius summarizes this development in two lines:

> Gott ist in mir das Feu'r, und ich in ihm der Schein:
> Sind wir einander nicht ganz inniglich gemein?

God in me is the fire, I am in him the clarity: / Are we not very closely united? (op. cit., p. 20).

85. Sermon "Justi vivent in aeternum," DW I, p. 111,7. The inquisitors translate *ein unglîch* by *unum, non simile:* RS 11,4 art. 1 (Théry, p. 177), a wording repeated by the Bull, art. 10, Denzinger-Schönmetzer n. 960: "sic ergo convertor in eum, quod ipse operatur me suum esse unum, non simile."

Expressions like "niht glîch, das selbe," "not alike, but the same," are frequent: Pf. 85, 26f, with regard to the relationship between Father and Son; Pf. 151,19 with regard to God in himself and God who is born in the mind; Pf. 163,33–38, with regard to God and the mind.

86. "Daz würken und daz werden ist ein. . . . Got und ich wir sint ein in disem gewürke; er würket und ich gewirde. . . ." Sermon "Justi vivent in aeternum," DW I, pp. 114,2–115,2.

87. Ἐνέργεια signifies neither "agent" nor "effect," but action inasmuch as it produces the effect, operation in progress. Aristotle, *De Anima,* III, 7,431 a 5; transl. R.D. Hicks, Amsterdam, 1965, pp. 139f.

88. " . . . daz ist ze nemende in der wirklichkeit der îngeberunge." Sermon

"Meister Eckhart sprichet," Pf. p. 193,16–20; with regard to the uncreated and uncreatable light "in" the mind and not "of" the mind, cf. Eckhart's statement at Cologne, quoted above, ch. 1, n. 44.

89. Sermon "Convescens praecepit eis," DW II, pp. 88,3–89,3.

90. "Niht in geslozzen, niht vereiniget, mêr: ez ist ein." Sermon "Et ecce, homo erat in Ierusalem," Pf. pp. 85,36–86,4.

91. Er gebirt mich sich und sich mich und mich sîn wesen und sîn natûre. . . . Dâ ist ein leben und ein wesen und ein werk." Sermon "Justi vivent in aeternum," DW I, p. 109,9–11.

92. Der grunt gotes unde der grunt der sêle sint ein wesen." Treatise "Daz ist swester Katrei," Pf. p. 467,15. Authenticity of this text is not universally recognized.

93. Sermon "Ave, gratia plena," DW I, p. 381,1. Angelus Silesius literally repeats this expression:

> In Gott wird nichts erkannt; er ist ein einig Ein,
> Was man in ihm erkennt, das muss man selber sein.

Nothing is known in God, he is a unique One, / that which is known of him, one must be oneself (op. cit., p. 35).

94. Meister Eckhart, quite like Heidegger today, understands this verb as being derived from *schicken*, to send. Eckhart uses it to designate the happening of identification: identity is "sent," "destined" to both God and Man. E.g.: "sô diu geburt geschihet . . . wan ez geschihet über zît in dem tage der êwicheit." Sermon "In diebus suis," DW I, pp. 166,11–167,2.

95. Sermon "Qui audit me," DW I, p. 199,1–6.

96. "Swaz in gote ist, daz ist got." Sermon "Nunc scio vere," DW I, 56,8; the censors of the Inquisition translated: "Omne quod est, hoc est deus!" RS II, art. 50 (Théry, p. 252). The sentence "Quidquid in Deo est, Deus est" was the solemn formulation by which the Synod of Reims in 1148 refuted the real distinction in God, a theory attributed to Gilbert de Poitiers, Mansi, *Sacrorum Conciliorum nova et amplissima collectio*, Paris-Leipzig, 1901–1927, vol. 21, col. 726E. See below, note 120. The accusation of pantheism is partly based on this erroneous translation of the statements of Meister Eckhart. Angelus Silesius writes:

> Ich muss ein Schein im Schein,
> Ich muss ein Wort im Wort, ein Gott in Gotte sein.

I have to be clarity in clarity, / I have to be a Word in the Word, God in God (op. cit., p. 19).

> In Gott ist alles Gott: ein einz'ges Würmelein
> Das ist in Gott so viel als tausend Gotte sein.

In God everything is God: the least little worm / Is no less in God than are a thousand gods (ibid., p. 132).

97. Sermon "Nunc scio vere," DW I, p. 55,4f.

98. Sermon "Surrexit autem Saulus," Pf. p. 83,17.

99. "Quaestiones Parisienses," LW V, p. 37,8.

100. "Expositio s. evangelii sec. Ioannem," n. 66, LW I, p. 55,2f.

101. Sermon "In hoc apparuit," DW I, p. 81,4f.

102.   Dies alles ist ein Spiel, das sich die Gottheit macht,
        Sie hat die Kreatur um ihretwilln erdacht.

All this is a play that the Godhead gives itself / It has conceived the creature for its own sake (Angelus Silesius, op. cit., p. 45).

103. Latin sermon VI, 53, LW IV, pp. 51,6–52,6. Angelus Silesius comments:

Dass du nicht Menschen liebst, das tust du recht und wohl,
Die Menschheit ists, die man im Menschen lieben soll.

That you do not love men, you are right: / For it is humanity that one should love in man (op. cit., p. 29).

104. B. Weiss, *Die Heilsgeschichte bei Meister Eckhart,* Mainz, 1965, pp. 109–134, has shown how much Meister Eckhart's ecclesiology is governed by his thought of identity beyond time. For Eckhart, the condition for participation in the mystical Body would be, according to Weiss, not faith, nor even the recognition of Christ as head of the Church, but detachment from time, and the identity between all men, God, and the world that follows from it.

105. Sermon "Omne datum optimum," DW I, pp. 71,4–72,3.

106. Sermon "Justi vivent in aeternum," DW I, p. 112,6–9. These lines have been incorporated as they stand into the Bull of condemnation, art. 9, Denzinger-Schönmetzer, n. 959. Cf. also RS II, 4, art. 10, (Théry, p. 181) and RS II, art. 40 (Théry, p. 244; Pelster, p. 1116).

107. Here is another distich by Angelus Silesius:

Der Mensch hat eher nicht vollkommne Seligkeit,
Bis dass die Einheit hat verschluckt die Anderheit.

Man has no perfect happiness, / Before unity has swallowed up otherness (op. cit., p. 55).

108. M. de Gandillac, "La 'dialectique' de Maître Eckhart," in *La Mystique rhénane,* pp. 59–94.

109. Sermon "Qui audit me," DW I, p. 199,8–11.

110. Sermon "Mulier, venit hora," text above, ch. 2. The parenthetical remark about the question "What Is Philosophy?" alludes to M. Heidegger, *Was ist Philosophie?,* Pfullingen 1960, p. 32: "Die Antwort ist keine erwidernde Aussage, die Antwort ist vielmehr die Ent-sprechung," "the reply is not an answer

in propositions, rather the reply is the co-respondence," transl. J. T. Wilde and W. Kluback, *What Is Philosophy?*, New Haven and New York, 1958, p. 69 (translation modified).

111. Franz von Baader remarks in his diary (Sämtliche Werke, ed. F. Hoffman, Leipzig, 1851–1860, vol. XV, p. 159): "Very often, at Berlin, I was in the company of Hegel. One day I read him some texts of Meister Eckhart, an author of whom he knew only the name. He was so delighted that he gave before me an entire course devoted to Meister Eckhart. At the end he also confided to me: 'Here we have found at last what we were seeking,'" quoted by I. Degenhardt, *Studien zum Wandel des Eckhart-Bildes,* Leiden, 1967, p. 114.

112. Sermon "In hoc apparuit," DW I, p. 90, 12. The best presentation of the Eckhartian "without a why" is found in Shizuteru Ueda, *Die Gottesgeburt in der Seele und der Durchbruch zur Gottheit. Meister Eckhart und der Zen-Buddhismus,* Gütersloh, 1965. Ueda makes use particularly of a well-known couplet by Angelus Silesius:

> Die Ros' ist ohn' warum, sie blühet weil sie blühet,
> Sie acht't nicht ihrer selbst, fragt nicht ob man sie siehet.

The rose is without why, it flowers because it flowers, / It pays no heed to itself, asks not if it is seen (A. Silesius, op. cit., p. 35). Martin Heidegger, too, comments on this verse by claiming the authority of Meister Eckhart: *Der Satz vom Grund,* Pfullingen, 1957, pp. 68–72. Cf. John Caputo, "The Rose Is without Why," *Philosophy Today,* 15 (1971), pp. 3–15.

113. Sermon "Quasi vas auri solidum," DW I, p. 274, 1–5. Cf. this text above, earlier in ch. 2.

114. Sermon "Got het die armen," Pf. 177,12. In Angelus Silesius, *Gelassenheit* receives the same meaning:

> Gelassenheit fäht Gott; Gott aber selbst zu lassen
> Ist ein' Gelassenheit, die wenig Menschen fassen.

Releasement grasps God, but to release God himself / Is a releasement that few people grasp (op. cit., p. 42).

115. "We must not know of any why or wherefore outside ourselves, neither of God nor of creature ... because whatever motivates us other than out of ourselves is thoroughly an act of mortal sin." RS II, art. 31, (Théry, p. 236).

116. Sermon "Justus in perpetuum vivet," DW II, p. 253,4f.

117. Sermon "Omne datum optimum," DW I, p. 69,2–4.

118. Sermon "In diebus suis," DW I, p. 171,12–15.

> Wo ist mein Aufenthalt? Wo ich und du nicht stehen.
> Wo ist mein letztes End, in welches ich soll gehen?
> Da wo man keines findt. Wo soll ich dann nun hin?
> Ich muss noch über Gott in eine Wüste ziehn.

Where shall I stay? Where you and I are not. / Where is the last end to which I should tend? / Where one finds none. Where then shall I go? / I must move still higher than God, into a desert (Angelus Silesius, op. cit., p. 61).

119. Sermon "Nolite timere eos," Pf. p. 180,18.

120. Ibid., p. 18, 15.

121. Ibid., p. 181,1–10.

122. DW I, p. 388,10–14.

123. DW I, p. 235,6.

124. "Lûter gotheit," DW I, p. 360,6.

125. "Das unbekantniss der verborgenen gotheit," DW I, p. 253,1.

126. The expression *got toeten* recurs in different contexts, e.g. DW I, pp. 73,12–74,1.

127. V. Lossky, *Théologie négative et connaissance de Dieu chez Maître Eckhart,* Paris, 1960, p. 343.

128. Sermon "Beati pauperes spiritu," DW II, p. 492, 3–4; 7–9. See the text of this sermon below at the end of ch. 3.

129. Ibid., DW II, pp. 205,6–504,3; Angelus Silesius writes:

> Dass Gott so selig ist und lebet ohn Verlangen,
> Hat er sowohl von mir, als ich von ihm empfangen.

That God be happy and live without desire, / He has received from me as much as I from him (op. cit., p. 20). See the text of the sermon "Blessed Are the Poor," below, ch. 3.

130. John 1:1 and 14:3.

131. M. Heidegger, "Das Ding," in: *Vorträge und Aufsätze,* Pfullingen, 1954, p. 175. Transl. A. Hofstadter, *Poetry, Language, Thought,* New York, 1971, p. 176. Translation slightly modified.

132. Shizuteru Ueda, "Über den Sprachgebrauch Meister Eckharts," in *Glaube, Geist, Geschichte, Festschrift Ernst Benz,* Leiden, 1967, pp. 266f. Ueda analyzes the texts in which this expression occurs.

133. ". . . Sîn nâtûre twinget in dar zuo." Sermon "Dilectus deo et hominibus," Pf. p. 231,13–16.

134. Treatise "Von abegescheidenheit," Pf. p. 484,18f. cf. DW V, p. 402,4f. The authenticity of this treatise is not certain.

135. Sermon "Intravit Jesus in templum," DW I, p. 20,3.

136. Treatise "Von der sêle werdikeit und eigenschaft," Pf. p. 409,29. The authenticity is not certain.

137. Sermon "Haec dicit dominus," DW II, p. 475,1.

138. Die Gottheit ist ein Brunn, aus ihr kommt alles her,
    Und läuft auch wieder hin, drum ist sie auch ein Meer.

The Godhead is a well, everything comes from it / And everything runs again into it: hence it is also a sea (Angelus Silesius, op. cit., p. 52).

Wenn ich in Gott vergeh, so komm ich wieder hin,
Wo ich in Ewigkeit vor mir gewesen bin.

When I lose myself in God, I return / To where I have been from all eternity, before me (ibid., p. 72).

139. Cf. above in the sermon "Mulier, venit hora": "The original outbreak of all goodness": "ein ursprunc alles guotes," DW II, p. 30,5.

140. "Commentary on the Book of Exodus," n. 16. LW II, p. 22,3-6. With these lines Meister Eckhart comments on the verse of John: "in ipso vita erat" (John 1:4). On the history of the translation "what has been created was life in him," cf. V. Lossky, op. cit., p. 115, note 65. The equivalence between "life" and "boiling" or "seething" goes back to an old Greek etymology according to which $\zeta\tilde{\eta}\nu$, to live, would derive from $\zeta\acute{\epsilon}\epsilon\iota\nu$, to boil, to seethe. This connection is attested, e.g., in Plotinus, *The Enneads* VI, 7,12: "There no indigence or impotence can exist but all must be teeming, seething, with life," op. cit., p. 570. Angelus Silesius takes up this teaching:

Gott gleicht sich einem Brunn, er fleusst ganz mildiglich
Heraus in sein Geschöpf und bleibet doch in sich.

God is like a fountain, he generously runs off / Into his creature, and still remains in himself (op. cit., p. 68).

Eh ich etwas ward, da war ich Gottes Leben,
Drum hat er auch für mich sich ganz und gar ergeben.

Before I became one thing, I was the life of God, / That is why he gave himself entirely up for me (ibid., p. 72). The author indicates in a note that he is referring to John 1:4; Silesius should therefore be added to Lossky's list of names.

141. Sermon "In hoc apparuit," DW I, p. 94,4f.

142. Ibid., p. 95,1-3.

143. Sermon "Homo quidam nobilis," DW I, p. 246,10f.

144. Sermon "Stetit Jesus in medio," DW II, p. 190,1-2.

145. Cf. my article on releasement in Meister Eckhart, Heidegger, and Suzuki, with an explanation of the *Ten Oxherding Pictures*, "Trois penseurs du délaissement," in: *J. Hist. Phil.* XII/4 (Oct. 1974), pp. 455-478, and XIII/1 (Jan. 1975), pp. 43-60. Also see below, the Appendix.

146. Sermon "In hoc apparuit," DW I, p. 91,3-7.

147. On this point, Nicholas of Cusa as well as Angelus Silesius is indebted to Meister Eckhart:

Wer nichts begehrt, nichts hat, nichts weiss, nichts liebt, nichts will,
Der hat, der weiss, begehrt, und liebt noch immer viel.

He who desires, has, loves, wishes nothing, / Still has, knows, desires, and loves
much (op. cit., p. 68).

148. The Middle High German text of this sermon has been published in DW
III, pp. 211-231.

CHAPTER 3

1. The Middle High German text of this sermon has been published in DW
III, pp. 310-329. In [1] we have followed the indications of translation given by
Joseph Quint, ibid. p. 311, n. 1.

2. The object known "must be in" the subject "somehow," cf. ch. 1, n. 12.

3. Aristotle, *Metaphysics*, X, 6; 1056b, 36; transl. W.D. Ross, in: *The Basic
Works of Aristotle*, R. McKeon, ed., New York, 1941, p. 845. See also V, 15;
1021a, 26, and 1021b, 4, ibid., p. 769.

4. "The creature's relation to God is founded upon the creature's being," *De
Quatuor Oppositis*, C. IV (ed. Perrier, I, n. 10).

5. "Any relation between the creature and the creator is in God according to
its reason (*secundum dici*), but in the creature according to its being (*secundum
esse*)," *Commentary on Saint John* n. 31; LW III, p. 25, 12f. "A relation owes its
whole existence to a mind; and as such it is a real category" (Relatio autem
totum suum esse habet ab anima, et ut sic est praedicamentum reale), *Parisian
Questions* I, 4; LW V, p. 40, 12f. *Master Eckhart, Parisian Questions and Prologues*,
transl. Armand A. Maurer, Toronto, 1974, p. 45.

6. Plato, *The Republic*, VI, 507b; transl. P. Shorey, Cambridge, Mass., and
London, 1970, vol. II, p. 97; Pseudo-Dionysius, *The Divine Names*, c. 3111, #2
(P.G. III, col. 980); Plotinus, *The Enneads* V, III, c. 12; transl. Stephen McKenna,
New York, 1969, p. 394; Proclus, *The Elements of Theology*, pr. 1: "Every manifold
in some way participates unity"; transl. E. R. Dodds, Oxford, 1963, p. 2. In his
commentary on The Book of Wisdom Meister Eckhart refers to this text of
Proclus. Where not otherwise possible we follow Dodds in the transitive use of
the verb "to participate"; cf. below, n. 17.

7. At the tribunal of Cologne, Eckhart expressly held this doctrine: "We are
heirs not insofar as we are many distinct Sons, but insofar as we are 'from him,
by him, and in him' who is the Son." Here his accusers understand a pure and
simple identification of created beings with the hypostasis of the only Son, RS
I, art. 1 (Théry, pp. 267-268 and 176-177).

8. "Intravit Jesus," [13] above, and the analysis in ch. 1, "The Divine Destiny
of the Ground of the Mind."

9. These corrections result, among other texts, from the sermon on "image"
which we have translated above, ch. 2, "Like a Vase of Massive Gold": "The
mind bears the image of God and is like God."

10. Cf. above our analysis of the sermon "Woman, the Hour Is Coming," ch.
2, "The Higher Part of the Mind and its Faculties."

11. We find in the works of Meister Eckhart "trinities" of evidently Augustinian inspiration: in the Latin writings "bodily activity—intellectual activity—divine activity"; in the German works "sense—reason—noble power of the mind," "sense knowledge—rational knowledge—spark of honesty," "bodily—spiritual—within the spirit," "created knowledge—spiritual knowledge—pure spiritual knowledge," etc. In each of these series the third term refers to a pure, not abstractive, operation of the mind.

12. *Commentary on the Book of Genesis,* II, n. 168; LW I, p. 314, 4f: the biblical author "wants to teach us that God is pure intellect, that his total being is intelligence itself."

13. Aristotle, *On the Soul,* III, 5; 430a 14; *Basic Works of Aristotle,* op. cit. p. 592.

14. *Commentary on the Book of Genesis,* I, n. 115; LW I, p. 270, 9–15.

15. Ibid., p. 272, 3–6.

16. Ibid., p. 271, 3–6.

17. Proclus, *The Elements of Theology,* prop. 101, op. cit., p. 90.

18. Affirmations "b" and "d" can be read correctly in Neoplatonism, but the theses "a" and "c" disturb the order of emanations. Ὄν and ζωή seem to designate the soul under the same relationship: they ground knowledge. The ancient masters of this school would say rather: to be, for the soul, is to live, and to live for the intellect is to know, so that the intellect is based only mediately in the being of the soul. This mediation by life, in Eckhart, is not clear. The intellectual school to which Meister Eckhart belongs knows this axiom especially in its Aristotelian form, where it simply means that animals and humans are living beings: "vivere viventibus est esse," Aristotle, *De Anima,* II, 4;415 b 13, *Basic Works of Aristotle,* op, cit., p. 561, and the commentary by Thomas, II, less. 7, no. 319; cf. *Nichomachean Ethics,* IX, 9; 1170 a 13ff: "Life is defined in the case of animals by the power of perception, in that of man by the power of perception and thought," ibid., p. 1089 ("esse enim erat sentire vel intelligere," a. 34) and the commentary by Thomas, IX, less. 11. In the Scholastics, this trilogy serves to defend the unity of the substantial form; in Meister Eckhart, to isolate in man the place of his divinization.

19. *Defense,* RS I (Théry, p. 263).

20. "The mind's being (essentia anime) is far remote from this realm and world as it is located in another one, beyond the faculties of intellect and will." Latin sermon XI, 2, n. 121; LW IV, p. 115, 3f.

21. In his *Commentary on Saint John* Eckhart links this passivity of the mind's being to his concept of detachment: "To the notion of passivity pertain nakedness and need, to the notion of activity pertain actual being and wealth," n. 181; LW III, p. 149, 12f.

22. The text from the Defense quoted in note 19 (Théry, p. 263) follows a reference to this passage from Augustine.

23. *Commentary on Saint John,* n. 709; LW III.

24. Latin sermon XXX, 1, n. 312; LW IV, p. 275, 8f.

25. 1 Cor. 12:14–26.

26. *Commentary on Saint John,* III, n. 403.

27. "Grace is not in the faculties of the mind, but in its substance; that is, in the core, or rather in the very being of the mind." Latin sermon XXV, 2, n. 267; LW IV, p. 242, 10f.

28. Vladimir Lossky, *Théologie négative et connaissance de Dieu chez Maître Eckhart,* Paris, 1960, p. 112: "The image and expression of the Trinity will be found whenever the concrete is identified with the abstract, the participating with the participated, the subject formed with the form, by the means of *inquantum.*" Martin Heidegger, *Was heisst Denken?,* Tübingen, 1954, p. 96, relates the expression "Spirit in the spirit" in Meister Eckhart to the "spark in the mind." Meister Eckhart's technical term "*sêle*" translates both the Latin *mens* and *animus.* The extension and comprehension of these two Latin terms is often the same since Augustine. Heidegger writes: "What the Latin word *animus* intends is designated more fully in the originary words 'memory' and 'thanc,'" transl. F. D. Wieck and J. G. Gray, *What Is Called Thinking?* New York, 1968, pp. 149–150. Eckhart's "*sêle*" should therefore be translated into English as "mind," not as "soul."

29. All expressions translated from the *Commentary on Ecclesiasticus* no. 10 & 11; LW II, p. 239, 1–241, 4.

30. Ibid., n. 10; LW II, p. 239, 11f.

31. Ibid., n. 10, p. 239, 13.

32. "According to the point of view of relation or order, God communicates or generates both in his own realm and in that of creatures," ibid., n. 12, p. 242, 2f.

33. J. Koch, *Meister Eckhart und die jüdische Religionsphilosophie des Mittelalters,* Breslau, 1928, pp. 1–15. According to Eckhart the relations in God—attributes or Persons—are extrinsic to the divine essence; in this, Koch argues, he follows the teaching of Maimonides on the divine substance above all distinction, quantity, or multiplicity. This doctrine was condemned by art. 23 of the Bull. In his defense, Eckhart produced a text from Maimonides: the substance of God, according to this text, is "one in whatever way you consider it; under any examination you will find it to be one, indivisible in all its modes and in all regards; and you will find multiplicity neither inside its intelligence nor outside its intelligence," quoted by Koch, op. cit., pp. 11–12.

34. Shizuteru Ueda, *Die Gottesgeburt in der Seele und der Durchbruch zur Gottheit, Meister Eckhart und der Zen Buddhismus,* Gütersloh, 1965, has devoted his entire book to the elucidation of these two themes in Eckhart. He concludes that there is a dichotomy of fact between "the motif of the breakthrough" and "the motif of birth." The first type is enounced like this: "the mind breaks through to the ground of God and seizes him as he is in himself, naked and one"; the second: "God begets his Son in the mind and thus begets the mind as his very Son," p. 24. C. F. Kelley, *Meister Eckhart on Divine Knowledge,* New Haven, forthcoming, declares the Word "identical with the all-inclusive Godhead," but fails to show how the two themes can be unified.

35. E.g., Thomas Aquinas, *Summa Theologiae,* part I, question 14, art. 8 c: "Suum esse est suum intelligere." In his *Parisian Questions,* ch. I, 5; LW V, p. 42, 1ff., Eckhart says on the contrary: "God is an intellect and understanding;

he is not being or existence," transl. A. Maurer, op. cit., p. 46. Further below we shall see some consequences of this identification between God and intelligence; see below, "The Limits of the Analogical Understanding of Being," section e.).

36. "To those who would condemn him as if, duped by his enthusiasm and also perhaps by his love, Eckhart had, in his claim of identifying creature with God, as it were exaggerated the feelings and ideas which suggested themselves to his 'mystical' soul, there would be lacking only one thing, the understanding of his thought," Michel Henry, *The Essence of Manifestation,* transl. G. Etzkorn, The Hague, 1973, p. 319.

37. Pierre Aubenque echoes this erroneous understanding of being in Eckhart when he writes: "It is not by chance, but by virtue of the same Platonizing logic, that Meister Eckhart reiterates a (Neoplatonic) univocal interpretation of analogy, understood as gradual participation of *esse," Le problème de l'être chez Aristote,* Paris, 1962, pp. 200–201, n. 4.

38. A. Lasson, *Meister Eckhart der Mystiker, Zur Geschichte der religiösen Speculation in Deutschland,* Berlin, 1868, constructs a "natural" opposition between mysticism and Christian Church: "The mystic will always feel anticlerical" (p. 16).

39. E. Bloch, *Atheismus im Christentum, Zur Religion des Exodus und des Reiches,* Frankfurt, 1968, remains faithful to his project of "reduction of the remote God to the subjectivity of man, as anthropologization of religion" (p. 94), when he states that Meister Eckhart "has claimed, at least in theory, the treasures alienated in heaven as man's own goods" (p. 95). See also H. Ley's works in the bibliography at the end of this book. All these non-Christian readings of Eckhart discover dimensions of his thought that must remain hidden to an orthodox theologian such as C. F. Kelley, whose purpose in reading Eckhart is "to recapture the spirit that dwells at the core of Christianity itself," op. cit.

40. S. Ueda, op. cit., compares Eckhart to the teachings of Rinzai Zen, and he concludes: "Eckhart crosses quite clearly the boundaries of the customary intellectual world of Christianity and moves in the universe of Zen," p. 48. See also below, the Appendix.

41. Bardo Weiss, *Die Heilsgeschichte bei Meister Eckhart,* Mainz, 1965, has shown the astonishing scarcity, in Eckhart's writings, of texts related to the traditional contents of Christian history and dogma.

42. Become *"ledic,"* above, ch. 1, "What Does It Mean 'To Be Virgin'?"; cf. also the example of the burning coal, above, ch. 2, n. 60.

43. See the sermon "Saul Rose from the Ground," above.

44. The two fanciful etymologies of "Zion" and "Israel" are borrowed from Isidore of Seville, *Etymologies,* XV, 1, 5: "This is 'Zion,' which in Hebrew means 'speculation,' as it is built on the heights and can be contemplated from afar." Eckhart writes: "Nathaniel is called a true Israelite, which means 'a God-seeing man,'" *Commentary on Saint John,* n. 250; LW III, p. 209, 3f.

45. See above, ch. 2, "Birth of the Son and Equanimity."

46. This is the opinion of H. Ebeling, *Meister Eckharts Mystik,* Stuttgart, 1941, p. 204. H. Hof has shown that this interpretation by Ebeling must be explained

as a misrendering of the metaphysics of Thomas Aquinas, *Scintilla Animae,*
Lund-Bonn, 1952, pp. 133-146.

47. "Analogice, exemplariter et per prius," *Commentary on the Book of Wisdom,*
quoted by Lossky, op. cit., p. 370, n. 166.

48. Ἐπειδὴ πολλαχῶς λέγεται τὸ ὄν, *Physics,* I, C. 2, 185 a 21. R. P. Hardie
and R. K. Gaye translate very loosely: " 'is' is used in many senses," in: *Basic
Works of Aristotle,* op. cit., p. 220.

49. *Categories* 4; 1 b 25; transl. E. M. Edghill, ibid., p. 8.

50. *Metaphysics,* IV, 2; 1003 a 33-34; W. D. Ross translates very loosely:
"There are many senses in which a thing may be said to 'be,' but all that 'is'
is related to one central point, one definite kind of thing, and is not said to 'be'
by a mere ambiguity," ibid., p. 732.

51. *Metaphysics,* VII, 1; 1028 a 31: the substance is called τὸ πρῶτον ὄν,
"the first being"; W. D. Ross translates the entire sentence: "There are several
senses in which a thing is said to be first; yet substance is first in every sense,"
ibid., p. 783.

52. *On the Soul,* I, c. 1; 402 b 8. J. A. Smith translates: "the 'universal' being
treated either as nothing at all or as a later product," and he explains in a
footnote: "i.e., as presupposing the various sorts instead of being presupposed
by them," ibid., p. 536. Neither the translation nor the note show that the
universal is here the concept that "follows from" an operation of the mind upon
the thing, to the exclusion of a preexisting first being.

53. *Commentary on the First Book of Sentences,* dist. XIX, question 5, art. 2, ad
1, ed. P. Mandonnet, vol. I, Paris, 1929, p. 212.

54. *On Truth,* question 2, art. 11: "Knowledge is predicated neither univocally nor yet purely equivocally of God's knowledge and ours. Instead, it is
predicated analogically, or, in other words, according to a proportion," transl.
R. W. Mulligan, Chicago, 1952, vol. I, pp. 112f.

55. *Summa Theologiae,* Part I, question 13, art. 5; transl. T. Gilby, New York,
1964, pp. 207f.

56. C. Fabro, *Participation et causalité selon saint Thomas d'Aquin,* Louvain-
Paris, 1961, p. 581. The author devotes a long chapter to the concept of analogy
in Eckhart (pp. 551-609), but he only quotes from Eckhart's Latin works. In
these texts, Fabro believes he has found the "most rigid Parmenidism," as a
result of which "Eckhart should no longer hold any analogy between substance
and accident, between God and creature" (pp. 564f.). The excess of Scholastic
dogmatism seems to have remained the same since the Inquisition's prosecu-
tions against Eckhart.

57. Eccles. 24:29. Meister Eckhart, *Commentary on the Ecclesiasticus,* n. 53; LW
II, pp. 281f: "It is noteworthy that some misunderstand this nature of analogy
and are still in error today. However, we speak the truth about analogy when
we say . . . that it is best expressed in this line: 'Those who eat me will hunger
still.' They eat because they are, they hunger because they are by someone else
(Edunt, quia sunt, esuriunt, quia ab alio sunt)." The two other places where
Eckhart develops his understanding of analogy are: *Book of Divine Consolation,*
DW V, pp. 8-61, *passim,* and *Commentary on Saint John,* nos. 14-22; LW III, pp.

13,1–19,2, where the paradigm of justice and the just is developed in sixteen points of argument.

58. "General Prologue" to the *Opus Tripartitum,* LW I, p. 156. A. Maurer translates "Existence is God," in: *Master Eckhart, Parisian Questions and Prologues,* op. cit., p. 77, but *esse* refers to the act of being, not to existence as opposed to essence. See also the sermon "Woman, the Hour Is Coming" above, ch. 2, "General and Individual Perfections."

59. E. Gilson, *History of Christian Philosophy in the Middle Ages:* New York, 1955, p. 441: "Being is, so to speak, imputed to beings by God without ever becoming their own being, about in the same way as in Luther's theology justice will be imputed to the just without ever becoming their own justice."

60. *Book of the Divine Consolation,* DW V, p. 37,5. Cf. also below, the last two paragraphs of the sermon "Proclaim the Word."

61. *Commentary on the Book of Ecclesiasticus,* n. 52; LW II, pp. 280f.

62. *Commentary on the Book of Wisdom,* n. 292; LW II, p. 652.

63. "Per modum passionis et transeuntis et fieri," *Commentary on Saint John,* n. 70; LW III, p. 59.

64. Sermon "Beati qui esuriunt et sitiunt justitiam," Pf. p. 148,9–26.

65. The act of accusation at Cologne points out the following definition of analogy, borrowed from the *Commentary on the Book of Ecclesiasticus:* "Equivocal relations are divided according to the differences between things signified; univocal ones according to the differences in a thing; but analogical relations are distinguished neither by things nor by the differences in things, but according to the modes of realization of one and the same thing," n. 52; LW II, p. 280; reprinted almost literally in RS I, art. 9 (Théry, p. 169).

66. "A good man, *qua* good, enters into all properties of goodness that God is in himself," RS I, art.7 (Théry, p. 23).

67. J. Koch, "Zur Analogielehre Meister Eckharts," in *Mélanges offerts à Etienne Gilson,* Toronto-Paris, 1959, pp. 347–350, has shown that this doctrine can call upon antecedents such as Otto of Freising, Gilbert of Porrée, and Augustine.

68. "All the just are so by justice which is one in number; that is, a number without number and one without one; or rather: a oneness above oneness by which all the just, inasmuch as they are just, are one." *Commentary on the Book of Wisdom,* n. 44; LW II, p. 366,4–7.

69. M. Galvano della Volpe, *Il misticismo speculativo di Maestro Eckhart nei suoi rapporti storici,* Bologna, 1930: "capziosità geniale," quoted by V. Lossky, op. cit, p. 308.

70. V. Lossky, op. cit., pp. 339f., stresses that the thought of Eckhart, if it remains above all analogical, results fundamentally from his spiritual attitude. Lossky adopts and develops further a phrase from Penido: "Analogy of attribution is agreeable to the mystics."

71. The Middle High German text of this sermon has been published in DW II, pp. 93–109.

72. Cf. above, ch. 1, the end of the section, "The Divine Destiny of the Intellect."

73. Cf. above, ch. 2, the section on "Identity."

74. We have presented this vocabulary in Chapter 2 at the beginning of the section "Dissimilarity.".

75. Goethe uses *Wesen* in this sense. In *Faust II*, Mephistopheles arranges for Faust's descent into the kingdom of Mothers: ". . . Dein Wesen strebe nieder. Versinke stampfend, stampfend steigst du wieder" (vv. 6303f.).

76. M. Lexer, *Mittelhochdeutsches Taschenwörterbuch*, Stuttgart, 1966, p. 315.

77. Sermon "Et ecce, homo erat in Ierusalem," Pf. p. 88,8.

78. Sermon "Laudate caeli," Pf. p. 300,7–11.

79. God is called the "essential being in simple unity without any distinction," die weselîche istikeit nâch einvaltiger einikeit âne einigen underscheit, sermon "Intravit Jesus in templum," DW I, p. 19,1–2.

80. Sermon "Renovamini," Pf. p. 319, 18–22.

81. Sermon "Justi vivent in aeternum," DW I, MS. P1, p. 97; p. 106, n. 2.

82. Josiah Royce's brief comments on the term *isticheit* present quite a clear picture of this complex matter, cf. his "Meister Eckhart" in *Studies of Good and Evil*, Hamden, Conn., 1898 and 1964, pp. 291f.

83. Sermon "Qui audit me," DW I, p. 197, 2–3. The censors of Avignon were even more embarrassed than we are by this text; they completely and simply suppressed the words *istic* and *isticheit:* "Paulus reliquit deum propter deum, et tunc remansit ei deus non secundum receptionem nec secundum dationem, sed secundum quod deus est in seipso," RS II, art. 17 (Théry, p. 287).

84. In insisting too much on the distinction between *Esse primum* and *esse secundum*, there is great danger of losing the unicity of *isticheit*. V. Lossky, op. cit., does not always escape this danger, cf., e.g., pp. 268f., 299ff. on "L'Etre et l'être" and "l'être et l'Etre."

85. *Parisian Questions*, question I, n. 6 and 8; LW V, pp. 42,7–45,5. English translation slightly modified from *Master Eckhart, Parisian Questions and Prologues*, op. cit., pp. 46–48.

86. Sermon "Proclaim the Word," above.

87. Sermon "Blessed Are the Poor," above.

88. See above, ch. 2, n. 111. Walter Schulz, *Der Gott der neuzeitlichen Metaphysik*, Pfullingen, 1957, quotes from the *Parisian Questions* on which we have based our remarks, and concludes: "God is no longer determined as a given Being, to which attributions with objective contents can be ascribed, rather God becomes a process (*Vollzug*)," (translated from p. 15).

89. Sermon "In hoc apparuit," DW I, p. 90,12.

90. Sermon "Blessed Are the Poor," DW II, p. 492,3–4, transl. above.

91. To my knowledge there have been two attempts at such a comparison, one by Käte Oltmanns, the other by John D. Caputo. Käte Oltmanns, *Meister Eckhart*, Frankfurt, 1935 and 1957, puts forth an interpretation of the notion of freedom which has generally been received with more reservation than approbation. Her developments have little ground in Heidegger and none whatsoever in Eckhart—as she recognizes herself: in Meister Eckhart, she says, "the word freedom plays no role" (p. 104). John D. Caputo, "Meister Eckhart and the Later Heidegger: The Mystical Element in Heidegger's Thought," in: *J. Hist. Phil.*, XII,

4 (Oct. 1974). pp. 479–494, and XIII, 1 (Jan. 1975), pp. 61–80, is more concerned with Heidegger than with Eckhart. The part of his study that deals with the early Heidegger, particularly with Heidegger's habilitation dissertation on Duns Scotus, is a precious complement to what I try to undertake in these pages. But I must confess that I am ill at ease with parallels between two thinkers so far apart from each other when these parallels become as specific as the following: Heidegger's "recollection into being" and mysticism at large (Caputo I, p. 483); Heidegger's analogy between Being and thinking, and Eckhart's analogy between God and the thinking within faith (ibid., p. 484); Heidegger's "Dasein," and Eckhart's "ground of the soul" (Caputo II, p. 61); Heidegger's "Event of appropriation" and Eckhart's "birth" (ibid., p. 62), etc. Such thematic comparisons tend to forget that the themes of modern philosophy, as Heidegger expressly states, arise with Descartes, not with Meister Eckhart. Cf. M. Heidegger, *What Is a Thing?* transl. W. B. Banton and V. Deutsch, Chicago, 1967, p. 98. Generally speaking, Caputo seems to me more reliable on Heidegger than on Eckhart.

92. Martin Heidegger, *Gelassenheit,* Pfullingen, 1959, pp. 26–28. J. M. Anderson and E. H. Freund translate: "Releasement toward things and openness to the mystery belong together.... Releasement toward things and openness to the mystery give us the vision of a new autochthony.... Releasement toward things and openness to the mystery never happen of themselves. They do not befall us accidentally. Both flourish only through persistent, courageous thinking.... If releasement toward things and openness to the mystery awaken within us, then we should arrive at a path that will lead to a new ground and foundation." M. Heidegger, *Discourse on Thinking,* New York, 1966, pp. 55–57. We shall not follow this translation.

93. This influence exists, however. Heidegger sometimes quotes from Meister Eckhart, and we learned personally from him that he developed his understanding of being as *An-wesen* (a verb, not a noun) in the years in which he also read Meister Eckhart's sermons.

94. *Gelassenheit,* p. 25; *Discourse on Thinking,* p. 54.

95. Diehls-Kranz, Fragmente der Vorsokratiker, frag. 93. G. S. Kirk and J. E. Raven, *The Presocratic Philosophers,* Cambridge, 1971, p. 211.

96. *Gelassenheit,* p. 26; *Discourse on Thinking,* p. 55.

97. Sermon "Proclaim the Word," DW II, p. 109, 1–2; transl. above.

98. "Auf solche Weise (wird) dasjenige, was den Horizont das sein lässt, was er ist, noch keineswegs erfahren," *Gelassenheit,* p. 39; *Discourse on Thinking,* p. 64.

99. See in the sermon "Like a Vase of Massive Gold," DW I, p. 272,2, the example of the blind man who "shows affection" for the master of the dog (der sînem herren heimelich waere). Transl. above.

100. M. Heidegger, *Vorträge und Aufsätze,* Pfullingen, 1954, p. 50; transl. W. J. Lovitt, *The Question Concerning Technology,* New York, forthcoming.

101. M. Heidegger, *Identität und Differenz,* Pfullingen, 1957, p. 62: "the Being of beings means Being which is beings. The 'is' here speaks transitively, in transition. Being here becomes present (*Sein west hier*) in the manner of a

transition to beings," transl. J. Stambaugh, *Identity and Difference,* New York, 1969, p. 64.

102. Cf. above ch. 3, "The Limits of the Analogical Understanding of Being," sections c.) and d.).

103. *Die Technik und die Kehre,* Pfullingen, 1962, p. 39. In this text Heidegger comments on a line from Meister Eckhart: "Those who are not of a vast essence, whatever they undertake leads to nothing (die nitt von grossem wesen sind, was werk die wirkend, da wirt nit us)" (Meister Eckhart, "Die rede der underscheidunge," n. 4; DW V, pp. 198,6f.). Heidegger continues: "We think the vast essence of man in that it belongs to the essence of being and is needed by it in order to preserve the essence of being in its truth." The translation by K. R. Maly, "The Turning," *Research in Phenomenology* I (1971), p. 7, is too loose as he translates "das grosse Wesen" as "the profound source."

104. "Our sole intention must be towards God, neither towards what is mine nor towards myself, quite as God's intention is towards nothing of his own but only towards what is useful for us," Latin sermon XXXI, n. 322; LW IV, p. 282,9–11. The same idea that property or attributes are "pure nothingness" is developed by the example of the burning coal in one's hand: what hurts you, Eckhart says, is nothingness, cf. DW I, p. 80,7–17, and above ch. 2, n. 60. If attributive determination is nothing, then not only the created will be nothingness, but also the Trinity. S. Ueda, op. cit., points out rightly that Meister Eckhart does not think nothingness as such, but the nothingness of determination: the particular is nothing, only the universal truly 'is.' In this, Ueda says, Eckhart differs radically from Zen teachers. A similar remark can be made about Heidegger: he does not think nothingness purely and simply, but being as nothing, as "no thing." "What is totally other than beings is not-being. But this nothingness is present as being (Aber dieses Nichts west als das Sein)," *Was ist Metaphysik?* Frankfurt, 1960, p. 45. Translation R. F. Hull and A. Crick in *Existence and Being,* Chicago, 1949, p. 353 (translation modified). Meister Eckhart thinks of nothingness in attributive schemes (the eye must be devoid of color to see color; likewise the mind must be virgin in order to receive and conceive God). In Eckhart as well as in Heidegger the understanding of nothingness is in the service of the understanding of being: the event of a presence that is never fixed, that remains without a name, beyond all representation, and that addresses man as a calling.

105. Martin Heidegger, address on the twentieth annivesary of the death of Rainer Maria Rilke, December 29, 1946, printed under the title "Wozu Dichter?" in *Holzwege*, Frankfurt, 1950, p. 283; translated by A. Hofstadter, *Poetry, Language, Thought*, New York, 1971, p. 128. See W. J. Richardson's explanations of how Heidegger comes to follow Eckhart in his choice of the word "heart": *Heidegger, Through Phenomenology to Thought*, The Hague, 1963, pp. 599f.

106. *Was heisst Denken?* Tübingen, 1954, p. 91; the English translation is a paradigm of scholarly irresponsibility. Not only do the translators omit this sentence, but they introduce five lines that are not in the text: "The Old English *thencan*, to think, and *thancian*, to thank, are closely related; the Old English

noun for thought is *thanc* or *thonc*—a thought, a grateful thought, and the expression of such a thought; today it survives in the plural *thanks*. The *thanc*, that which is thought, the thought, implies the thanks." *What Is Called Thinking?*, transl. F. D. Wieck and J. G. Gray, New York, 1968, p. 139. Also in *Gelassenheit*, pp. 66f.: "Noble-mindedness would be the nature of thinking and thereby of thanking. . . . In the nature of thinking so understood, we may have found what we seek," transl. J. M. Anderson and E. H. Freund, *Discourse on Thinking*, New York, 1966, p. 85.

107. *Gelassenheit*, p. 27; *Discourse on Thinking*, p. 56.

108. *Der Satz vom Grund*, Pfullingen, 1957, p. 188.

109. Cf. above, ch. 2, n. 110; with regard to the *grunt* in Eckhart we have seen that it does not mean "foundation" in the metaphysical sense: the ground of the mind is rather *abegrunt*, abyss, cf. above ch. 1, n. 62. Heidegger's commentators have noticed that on this point Heidegger "can claim for himself the mystical tradition" that teaches living without why. O. Pöggeler, *Der Denkweg Martin Heideggers*, Pfullingen, 1963, p. 157.

110. Sermon "Proclaim the Word," DW II, pp. 107, 4–108, 1; translation above.

111. Text quoted above, ch. 1, n. 61. The scholar's objection has to be balanced by a reminder that the ground of the mind is "naturally" released. In Eckhart, the sole task of the will is to reintegrate the natural state and to make the soul become what it has been from its very origin.

112. Sermon "See What Love," Pf. 42, 2: "Unde bin ich wol übersatzt in daz gotlich wesen, so wirt got min"; and ibid., p. 40, 25–28.

113. "Der Spruch des Anaximander," in *Holzwege*, Frankfurt, 1950, p. 312: "translate ourselves to what is said in the fragment," transl. D. F. Krell and F. A. Capuzzi, "The Anaximander Fragment," in *Early Greek Thinking*, New York, 1975, p. 27. "It is essential that we translate ourselves to the source of what comes to language in it," ibid., p. 313 (transl. p. 28). This translation, in Heidegger's view, is essentially the work of the poet, ibid., p. 317 (transl. p. 32), and the entire interpretation of Hölderlin's ode *Heimkunft/An die Verwandten*, in *Erläuterungen zu Hölderlins Dichtung*, Frankfurt, 1951, pp. 9–30; transl. R. F. Hull and A. Crick, *Existence and Being*, Chicago, 1949, pp. 239–269.

114. *Gelassenheit*, pp. 27 and 31; *Discourse on Thinking*, pp. 56 and 58. For Heidegger, letting-be is the essence of thought in which in turn the essence of man becomes manifest.

115. *Holzwege*, Frankfurt, 1950, p. 193. Transl. W. J. Lovitt, *The Question Concerning Technology*, New York, forthcoming.

116. *Nietzsche*, Pfullingen, 1961, 2 vol., esp. vol. 2, pp. 350–355.

117. *Gelassenheit*, pp. 58–61: "Geschichte der Gegnet"; *Discourse on Thinking*, pp. 78f.

118. *Gelassenheit*, p. 65. The words "nature," "essence," and "achieve" all translate the German *Wesen*. *Discourse on Thinking*, p. 82 (translation modified).

119. "Detach yourself, so that you neither be nor possess anything, then you will be and you will possess all things." Sermon "See, I Send My Angel," Pf. p. 162, 16f., with the corrections of Quint, *Überlieferung . . .*, p. 481. *Scheide abe,*

abegescheidenheit, Abgeschiedenheit: Heidegger uses this word especially in his commentary on a poem of Trakl: "Die Sprache im Gedicht," in *Unterwegs zur Sprache*, Pfullingen, 1959, pp. 35–82; transl. P. D. Hertz, *On the Way to Language*, New York, 1971, pp. 159–199. *Der Abgeschiedene* is the stranger, separated from his congeners (p. 51), the fool always on the way to elsewhere (p. 53) who from the beyond summons the poet in order that his poem make the human race return to its peaceable origins (pp. 73f.). The word uttered out of *Abgeschiedenheit* gathers together, it institutes the locus from which a new era arises (pp. 66f. and 76f.). In Heidegger, *Abgeschiedenheit* says the event where the word makes a new period dawn. This temporal aspect is absent from Meister Eckhart (see our remarks above, ch. 2, introductory remarks to "Intensities of Releasement"). In both authors, though, *Abgeschiedenheit* has a radical meaning: it indicates the root in which all things are gathered together as in an event.

120. See above, "The Limits of the Analogical Understanding of Being," sections b.) and e.).

121. This *Conclusion* had appeared earlier as part of my article "Heidegger and Meister Eckhart on Releasement," *Research in Phenomenology*, III, 1973, pp. 115–119. Reproduced here by authorization from the Humanities Press.

122. Martin Heidegger, *Zur Sache des Denkens*, Tübingen, 1969, p. 5, transl. J. Stambaugh, *On Time and Being*, New York, 1972, p. 5.

123. Ibid., p. 9; translation, p. 9.

124. See above, ch. 3, n. 28 and n. 103.

125. *Zur Sache des Denkens*, p. 33; *On Time and Being*, p. 31.

126. Ibid., p. 47; translation, p. 43.

127. Ibid., p. 5; translation, p. 5.

128. Ibid., p. 48; translation, p. 45.

129. See our commentary on this quote above, ch. 2, n. 128f. To claim the ultimacy of the "there is," understood as an event, obviously runs counter to all efforts to read Eckhart in a theistic perspective, as does, for instance, C. F. Kelley: "The Principle itself necessarily, objectively and really is; it is transcendentally distinct from the entire order of manifestation and every modality thereof, and God is that Principle." In *Meister Eckhart on Divine Knowledge*, New Haven, forthcoming.

130. The Middle High German text of this sermon has been published in DW II, pp. 486–506.

APPENDIX

1. Daisetz T. Suzuki, *Mysticism: Christian and Buddhist*, New York, 1957. All quotations except those of n. 8 are taken from the first contribution, "Meister Eckhart and Buddhism." The text of our *Appendix* was originally published in French in "Trois penseurs du délaissement: Maître Eckhart, Heidegger, Suzuki," *J. Hist. Phil.*, XIII (1975), pp. 56–60. Copyright by Journal of the History of Philosophy, Inc.

2. See the sermon "Jesus Entered" above, and the commentary, "A New Commerce with Things: Detachment."

3. See the references above, ch. 1, notes 25–37.

4. Suzuki, op. cit., p. 7.

5. See above, ch. 2, n. 45, and ch. 3, "The Limits of the Analogical Understanding of Being," section d.).

6. The expression is that of Hans Hof, *Scintilla animae*, Lund and Bonn, 1952, p. 16.

7. Suzuki, op. cit., p. 9.

8. Ibid., p. 8.

9. Ibid., p. 12.

10. Ibid.

11. See the characterization of Eckhart's type of thinking as opposed to that of late Scholasticism, above, ch. 1, notes 46–51.

12. Suzuki, op. cit., p. 14.

13. Suzuki, op. cit., pp. 18f.

14. D. T. Suzuki, *Essays in Zen Buddhism, First Series*, London, 1941, and New York, 1961, p. 268.

15. *Mysticism: Christian and Buddhist*, p. 32.

16. Ibid., p. 32.

17. *Essays in Zen Buddhism, First Series*, pp. 371–376.

18. Ibid., p. 63.

19. Ibid., p. 230.

20. Ibid., p. 235.

Selected Bibliography

A. Text editions:

Meister Eckhart, *Die deutschen und lateinischen Werke,* ed. for the Deutsche Forschungsgemeinschaft by Joseph Quint, Stuttgart, 1936–. DW I, 607 pp.; DW II, 930 pp.; DW III, 695 pp.; DW V, 622 pp.; LW I, 759 pp.; LW II (fasc. 1–10) 512 pp.; LW III (fasc. 1–4), 304 pp.; LW IV, 479 pp.; LW V (fasc. 1–2), 128 pp. The volumes followed by a reference to fascicles are incomplete.

Jundt, A., *Histoire du panthéisme populaire au Moyen Age et au XVIe siècle,* Paris, 1875, Appendix II, pp. 231–280: Sermons et pièces diverses de Maître Eckhart.

Pelster, Franz, "Ein Gutachten aus dem Eckehart-Prozess in Avignon," in *Aus der Geisteswelt des Mittelalters, Festgabe Martin Grabmann,* Münster, 1935, pp. 1099–1124.

Pfeiffer, Franz, Deutsche Mystiker des vierzehnten Jahrhunderts, 2 vol.; vol. 2, *Meister Eckhart, Predigten und Traktate,* Leipzig, 1857, and Aalen, 1962, 686 pp.

Quint, J. (ed. and transl.), *Meister Eckhart, Predigten und Traktate,* Munich, 1955, 547 pp.

———, *Die Überlieferung der deutschen Predigten Meister Eckeharts,* Bonn, 1932, 958 pp.

Schaefer, E., *Meister Eckharts Traktat 'Von Abgeschiedenheit', Untersuchung und Textneuausgabe,* Bonn, 1956.

Théry, Gabriel, "Edition critique des pièces relatives au procès d'Eckhart contenues dans le manuscrit 33 b de la bibliothèque de Soest," in *Archives d'histoire doctrinale et littéraire du Moyen Age,"* vol. I, 1926–27, pp. 129–272.

———, *Le Commentaire de Maître Eckhart sur le Livre de la Sagesse,* ibid., vol. III (1928), pp. 321–443; vol. IV (1929), pp. 233–394.

B. English Translations:

Blakney, Raymond B., *Meister Eckhart, A Modern Translation,* New York and London, 1941. (Contains: Talks of Instruction, The Book of Divine Comfort, The Aristocrat, About Disinterest, a selection of twenty-eight Sermons, Fragments, and the Defense.) A highly interpretive and misleading translation.

Clark, James M., *Meister Eckhart, An Introduction to the Study of His Works, with an Anthology of His Sermons,* London, 1957. A small selection, same qualities as above.

Clark, James M., and Skinner, John V., *Meister Eckhart, Selected Treatises and Sermons,* transl. from the Latin and German with an Introduction and Notes, London, 1958. A good selection and intelligible, mostly correct, translation.

Evans, C. de B., *Meister Eckhart by Franz Pfeiffer,* vol. I, London, 1924; vol. II, London, 1931. A complete but hardly readable translation of Pfeiffer's outdated text edition, in archaic English.

Maurer, Armand A., *Master Eckhart, Parisian Questions and Prologues, with an Introduction and Notes,* Pontifical Institute of Medieval Studies, Toronto, 1974. A good, sometimes interpretive translation of important Latin treatises.

C. Studies:

Ancelet-Hustache, J., *Master Eckhart and the Rhineland Mystics,* transl. from the French by H. Graef, New York, 1957. An excellent introduction.

Brunner, F., *Maître Eckhart* (coll. "Philosophes de tous les temps"), Paris, 1969. Good introduction to Eckhart's philosophy with selection from some Latin works.

Clark, J. M., *Meister Eckhart, An Introduction to the Study of His Works, with an Anthology of His Sermons,* London, 1957. A recommendable synthetic presentation of Eckhart's thought.

———, *The Great German Mystics, Eckhart, Tauler, and Suso,* Oxford, 1949. Same qualities as above.

Dempf, A., *Meister Eckhart, Eine Einführung in sein Werk,* Leipzig, 1934. A lecture series insisting on Eckhart's philosophy of the mind.

———, *Meister Eckhart,* Freiburg, 1960. The author sees four "innovations" in Eckhart's philosophy: a new philosophy of the mind, grace understood as spiritual being, essence and existence located in reason, and the union between the One in the soul and One in God.

Hof, H., *Scintilla Animae. Eine Studie zu einem Grundbegriff in Meister Eckharts Philosophie,* Lund and Bonn, 1952. The title is misleading: the book deals less with the "spark in the soul" than with a confrontation between Neoplatonic and Scholastic elements in Meister Eckhart. The author's judgments on medieval thinking are uncertain.

Kelley, C. F., *Meister Eckhart on Divine Knowledge,* New Haven, 1977. The author defines his project as "expanding the doctrine of Scriptures from the standpoint of formless and unrestricted knowledge, which is incommunicable in human terms." By such knowledge he means Eckhart's thesis of the identity of being and knowing in God. His project is directed against "those whose cognitional horizon is grossly limited by their education in modern philosophy."

Kelly, P., "Meister Eckhart's Doctrine of Divine Subjectivity," in *The Downside Revue,* 1958 (76), pp. 65–103.

Kertz, K. G., "Meister Eckhart's Teaching on the Birth of the Divine Word in the Soul" in *Traditio,* 1959 (15), pp. 327–363.

Koch, J., "Zur Analogielehre Meister Eckharts" in *Mélanges offerts à Etienne Gilson,* Toronto and Paris, 1959, pp. 327–350. An extremely well-informed and reliable presentation of the analogy of being with reference to Eckhart's Scholastic and pre-Scholastic sources by the editor of the Latin works.

———, "Kritische Studien zum Leben Meister Eckharts" in *Archivum Fratrum Praedicatorum,* 1959 (29), pp. 1–51, and 1960 (30), pp. 1–52. Reprinted in J. Koch, *Kleine Schriften,* vol. I, Rome, 1973, pp. 247–347. The only piece of thorough scholarly research on Eckhart's life that we possess. The source from which all other biographical presentations borrow.

Kopper, J., *Die Metaphysik Meister Eckharts,* Saarbrücken, 1955. An interpretation of Eckhart's metaphysics out of Kantian transcendental criticism.

Lossky, V., *Théologie négative et connaissance de Dieu chez Maître Eckhart,* Paris, 1960, 450 pp. The most valuable contribution to the study of Eckhart's philosophy since the war, although it is based nearly exclusively on the Latin texts in the not-quite-reliable manuscript of the *Codex Cusanus.* Also, Lossky interprets Eckhart in the light of the Greek Fathers of the Church and of Neoplatonic philosophers, which leads him to neglect the most innovative ideas in the German sermons.

Meister Eckhart der Prediger. Festschrift zum Eckhart-Gedenkjahr, herausgegeben von U. Nix und R. Öchslin, Freiburg, 1960, 284 pp. A collection of uneven essays by J. Koch, H. Fischer, H. Kunisch, R. Öchslin, H. Piesch, B. Dietsche, U. Plotzke. The contributors are more interested in theological than in philosophical questions.

Moody, H., "Participation and Perfection in Meister Eckhart's Doctrine of Man," Ph.D. dissertation, Columbia University, 1973. Relies on V. Lossky and shares his perspective.

Muller-Thym, M., *The Establishment of the University of Being in the Doctrine of Meister Eckhart of Hochheim,* New York, 1939.

La Mystique Rhénane. Colloque de Strasbourg, May 1961. Paris, 1963, 289 pp. Papers and discussions on Meister Eckhart, the most valuable of which is M. de Gandillac's "La 'dialectique' de Maître Eckhart," pp. 59–94.

Petry, R. C., *Late Medieval Mysticism,* Philadelphia, 1957.

Royce, J., "Meister Eckhart" in *Studies of Good and Evil,* Hamden, 1898 and 1964, pp. 261–297. A study by the American Idealist which turns out to be less Hegelian and less original than one would expect.

Schmoldt, B., *Die deutsche Begriffssprache Meister Eckharts,* Heidelberg, 1954. The author indicates the Latin counterparts of Eckhart's German technical terms and explains his philosophy according to these Scholastic equivalents. A useful philological aid which neglects, however, the broader context and history of the words analyzed.

D. Comparative Studies:

Bracken, E. von, *Meister Eckhart und Fichte,* Würzburg, 1946. By far the larger space (pp. 10–407) is dedicated to Eckhart's philosophy, with particular emphasis on the problem of universals, and on the debate between nominalism and crude realism. The comparison with Fichte's *Science of Knowledge* (pp. 408–579) isolates common themes in both authors and should be evaluated as a study in the history of philosophy.

Caputo, J. D., "Meister Eckhart and the Later Heidegger: The Mystical Element in Heidegger's Thought" in *Journal of the History of Philosophy,* 1974 (12), pp. 479–494, and 1975 (13), pp. 61–80. A suggestive comparison with the later Heidegger which pushes, however, the syncretism into questions of detail where it serves neither of the authors considered. Caputo has now expanded this article into a book, *The Mystical Element in Heidegger's Thought,* Athens, Ohio, 1978.

Degenhardt, I., *Studien zum Wandel des Eckhart-Bildes,* Leiden, 1967, 349 pp. Shows in brief sketches the influence of Eckhart on later medieval mystics, on Nicholas of Cusa, Franz von Baader, Hegel, Schopenhauer, and others.

Dumoulin, H., *Östliche Meditation und christliche Mystik,* Freiburg, 1966. By far the best-informed and most reliable of all comparative works on Eckhart and Buddhism.

Enomiya, H. M., *Zen-Buddhismus,* Cologne, 1966.

Gilson, E., "Maïmonide et la Philosophie de l'Exode," *Medieval Studies,* 1951 (XIII), pp. 223ff.

Haas, A., *Wirkendes Wort,* 1972 (XXII), pp. 123–133. Draws on contemporary Marxists such as Ernst Bloch to discuss whether Eckhart was a "mystic of the Left."

———, "Maître Eckhart dans l'idéologie marxiste" in *La Vie Spirituelle,* 1971 (LIII), pp. 62–79. Same survey as above.

Heinrich, W., *Verklärung und Erlösung im Vedanta, bei Meister Eckhart und bei Schelling,* Munich, 1962.

Ley, H., *Geschichte der Aufklärung und des Atheismus,* Berlin, 1966—.

———, *Studie zur Geschichte des Materialismus im Mittelalter,* Berlin, 1957. The most knowledgeable and scholarly among the Marxist interpretations of Eckhart. In both of these works Ley sees Eckhart as the theoretician of revolutionary peasant groups, and his philosophy as a continuation of the progressive Arabic Aristotelianism of Averroës and Avicenna. The large audience that Eckhart found in his time, as well as the Inquisition's suspicions, were due to his attacks on the authority of church, state, and the feudal system. Ley also links Eckhart to the Begards. The author denounces the intellectual annexation of Eckhart's philosophy by German Idealism.

Merton, T., *Zen and the Birds of Appetite,* Gethsemani, 1968. A collection of articles on mysticism, Christianity, and Zen whose main purpose lies in raising a "new consciousness."

Nambara, M. "Die Idee des absoluten Nichts in der deutschen Mystik und ihre Entsprechungen im Buddhismus" in *Archiv für Begriffsgeschichte,* vol. VI, Bonn, 1960, pp. 143–277. A survey article on the notion of Nothingness which, as such, remains necessarily superficial.

Oltmanns, K., *Meister Eckhart,* 2. Auflage, Frankfurt, 1957. A comparison between Meister Eckhart's and Heidegger's understanding of freedom which, although "it owes more to the philosopher Heidegger than can be said," seems to have left both Eckhartian and Heideggerian scholars perplexed.

Otto, R., *Mysticism East and West. Sankara and Meister Eckhart,* 1932.

Rahner, H., "Die Gottesgeburt. Die Lehre der Kirchenväter von der Geburt Christi im Herzen der Gläubigen" in *Zeitschrift für katholische Theologie,* 1933 (LIX), pp. 333–418, and in *Symbole der Kirche,* Salzburg, 1964, pp. 1ff. A highly informative article on the Patristic origins and the history of the doctrine of the birth of Christ in the heart of the faithful.

Ralfs, G., "Lebensformen des Geistes. Meister Eckhart und Hegel," in *Kantstudien,* Supplement No. 86, Cologne, 1964.

Schomerus, H. W., *Meister Eckhart und Manikka-Vasagar, Mystik auf deutschem und indischem Boden,* Gütersloh, 1936.

Schrimpf, G., "Des Menschen Seligkeit. Ein Vergleich zwischen Plotins 'Peri Eudaimonias,' Meister Eckharts 'Buch der göttlichen Tröstung," und Fichtes 'Anweisungen zum seligen Leben' " in *Parousia,* Festgabe J. Hirschberger, Frankfurt, 1965.

Schürmann, R., "Trois penseurs du délaissement: Maître Eckhart, Heidegger, Suzuki" in *Journal of the History of Philosophy,* 1974 (XII), pp. 455–477, and 1975 (XIII), pp. 43–60.

———, "Heidegger and Meister Eckhart on Releasement" in *Research in Phenomenology,* 1973 (III), pp. 95–119.

Siewerth, G., *Das Schicksal der Metaphysik von Thomas zu Heidegger,* Einsiedeln, 1959. An attempt to verify the "forgetfulness of Being" in Western metaphysics by one of the founders of neo-Scholasticism. The result can only be a restatement of well-known elements in the philosophy of *esse,* with some simplifications in the chapter on Eckhart (pp. 88–92).

Suzuki, D. T., *Mysticism: Christian and Buddhist,* New York, 1957. A collection of articles that are probably more reliable on what they say of Rinzai Zen than on Eckhart. Suzuki wants to overcome philosophic and religious divisions among men by pointing to the Zen element contained in every authentic and advanced spiritual experience.

Ueda, S., *Die Gottesgeburt in der Seele und der Durchbruch zur Gottheit. Meister Eckhart und der Zen-Buddhismus,* Gütersloh, 1965. A not-very-innovative study of the main concepts in Eckhart followed by a brief and somewhat meager confrontation with Zen (pp. 145–169).

Welte, B., "Meister Eckhart als Aristoteliker" in *Auf der Spur des Ewigen,* Freiburg, 1965, pp. 197–210. A thoughtful analysis of the Aristotelian models of thought in Eckhart, particularly of the "active" and "passive" intellect.

———, "Rückblick auf die Metaphysik. Thomas von Aquin und Heidegger's Gedanke von der Seinsgeschichte" in *Wort und Wahrheit,* 1967 (XXII), pp. 747–757. A powerful and thoughtful attempt to illustrate concretely Heidegger's understanding of the "history of being." Eckhart "has freed himself from metaphysics, that is, from representation, from concept, and from the grip on beings," the author writes. He concludes that Eckhart has opened up future possibilities for thought.

Index of Technical Terms